Also available from Continuum

Continuum Companion to Discourse Analysis, edited by Ken Hyland and Brian
   Paltridge
Discourse and Politeness, Naomi Geyer
Forensic Linguistics Second Edition, John Olsson
Language and the Law, Sanford Shane
Wordcrime, John Olsson

Analysing Police Interviews

Laughter, Confessions and the Tape

Elisabeth Carter

continuum

Continuum International Publishing Group

The Tower Building
11 York Road
London SE1 7NX

80 Maiden Lane
Suite 704
New York NY 10038

www.continuumbooks.com

British Library Cataloguing-in-Publication Data
A catalogue record for this book is available from the British Library.

ISBN: 978-1-4411-7973-9 (hardcover)

Library of Congress Cataloging-in-Publication Data
A catalog record for this book is available from the Library of Congress.

Typeset by Fakenham Prepress Solutions, Fakenham, Norfolk NR21 8NN
Printed and bound in Great Britain

The apple doesn't fall far from the tree

Contents

List of figures   x

List of extracts   xi

1 Overview   1

2 An Introduction to Police Interview Research, Policing and
  Recorded Evidence   4

3 An Introduction to Conversation Analysis: History and Practice   15

Part 1 Laughter   35

4 Buttressing Innocence and Challenging the Officer: Suspect
  Laughter in the Interview   41

5 Officer Laughter: Challenging the Suspect and Breaking the
  Rules   54

Conclusion to Part 1   65

Part 2 The Silent Participant   69

6 The Silent Participant: Institutional Constraints, Semantic and
  Legal Redundancy   74

7 The Silent Participant: Uninitiated Third Turns   90

Conclusion to Part 2   103

Part 3 Confessions   106

8 Confessions: Knowledge Claims   116

9 Confessions: Minimization   129

Conclusion to Part 3   141

10 Conclusion   144

Appendix I Transcription Conventions   164

Appendix II Additional Transcript Extracts   167

Contents

Appendix III Glossary of Technical Terms   178

Appendix IV Extract from *The Bill* Script   182

References   184

Notes   197

Index   201

Acknowledgements

Thanks to Goldwave Inc. for their permission to include GoldWave screen-shots, and to A. P. Watt Ltd on behalf of P. G. Morgan for the permission to include parts of the script from Episode 513 of The Bill: 'A perfect murder Part 2'.

Thanks to the very many friends and colleagues who their gave time and insight in reading and reviewing this work in its many stages of completion: Professor Elizabeth Stokoe, Dr Hannah Mason-Bish, Dr Bethany Morgan Brett, Dr Lynne Pettinger, Dr Chrissie Rogers, Dr Katy Wheeler, Ian Carter, Annelies Clovis, Alison Day, Dave Day, Paul Day, Christopher Holden, Alison Mirpuri, Victoria Russell, Ragnhild Tveiten and Laura Wilkinson. All mistakes and errors are my own.

Thanks also to Dr Robert Wenn, Andrew Wenn, Leo Jayawardena, Commander Messinger, DS Conway, Clive Rees and Mark Fox for their help in accessing the tapes.

Special thanks to Professor Eamonn Carrabine, who was my PhD supervisor and still remains a great source of support and encouragement, even though he no longer has to! Thanks also to the Department of Sociology at the University of Essex, my academic home.

Lastly special thanks to my family for being them, and to Tim Day who has been there cheering me along every step of the way.

List of figures

Chapter 3

Figure 1.1 The silence episode in talk-in-interaction   25
Figure 1.2 The silence episode in talk-in-interaction – close-up 1   25
Figure 1.3 The silence episode in talk-in-interaction – close-up 2   26
Figure 1.4 Establishing the start of the silence   26
Figure 1.5 The silence captured   27
Figure 1.6 Silence and background disturbances   27

List of extracts

Chapter 3

1.1) CA transcription in situ

Part 1

Chapter 4

1) Drugs in the wardrobe
2) Hit on the head with a statue
3) Nah
4) Anywhere near there
5) Drugs in the wardrobe ii
6) No deal

Chapter 5

7) No comment to that
8) What's the catch?
9) What shall I call you?
10) Very annoying
11) You're not a garage
12) Offshore boating
13) Complete idiot

Part 2

1.2) The uninitiated third turn in the question-answer sequence

Chapter 6

14) Free legal advice
15) As has been explained
16) Your representative
17) The benefit of the tape
18) Heard it all before
19) Presence of the tape

Chapter 7

20) Describe it to me
21) Don't know
22) Didn't see
23) Time away
24) Green lane
25) Herbal substance
26) Ten pound

Part 3

Chapter 8

27) I'll tell you what I did do
28) Got anything to say about that?
29) I put it to you
30) Rat your mates out?
31) Innocent party

Chapter 9

32) The gentleman
33) I will take them back
34) Not nicked for that as well
35) In a sense yeah

Chapter 10

36) Let me finish
37) Too much TV

Chapter 1

Overview

This book explores the interaction between officers and suspects in the police interview. The police interview has become a mainstay of popular culture through television programmes such as *The Bill* and *A Touch of Frost*, but there are few academic explorations that look at the reality of interaction in this setting. Here the detail of the interview is explored using real cases and the methodology of conversation analysis (CA) to reveal the reality of police interviews in action. Each analytic chapter will investigate a different area – laughter, the effect of the tape, and the confession. These areas will reveal hidden layers of communication in the line-by-line, in-depth investigations of real police interviews, and the delicate co-construction and negotiation involved in their success.

A selection of extracts from a corpus of 150 police interviews from the UK are used as empirical evidence which show how the officer and the suspect navigate and negotiate in this specialist setting and how they form and shape their identities as officer and suspect. The aim is to provide innovative insights into the police interview by exploring the interactional phenomena, illustrating how they present, and offering a range of specialist hidden tools that can be operated by officers and suspects in a range of ways specifically aligned to the strategic requirements of their roles. For example, utterances that are of no benefit to the suspect during the interview can be used by officers to secure the admissibility of the interview as evidence, claims to knowledge that contradict the suspect's version of events can yield a confession, and laughter can be used by officers to circumvent the rules of police interviewing without reprimand, or by suspects to reinforce their story or to challenge an officer's version of events. Broader insights into the myths and practices surrounding the police interview are revealed by juxtaposing them with common myths of police interviewing that prevail by being passed down from senior to junior officer, presented in media representations of policing, or described as good techniques in interrogation manuals and research.

Despite being a central component of the police role, much research into policing and the criminal justice system focuses on aspects other than the police interview. Where research does focus on police interviewing, it tends to focus on the confession. Interest in this subject is bolstered by media representations of policing and the public perception of, and fascination with, this aspect of the interview. However, these explorations rarely use police interviews as data, and detailed line-by-line analysis of the structure of confession elicitation is relatively scarce. As a result, research in areas considered 'less interesting' or central to the police interview remain under-represented. This then perpetuates the popularity of more commonly explored areas by keeping those other elements of the police interview either out, or to the fringes of, the public, practitioner and academic realms. Here the focus is on these details of the interview by exploring both conventional and unconventional areas of police interview interaction on a further level. This means the research presented here can address current gaps in knowledge, both theoretical and practical, and through the conversation analytic approach, provide real insights into the very constitution of this talk and potential benefits to existing training and techniques.

The introductory chapters provide a brief overview of the range of literature surrounding policing and the sociology of the police, and touch on the communicative patterns of the phenomena under investigation in ordinary interaction and in other contexts. This is not designed to be exhaustive; rather, it's an overview of the field within which this research is situated. (Readers seeking a more comprehensive review of the literature in these fields are directed to specialist volumes dedicated to that purpose.) Various sources are considered to identify and frame the under-explored and unexplored areas of the police interview; academic research, policing and law enforcement training manuals and handbooks, the Police and Criminal Evidence Act (1984, hereafter the PACE Act 1984 or the Act 1984) and fictional representations of policing. The myths of the police interview are examined, and how they are spread through both officer training and fictional representations of the police. The introduction to CA and its practical applications are then illustrated, and the access of and approach to the data used are discussed. The roots of CA are outlined alongside its basis in broader sociological traditions. It details conversation analytic techniques, the transcription process and the potential difficulties associated with this type of approach. Both introductory chapters provide the framework by which the order and sequential nature of officers' and suspects' navigation of interaction are later explored.

The first analytic part (Chapters 4 and 5) investigates the uses of laughter, and explores how it can be used as a tool by the officer and the suspect in the interactionally restricted setting of the police interview. Understandings of laughter in both ordinary conversation and in other institutional contexts are drawn on to frame the analysis of laughter in the police interview. Although the presence of laughter in this heavily constrained institutional environment may seem unexpected, its systematic and structured accomplishment of a variety of actions in other settings is shown to be mirrored in police interview interaction.

Part Two (Chapters 6 and 7) investigates how the tape recording of the police interview can affect the shape of officers' talk. The effect of overhearers of talk in other institutional settings has been well documented; it often shows in the participants making alterations to their talk in order to orientate to subsequent listeners or those who cannot contribute to the interaction. Such orientation by police officers in recognition of their talk being 'overheard' by the recording device in the interview is not as well documented. Research in other institutional contexts is used in establishing how the effect of the silent participant may manifest in the police interview. The police interview data reveals the practicalities of how the structure of officers' talk in the interview is designed to maintain a communicative channel with the later overhearers of that interaction, and the difficulties that can occur in doing so.

Finally, Part Three (Chapters 8 and 9) reveals the reality of police interview confessions alongside the myths and mystique that prevail about how they are drawn from suspects. This is one of the more popular topics one would expect to encounter in discussions of the police interview. If general perceptions, criminological assertions and fictional representations were to be believed, no police interview would be complete without a confession. Part Three exposes the reality behind some of those myths, revealing quite a different relationship between officer and suspect from what is traditionally understood through media representations of confession elicitation. It unravels the structure of the elicitation of confessions in line-by-line analyses of the interaction immediately prior to a confession, and provides insights into the officers' and suspects' construction and negotiation of their production. The concluding chapter draws the findings together, discusses the academic implications and practical applications of the analytic findings to policy and interview practice, and suggests some potential future directions and explorations for the data and analytic techniques.

Chapter 2

An Introduction to Police Interview Research, Policing and Recorded Evidence

A wealth of police interview research focuses on the officer in the police interview and on aspects that satisfy the perceived agenda of the officer. This is illustrated by the serious analytic attention given to techniques for the elicitation of confessions and methods by which officers can detect a suspect's deception, discussed further in Chapters 8 and 9. However, the research presented in this book examines the interaction and roles of both the suspect and the officer and provides an insight into their joint construction of the police interview.

The analyses explore ways that both the suspect and the officer negotiate their roles and the contextually defined constraints of their interaction, revealing and discussing the self-imposed and other-imposed constraints of their respective positions. This investigation strives to be uninfluenced by police requirements, interview myths or judgements of truth or deceptiveness. It aims to provide, and be led by, detailed, data-driven empirical insights into the police interview that contribute to knowledge by addressing current gaps in the literature and the contrasting accounts of the police interview. It is designed to explore the real-time interaction in the police interview, making the reality of this exchange, commonly closed to all but police personnel, accessible.

The police interview can be seen as the institutional and interactional manifestation of the social 'battle' between the police and suspects; the social and perhaps moral barrier between the participants could be likened to 'set pieces of social control, which are almost by definition wrapped in symbols and ritual' (Holdaway and Rock 1998: 156). A large and rapidly growing body of literature focusing on the criminal justice system varies from the analysis of police emergency calls (Sharrock and Turner 1978) to the interaction in courtrooms (Drew 1992), offenders' neutralization of crimes (Sykes and Matza 1957), policing (Reiner 2010) and the criminal justice system in general. The police interview itself has been approached from a variety of perspectives such as interview techniques (Baldwin 1993; Moston and Engelberg 1993; Heydon 2005; Kidwell and González Martínez 2010), defining and describing question types in police interviews (Oxburgh *et al.* 2010) and officer interview training (Memon *et al.* 1995; Powell 2002).

As noted by Davis *et al.* (2005), much research in this field has relied on laboratory-generated rather than empirical data – for example, conducting interviews with suspects about their experience after they have been interviewed by the police (Sykes and Matza 1957), interviewing officers regarding their own performance (Kebbell and Wagstaff 1996), or in experiments to examine the propensity for interviewees to produce false confessions (Kassin and Kiechel 1996; Bain and Baxter 2000; Horselenberg *et al.* 2006). Redlich *et al.* (2008) used university undergraduates to assess the credibility and suggestibility of child victims and suspects through reading transcripts of police interviews. Although laboratory-based research provides a valuable resource for examining aspects of the police interview that practicalities render inaccessible (such as the production of false confessions), it still cannot replicate the communicative environment, real crimes, intrinsic responsibility of the officer, and the high stakes of the police interview setting. The research in this book explores the real-time processes of the police interview-in-action through the use of empirical data and CA to examine the participants' underlying communicative orientations, restrictions and capabilities.

Despite the growing number of empirical investigations into the police interview, it still remains comparatively rare in both conversation analytic research and in research into the criminal justice system. This is probably associated with the difficulty in gaining access to police interview tapes, compounded by the detailed and particular methodological requirements of CA. The following chapter provides an introduction to CA and its procedures, together with a more detailed discussion of CA and an account of the practical and methodological challenges encountered during the course of this research.

Policing and Recorded Evidence

The tape recording of police interviews was standardized in the UK in 1992, enabling members of the criminal justice system to hear the interaction that had taken place, rather than having to rely on the transcript of interaction written by an officer during the interview. This turn from using written records to tape recording practices meant that the real-time interaction in interviews has only relatively recently been made accessible to those outside the criminal justice system. The tape recording of police interviews created an unprecedented transparency of the interaction as it enables the listener of the tape access to the talk-in-action as it unfolded, as if a 'silent participant' in that interview.

On an operational level, the introduction of tape recording 'meant that any flaws in techniques or procedures could no longer be ignored or concealed' (Moston and Engelberg 1993: 223). This is reflected in the reduction of known cases of miscarriages of justice since its introduction, although further technological advances beyond tape recording, such as video recording technology, make little additional difference (Baldwin 1992b). Prior to the change in legislation, written records could result in errors in representing what occurred in the interview, due to (among other difficulties) the inability to accurately represent tone of voice (Mirfield 1985). It follows that using recording equipment in police interviews signals both the additional protection of suspects' rights, and also the protection of the officer against claims of manipulation or misrepresentation. 'The new technology ... helps police in gathering evidence at the same time as it *adds to* the protection of the rights of the accused' (Law Reform Commission of Canada 1988, emphasis added).

This technological advancement may have other implications. Discussed in more detail in Part Two, the participants' orientation to the presence of the tape as a silent participant to that interaction can alter its very shape in the way the officer communicates with the suspect. The investigation into the detail of the police interview this book provides takes into account and explores both the legally and interactionally defined boundaries of that talk. The interactional boundaries are fluid and negotiated through the course of the talk-in-action; their characteristics, construction and maintenance by the participants is revealed in the analytic chapters that follow. However, the legal boundaries, in the form of the PACE Act 1984, differ from those interactional boundaries as they are legally enforceable, non-negotiable and set prior to the interview.

The PACE Act 1984 is the legislative framework in England and Wales which documents the powers of the police and other authorized officers (such as enforcement officers of local government), and outlines the protocols that govern their conduct. The Act was created to standardize police practices and balance the concerns of the officer with the needs of the suspect. It was developed to inform and protect the rights of the public in their contact with the police and authorized officers, and provide officers with a statement of the requirements and regulations of their role. Currently the Act comprises eight codes of practice, lettered from A to H, each relating to a different aspect of the criminal justice process. The most recent addition is code H, introduced in 2006, which relates to the detention, treatment and questioning of suspects arrested under Section 41 of The Terrorism Act 2000 (the PACE Act 1984, 2006 edition, Code H Section 1, paragraph 1.1). The codes relevant to the research in this book are code C, which deals with the 'detention, treatment and questioning of persons by police officers' (PACE Act 1984, 2006 edition: vi) and Code E, which is the 'code of practice on audio recording interviews with suspects' (the PACE Act 1984, 2006 edition: xi). The most recent version of Code E came into effect in April 2010.

The PACE Act 1984 has undergone many revisions (most recently in 2005, 2006, 2008 and 2010) and modifications in line with legislative changes, such as the Police Reform Act 2002. The introduction of the Serious Organised Crime and Police Act 2005 altered the police powers of arrest, and changes to the suspects' right to silence meant that inferences could now be drawn from a suspect's silence in the interview (Criminal Justice and Public Order Act 1994, section 34). Despite the many changes and additions subsequent to its inception, the central premise of the Act (1984) has remained to 'provide a clear statement of the rights of the individual and the powers of the police' (the PACE Act 1984, 2006 edition: iv).

While not an investigation into the powers of the police or their ability to adhere to the protocols of the Act (1984), the research in this book uses the legislative framework of the Act as a frame of reference for particular behaviours in the police interview. For example, the officers' orientation to the silent participant examined in Chapters 6 and 7 may be linked to enacting protocols required by the Act. Similarly, the management of episodes of laughter examined in Chapters 4 and 5, and the types of techniques used by officers in drawing confessions from suspects explored in Chapters 8 and 9 will inevitably rely on, or be shaped by, these protocols and requirements. It is in this way the analyses also provide insights into the workings of these legislative mechanisms in action, their efficacy and the participants' management of their requirements.

Police Sociology and Criminology

By investigating the police interview, an integral component of the police investigative process and the criminal justice system, this research is firmly based in part of a tradition that explores policing and police work. It has been approached from various angles, many based on type of crime – for example, cyber crime (Jewkes 2003; Jaishankar 2007), white collar crime (Sutherland 1949) and terrorism (Matassa and Newburn 2003). Research also concentrates on the wider structure of the police (Clark and Sykes 1974), politics (Reiner 2000), corruption (Maguire 2003) and policing and the media (Reiner 2003). A considerable body of literature has also been published on areas such as police and gender, an overview of which is provided by Heidensohn (2002, 2003). Insights include the importance of gender on the institution (Martin 1980; Westmarland 2001), the threat female officers pose to the masculinity, aggression and physical strength deemed central to the police role (Walklate 1995), and an insider's perspective of sexual discrimination (Halford 1993). The history, corruption and ethical improprieties of the police and institutional changes and solutions (Reiner 1992; Maguire 2003) demonstrate how the shifting climate of policing can bring solutions to past problems. For example, introducing the tape recording of police interviews worked towards reducing the presence of oppressive police interview questioning practices.

Reiner (1992, 2000) and Newburn (2003b) provide comprehensive accounts of the changing sociological and political climate and trends of police research from the 1960s. Clark and Sykes (1974) focused on the structure of policing as part of the institutional makeup of the criminal justice system, rather than on particular aspects of that structure, such as the police interview. Using data from calls to the police, Shearing (1998) studied policing from 'outside the police' in order to challenge the existing paradigm of viewing police work through the institution, which he criticized as sidelining police practices (Holdaway and Rock 1998). However, in examining policing as an activity of other agencies, areas of police work such as the police interview, itself arguably at the core of the police role, remain under-investigated. This focus on alternative, extra-constabulary policing still prevails. Newburn's (2003a) volume reflects the 'fragmented and plural nature' (Newburn 2003b: 5) of contemporary policing, indeed its 'intention ... to cover all the major aspects of policing' (Newburn 2003b: 6) illustrates criminology's focus on types of crimes (with chapters on cyber crime, drug crime and terrorism) and processes (such as under-cover policing) rather than overarching and non-crime specific police practices such as police interviewing. This book does not focus on the type of crime of the suspect, as methodologically it holds little importance in the roles of, regulations imposed upon and the fundamental maintenance of communication between the two parties. (A discussion of this methodological position follows this chapter.)

Police culture and the policing role throughout history change along with the shape and expectations of the society they watch over. The disparate media representations of policing can reflect the different social perceptions of the police (Newburn 2003b), the changing policing strategies and the attitudes towards policing through history. Recent televisual representations of policing reflect both honest and corrupt aspects of the police, from *Heartbeat*, set in 1960s Yorkshire, which poses the village policeman as the heart of the picturesque local community, to *Life on Mars* and *Ashes to Ashes*, based in 1970s Manchester and 1980s London respectively, where corruption and violence are portrayed as a normal part of the police role. For a review of fictional and non-fictional media representations of policing, see Reiner (1992: 171–203) and Carrabine (2008).

Examining police subculture provides an insight into the outlook, structure and working practices of the police. Waddington (1999) discusses 'canteen culture' as a reflection of officers tailoring their undesirable talk by directing it towards their peers rather than it showing in their public, overt policing role on the streets (Holdaway 1983; Uildriks and Mastrigt 1991). Despite much research centring on less desirable police traits such as aggression, sexism and racism, these traits do not necessarily translate to the streets (Black 1970, 1971). They do, however, appear in social activities through which relationships are negotiated, and through which those with different values are inherently excluded, such as Muslims from the police culture of drinking (Manning 1980; Holdaway 1996, 1997). Rafky (1973) found that police officers are either equally or more tolerant of civil rights than the general public, while Waddington (1999) cites studies that claim police officers are equally tolerant across academic ability and rank are more tolerant than firemen and less aggressive than social workers. The picture of police officers as covertly racist and sexist is a bleak one, with little comfort from the apparent lack of transference of these traits to their professional persona, or that such negative traits are not the sole reserve of the police (Bucke 1994; Waddington 1999).

The public have greater access than ever to the police on many levels, with access to aspects of the police through government reports and enquiries, increased transparency in policy and practice through news media (for example, 'leaked' documents (Garret 2006) and public commentary of the progress of the shooting and death of Jean Charles de Menezes in London in 2005). Additionally there have been technological advances (such as the internet as a resource, 'real-life' police documentaries on television and advances in disclosure with the Freedom of Information Act 2000 versus the Data Protection Act 1998). However, many of these sources may not be wholly accurate, as they may be edited for the purposes of entertainment, or carefully managed for damage limitation and political means, borne from the 'constant organizational need ... to maintain good relations with the public' (Clark and Sykes 1974: 463). This 'need' was famously put ahead of justice at the Court of Appeal in November 1979 where the Birmingham Six, accused of pub-bombing, appealed their wrongful imprisonment and Lord Denning (1980) judged that it would be better to maintain society's faith in the veracity of the police, had they been hanged upon their guilty verdicts, than their conviction be later proven unsafe and overturned. The following quote is from Lord Denning's (1980) judgement at the appeal of the Birmingham Six.

> Just consider the course of events if this action is allowed to proceed to trial. If the six men fail, it will mean much time and money will have been expended to no good purpose. If the six men win, it will mean that the police are guilty of perjury, that they are guilty of violence and threats, that the confessions were invented and improperly admitted in evidence and the convictions were erroneous ... This is such an appalling vista that every sensible person in the land would say that it cannot be right that these actions [the appeal against their convictions] should go any further.

Their convictions were declared unsafe in March 1991. Reiner (2003) argues the media publicize the police as bastions of social order, justice and stability. Public inquiries (such as the inquiry into the stabbing and subsequent death of Stephen Lawrence (Macpherson 1999), and the Independent Police Complaints Commission investigations into the death of Jean Charles de Menezes), and miscarriages of justice, such as those of the Birmingham Six and following the murder of Maxwell Confait (Price and Caplan 1977), suggest otherwise. In the absence of personal involvement with the police such as having been interviewed or arrested before, the fictional representations of these situations are likely to form the lay person's main experience of the police. Indeed, representations of the police are 'a potent source, reproduction and reinforcement of the myth and mystique that surround policing' (Newburn, 2003b: 4). Chapters 8 and 9 will explore one of the aspects of policing arguably most wrapped in this myth and mystique; the practices or techniques of an officer prior to a confession, and Chapters 4 and 5 challenge the more general perceptions or expectations of police interview behaviour in its investigation of laughter in this setting.

Police Interview Techniques, Training and Myths

In addition to the interactional structure epitomized in the organization of turntaking,[1] the police interview is also influenced by the legally imposed, standardized and structured procedures under the PACE Act 1984 to which the officer must adhere, or risk the interview, in part or as a whole, being ruled inadmissible. The techniques available to the officer upon interviewing suspects, however, and the training they receive to do so, are not as strictly standardized. As explored later, officers' interactional expertise can often be informed by folklore and techniques handed down from senior to junior officer. This section addresses some of these myths, explores interview techniques across different contexts, and the application and perception of police interview training. For a comprehensive exploration of the history and development of interrogation practices in the USA, see Leo (2008). Chapters 8 and 9 will then focus on more specific techniques used in the elicitation of confessions.

The 'essential elements of an investigative interview' (Powell 2002: 45) are the officers' rapport, open-mindedness and the ability to match their communicative abilities to that of the suspect's (Powell 2002). According to Baldwin (1993), an officer with a good interview technique is one that prepares, explains procedures, is even-handed, listens and responds, is flexible and in control. To be successful they have to display certain personal qualities such as intelligence, motivation, tact, self-control, an interest in and understanding of human nature (Inbau *et al.* 1986, Field Manual 1987) (hereafter FM 1987). To obtain an unhindered free-flowing response from the suspect, the officer must use open-ended questions and avoid leading or closed questions (Fischer and Geiselman 1992). Agnew *et al.* (2006) constructed a simulated police interview to examine the techniques of officers and care-givers in interviewing intellectually challenged children. It found that although officers interrupted frequently and provided few minimal responses, the use of open, non-leading questions elicited fuller responses (Agnew *et al.* 2006). This is echoed by Powell's (2002: 46) claim that 'there is no doubt among memory researchers that the mastery of an open-ended questioning style needs to be a major focus of interviewer training'.

The use of open-ended questions can also yield more accurate responses

(Dent and Stevenson 1979). Specific questions increase the rate of errors in suspects' memory recall (Powell and Roberts 2002), inhibit memory and event recall (Powell 2002), and can reduce the likelihood of eliciting accurate responses from the suspect (Dent and Stevenson 1979). Powell (2002) claims that using a specific and closed questioning technique may actually mislead the suspect, despite it being a favoured and commonly used technique of officers. Powell (2002) suggests that officers use these dysfunctional techniques because of an inability to use alternative or enhanced ones. Although there is a wealth of literature on interviewing techniques, this suggests there is a lack of standardized, evidence-based interview training, and officers receive 'remarkably little training in techniques of questioning' (Moston and Engelberg 1993: 223). Research into the 'typical' interviewing technique of the police officer (see Fischer *et al.* 1987; Baldwin 1992b; Moston and Engelberg 1993) also found officers employing a range of non-specialist techniques in training and in practice, rather than a more cohesive approach.

In Powell's (2002) review of police interview training, she revealed 'best practice guidelines' (Powell 2002: 44) are not used and posits the standardization and stricter enforcement of techniques as a solution to the various (and often poor) techniques used by officers. However, improvements in training are 'no panacea for poor interviewing standards' (Baldwin 1992b: 11), or a culture of malpractice (Maguire and Norris 1994). Baldwin found little correlation between officers' training and interview performance and that officers lack awareness of serious deficiencies and what construes a bad technique. Despite its importance, police interview training is often limited to officers learning interviewing techniques and relying on myths passed down from officer to officer (Baldwin 1992b), rather than through training in, and practicing, evidence-based techniques. Inbau *et al.* (1986) claim that traits that are beneficial to police interviewing are not necessarily encouraged or useful in other aspects of police work, which suggests that training in these techniques may not be considered a priority. 'Part of the reason for a lack of interest in training police officers in interviewing skills has been the assumption that questioning plays only a limited part in the detection of crime' (Moston and Engelberg 1993: 224).

Based on 'shared misunderstandings and tacit notions about policing' (Manning 1997: 4), popular opinions of the confession (Baldwin 1992b) are that they tend to mirror fictional representations on television shows.[2] The officer in this scenario wears the reticent suspect down with a number of elicitory steps (Inbau *et al.* 1986) including repeated questions, accusations and threats until the suspect 'turns' and the truth is eventually gleaned. Common interviewing myths include the expectation of a high proportion of suspects to be 'difficult', and that highly skilled psychological approaches are required to 'crack' difficult suspects and get a confession (Baldwin 1992b, 1993). In reality, police interview confessions are rare (Baldwin 1992b, 1993; Napier and Adams 2002), increasingly at the periphery of the interview focus (Greer 1994), and are unlikely to result from specific interviewing techniques (Baldwin 1992b). Indeed, 'a confession is often despite the officers efforts to elicit one, not because of it' (Baldwin 1992b: 14). In the same way that some criminals commit crimes simply for the thrill or the excitement of it (Katz 1988; Presdee 2000; Hayward 2004), some suspects confess in order to display their dexterity and ability to 'carry off' a crime (Ekman 1985; Shuy 1998).

Despite this, the confession remains highly sought in the police interview, even described as 'the primary purpose of most interrogations' (Hodgson 1994: 91). Hester and Eglin (1992: 135) state, 'Obviously the main aim of interrogation from the point of view of the police is to obtain a confession.' Moston, Stephenson and Williamson's (1993) research, which surveyed police perceptions pre- and post-interview, found 80% of the sampled officers declared their main purpose of interviewing was to obtain a confession, a finding echoed by Plimmer (1997). According to Moston *et al.* (1993), 75% of officers (64% according to Walsh 2006) believe the suspect is guilty before the interview has started. This turns the interview into a 'guilt presumptive process' (Kassin 2006: 214) and suggests it is often characterized by a presupposition of guilt and an insistence that protestations of innocence are lies (Hodgson 1994; Kassin 2006). Not only can an officer's presupposition of guilt have an influential effect on the interview and its outcome (Mortimer and Shepherd 1999; Kassin 2006); it challenges the presumption of innocence on which the British and American criminal justice systems depend. It also lies in stark contrast to its central premise as an information interview, and has serious implications for the protection of suspects' rights. Where innocent suspects do not confess, the officer who harbours a pre-held notion of guilt may pressurize the suspect into a false confession, or be compelled to manufacture evidence to make their assumption fit (Maguire and Norris 1994) rather than re-evaluate their original presupposition (Kassin *et al.* 2003), leaving the suspect vulnerable to an officer's unwavering insistence of their guilt. Shuy (1998) identified part of the interrogators role to identify smaller or 'part-confessions' as part of a wider confession that remains to be drawn, rather than their production being seen as discrete elicited utterances. This suggests that the officer should remain unsatisfied with the suspect's story and convinced the suspect is withholding further insights.

This final section has explored some problems in police interview training and techniques such as the lack of emphasis on training and the reliance on myths and on techniques handed down from officer to officer. The lack of wholly standardized training and the proliferation of police interviewing myths must in some way affect officers' ability and performance. In addition to many officers holding an inaccurate view of their own ability and of the premise of the interview itself, the protection of suspects' rights and the presumption of innocence are surely compromised in light of presuming guilt and focusing on extracting a confession. The other analytic chapters will explore this further; Chapters 4 and 5 illustrate how these issues present in the way laughter can facilitate deviations from the PACE Act 1984, in the officers' administrative rather than supportive provision of suspects' rights in Chapters 6 and 7, and the reality of confession elicitation techniques is explored in Chapters 8 and 9.

This chapter has outlined various sociological and criminological contributions to policing, approaches to investigating policing policies and practices from political motivations, corruption and media representations, to the history and growth of the police as an organization. Although not a major focus of police research, a considerable amount of literature has also concentrated on various aspects of the police interview. Of those there are few empirical, in-depth explorations of the verbal communicative practices of the participants in the police interview which disregard notions of innocence, guilt, deceptiveness or other value-laden phenomena. This book aims to develop understandings of the police interview, and uses CA to satisfy the demands this type of analytic focus creates.

Chapter 3

An Introduction to Conversation Analysis: History and Practice

Conversation analysis is the detailed and systematic analysis of naturally occurring recorded audio interaction which can reveal the social and organizational processes behind the creation and accomplishment of talk. The construction of talk-in-interaction reveals participants' orientations to each other, the local context in which the talk is based (such as in a police interview or a doctor's waiting room) and to the wider social context in which the local context is based. The production and management of talk is an achievement mutually produced, universally ordered and locally managed within contexts and between participants. The use of conversation analytic techniques to explore the talk in the police interview enables this research to provide a detailed and structured local investigation of phenomena within it, while maintaining a wider exploration of the real-time production and negotiation of talk in action.

CA is an inductive approach to data – that is, a bottom-up approach that does not view the data with specific questions or hypotheses in mind. Other approaches – for example, content analysis – can be applied in a deductive or top-down fashion, to test hypotheses or research questions. CA does not rely on a hypothesis or a research question; rather it is the data itself that informs the point of interest or phenomenon for analysis:

> When we start out with a piece of data, the question of what we are going to end up with, what kind of findings it will give, should not be a consideration. We sit down with a piece of data, make a bunch of observations, and see where they will go.
>
> (Sacks 1984: 27)

CA is characterized by its method of approaching data and analysis, and requires naturally occurring, recorded audio data on which particular transcription and analytic techniques are applied. The close and detailed transcription of the data is an important feature of CA, and creating a conversation analytic transcription of the data requires repeated plays of the audio in order to render as much of the detail as possible into written form.

CA has been used to explore a wide spectrum of phenomena within ordinary, institutional and multiparty interaction, from that between a stand-up comedian and an audience (Rutter 1997) to that between a doctor and a patient (Haakana 2001). Although the beginnings of CA lie in the ordinary interaction of telephone conversations (Sacks 1992) the methodology can be applied to any interactional setting. That details of the interview still remain under-explored through a conversation analytic lens could be a reflection of the complexity of the analytic procedures such as the lengthy and detailed transcription requirements and the consequent necessity to focus on smaller sets of data. The conversation analytic requirement for data to be naturally occurring and audio recorded may also have been a restricting factor in its use, as police interviews have only relatively recently been available as potential data for research purposes. Further, a historical misconception of CA as a purely linguistic methodology may have restricted its use in some areas of sociology and criminology.

CA enables the deep and detailed analysis of interaction, relying on audio-recorded talk to facilitate the repeated listening required to transcribe and analyse its prosodic intricacies, such as intonation and volume. Police interviews are a type of data that match CA's requirement for naturally occurring (defined here as not produced for the purposes of research) and repeatable audio data. Using this method also provides an innovative way of exploring aspects of police interviews that have neither been seen as areas to research, nor been analysed in this particular way. This interactional exploration of the police interview situates this research at the intersection between linguistics and sociology, and between the traditions of ethnomethodology and of the sociology of the police. The findings of this book are empirical insights into the police interview-in-action, which aim to broaden current academic, institutional and general understandings of the police interview, and aim to advance police interviewing in practice. Situating this book in a conversation analytic approach is part of its contribution to the field of policing and provides a multidisciplinary perspective which has the potential to inform areas of police interview policy, training and practice.

CA History

This empirical approach was created in the 1960s by Harvey Sacks, and developed with Gail Jefferson and Emanuel Schegloff (Schegloff and Sacks 1973; Sacks *et al.* 1974; Jefferson *et al.* 1987). Although CA began with the analyses of telephone calls to suicide help lines[3] (Sacks 1992, Vol. 1) and in the analysis of ordinary conversations, its methodological techniques can be applied to any instance of naturally occurring recorded talk in any context. Based in the ethnomethodological tradition, 'an approach that [claims it] does not appropriately fit within conventional sociological categories of either theory or method' (Roberts 2006: 90), it draws upon the 'impressive array of concepts' through which members' methods of constructing their social reality can be elucidated. Ethnomethodology challenged the orderliness of society posed by traditional sociology by claiming the *behaviour* of members, rather than their interactive contexts, are ordered and systematic, and that they are not static but accomplished through members (Goffman 1959), and that they both shape and are shaped by the interactional context (Garfinkel 1967). As Aaron Cicourel (1968: 111) explains, the '*sense* of social structure [is] contained in the actor's definition of the situation'.

Ethnomethodology arose from Garfinkel's 'self-conscious critique' (Marshall 1998: 203) of sociology at that time. Sacks and Garfinkel (1970) described the then-current trend of conventional sociological research methods as ironic, as knowledge of society was seen as the domain of the sociologist while its lay members remained 'merely players' (Shakespeare 2000: 7) in society, unable to comprehend it. The influence of ethnomethodological perspectives on traditional linguistic approaches is clear in the linguistic turn towards viewing language as a means of creating understandings of social interaction, and the use of empirical data rather than fictional exchanges. This grew from the awareness of the orderly and structured nature of ordinary, 'taken-for-granted' talk, rather than these exchanges being overlooked as unimportant and essentially a 'degenerate form of linguistic competence' (Chomsky 1965). The common-sense perceptions of society by those in it, and the emphasis on the everyday construction of members' own social being in Goffman's (1959) sociology of interpersonal interaction are epitomized by Garfinkel's (1967) breaching experiments, where those common-sense 'rules' were exposed through their purposeful violation.

Garfinkel's (1967: vii–viii) pursuit of making 'practical sociological reasoning analysable' remains at the core of CA, as does the serious attention given to the 'common-sense knowledge of social structures' (ibid.) and the ritual management and understanding of the 'performance' (Goffman 1959). This is explored on two levels in CA: through the speaker's knowledge of the interaction and its context; and also in the knowledge and interpretation of that talk by the listener (signalled through the structure of their response). This reflects the methodological concern that it should be both context-sensitive and context-free (Sacks *et al.* 1974). That is to say, while analyses of talk are not necessarily contextually related and can be reproduced across any naturally occurring data, it is acknowledged that patterns of interaction also alter according to their local parameters and the individual interaction across contexts.

The interactional 'order at all points' (Sacks 1984: 22) is reflected in the production and reproduction of social practices through talk. The premise of 'face' in conversation stems again from Garfinkel's (1967) breaching experiments, which performed early analyses of the structures of social actions. It is also informed by Goffman's (1959) work on stigmas, which showed that people cover up stigmas such as baldness or bad teeth by wearing wigs or not smiling in photos in order to align themselves with being 'normal'. Such accountability to society is reflected in the construction of accounts of actions so that those on the 'outside' can make sense of them in the way that the member intends. An example of this is somebody tripping up in the street, and then turning to look at the pavement they had just walked on to justify their stumble as part of an external impetus (the pavement) rather than a product of their own incompetence or idiocy. Such a display signals to onlookers the normality of that member of society – and this, according to Sacks (1984), is 'one's constant preoccupation, doing "being ordinary"' (414–415). So CA approaches accountability in conversation as a reflection of, and an insight into, the participants' orientation to the interaction itself and to the wider societal context in which it is produced. Indeed, 'the way that somebody constitutes oneself ... [is] a job that persons ... may be cooperatively engaged in to achieve that each of them ... are ordinary persons' (ibid.).

Sacks' analyses of such detailed occurrences in talk provided a new emphasis on the small rather than the 'big issues' (Hutchby and Wooffitt 1998: 21) in the social sciences. This gave rise to a host of research into ordinary conversation and its structure (Sacks *et al.* 1974) through the analysis of phenomena such as laughter (Jefferson 1979, 1984, 1985), silence (Jefferson 1989) and repair[4] (Schegloff 1992). This substantial attention to the mundane then sidelined, to some extent, 'extraordinary' interactional exchanges. The use of CA has broadened since these beginnings and has now been used to provide insights into wider and more specialized contexts. This is illustrated by conversation analytic explorations of a variety of contexts such as the courtroom (Komter 2003), doctor–patient interaction (Heath 1981; Have 1989;Haakana 2001) and police work (Heydon 2005; Haworth 2006; Johnson and Newbury 2006; Jones 2008; Stokoe and Edwards 2008; and Stokoe 2009a). There have been recent advances in exploring the police interview in other areas such as the conversation analytic investigation of storytelling in this context (Holt and Johnson 2006) and the discourse analytic examination of questioning strategies of the police (Johnson and Newbury 2006; Oxburgh *et al.* 2010). These include areas such as the reproduction of racial insults by officers in police interviews as quotes from witness statements (Stokoe and Edwards, 2007), and analysing the construction of denials of male suspected perpetrators of domestic violence (Stokoe, 2010).

Unlike other methodological approaches, it is central to CA that it is the participants' interaction, and not the researcher's imposed interpretation of the interaction, that forms the analysis. This difference is illustrated by Krippendorff's (2004) claims that different interpretations of the same data by different readers are *expected* to be found by different readers in their use of content analysis, stating 'an analyst's reading must never be taken as the only legitimate one' (Krippendorff 2004: 31). The strict transcription and analytic procedures involved in the application of CA mean that it can be replicated across data and contexts, and the analysis is both repeatable and open to testing by its readers. The emphasis is on the co-constructed nature of interaction, rather than on the semantics of individual words or the syntax of an isolated string of utterances. As such, it looks at the accomplishment of talk through the strategies used by the participants in their construction and maintenance of it, rather than primarily through analysing the verbal content. 'The objective of CA is to uncover the tacit reasoning procedures and sociolinguistic competencies underlying the production and interpretation of talk in organized sequences of interaction' (Hutchby and Wooffitt 1998: 14).

CA in Practice: Data, Acquisition and Ethical Considerations

The corpus of data drawn on for this research comprises 150 pre-recorded audio tapes of interviews in which one or more police officers interview a suspect arrested on suspicion of committing a criminal offence. The interviews were conducted by police officers in custody suites of UK police stations, range from 1 to 42 minutes long, and cover a wide assortment of alleged offences against person and property, from public urination and possessing a forged MOT certificate to serious sexual assault and murder.

The tapes were created between 1993 and 1996 in fulfilment of the legal requirement (PACE Act 1984, Code E, section 3) of the police to create an audio record of interviews with suspects, and not created or conducted for the purpose of research. They were from police investigations which had been concluded, and more than three years had elapsed between the date they were recorded and their release for use as research data, which is the statutory period of time the police are required to maintain the records in accordance with the Data Protection Act 1998. Police interview tapes are kept sealed (unless required for evidence in court) and are protected from release to those unconnected with the case, the chain of custody, and to those outside of the criminal justice system, for three years after they are created. At this point the tapes are destroyed. In accordance with this legislation, the tapes that were made available were destined for incineration until they were released into my possession for this research. As the tapes remain the property of the police authority in which they were created, the consent of the individual police interview participants was not required. All identifying features from the tapes were fully anonymized upon transcription, making it impossible for any people, property or places referred to in the tapes to be identified through the extracts shown in this book. All spatial and temporal references have also been changed; however, all relative times and distances remain intact in order to preserve the semantic cohesiveness of the interaction. As a further measure, the linguistic integrity of the data was preserved through ensuring all replacement words had a similar syllabic structure from the originals and that the pronunciation and production of the original words were transposed onto the anonymized versions chosen so as not to affect the intonational or prosodic features of the interaction.

The relative scarcity of empirical police interview research reflects the difficulty in accessing police interview data of this nature for academic research. The acquisition of police interview tapes for this research was a product of persistence and, as often in sociological research, serendipity (Merton and Barber 2004). It involved several months of writing letters to law enforcement agencies, telephone calls to individual police stations and ultimately calling on my legal contacts in order to secure the tapes; further details will not be made available due to considerations of confidentiality. Acquiring pre-recorded taped interviews as a data source was a release from any responsibility of deciding who or what to record, and from having any effect on the participants that may have arisen from being present, as a researcher, at the interview.

Using the conversation analytic premise, the data was approached in an inductive, rather than deductive, manner by listening to each of the tapes for any particularly interesting interactional sequences or phenomena, and then reviewing their presence in the literature. During this process I became intuitively interested in how often laughter featured in the interviews, and noted each occurrence. The 13 extracts presented in Part One were selected by first eliminating the least clear recordings, and then transcribing the remaining tapes where laughter was present, using the conversation analytic cyclic process of transcription and analysis to gain a deeper insight into the interaction (as discussed in Hutchby and Wooffitt 1998; Have 2007; and Liddicoat 2007). The final selection of extracts from those transcribed were chosen to reflect the range of laughing episodes present in the corpus, in order to maximize the ability of this research to yield results based on an as representative and as wide a range of instances of laughter as possible, rather than on the analysis of a narrow range of similar extracts. This reflects the conversation analytic premise of giving serious attention to deviant cases (Hutchby and Wooffitt 1998).

Through this process, the presence officers' orientations to the silent participant (the later listeners of the tape), and the gap in the analysis of this phenomenon in police interview literature also became apparent. References to the silent participant in the data provided an opportunity to explore this detail of the interview and gain a similar understanding of the police interview to that achieved by Drew (1992) and Greatbatch (1992) in their analyses of courtroom and news interview interaction respectively. Conducting a similar reduction of the data as discussed above, I selected as wide a range of instances as possible of the officer orienting to the silent participant. The final data for Part Two therefore consists of the 13 extracts best able to explore the range of effects of the silent participant in the police interview talk in the corpus.

The confession was chosen as a potentially analytically interesting episode in the data as a reflection of the interest in this particular aspect of the police interview by criminologists, law enforcement officers and agencies, the media and the general public. Listening to the tapes, I was struck by the rarity of confessions by suspects and also became interested in the composition of instances where, although a traditional confession in which a suspect admits to a crime was not produced, the suspect does 'confess' to something they had previously withheld or denied in the interview. This is referred to in this book as a 'confessionary turn', a fuller definition of which is detailed in Part Three. Their rarity – a total of nine confessions or confessionary turns were present in seven tapes out of 150 – necessitated the use of every example. This selection process resulted in the use of 21 tapes from the corpus overall, from which 35 extracts are presented and analysed in this book.

CA in Practice: Transcription

Creating a conversation analytic transcription is an exercise that demands repeated replaying of the data in order to accurately capture and represent fine details of intonation, volume, and other prosodic features in the talk, in addition to the utterances themselves. The transcription of the police interview data was a lengthy process; the transcriptions used in this book took approximately one to two hours for every audio minute. However, this process has been described as taking as long as five to eight hours for every audio minute (Smith and Osborn 2003) and therefore requires 'the *patience* to work laboriously for hours on end at the production of detailed transcriptions' (Have 2007: 19, emphasis in original) that provide the analyst with a written representation of the talk and the way it was spoken. The close and repeated listening of the data required to create those transcriptions also offers the analyst a deep understanding of the nuances of the data, and this itself forms part of the analytic process (Have 2007). The importance of the accuracy of the CA transcript is reflected in the rigorous transcription conventions characteristic of this approach, and this rigour makes the research repeatable and comparable to other conversation analytic research across and between interactional contexts. Transcriptions also provide the researcher with access to the intricacies of the talk without having to continually navigate the audio record.

The following extract (1.1) has been transcribed using CA techniques. It illustrates how some of the transcription conventions look in situ as part of a transcript. The full list of transcription conventions used in this book is in Appendix I. The numbering to the left of the transcript is used to identify which line of talk is being referred to, while the lettering 'S' and 'P1' show where each participant (the suspect and police officer respectively) take their turn to talk. The pauses between and within turns are shown in brackets and are measured in tenths of seconds; a full stop in brackets signifies a pause of less than two-tenths of a second. The importance of timing in CA is discussed later. Other symbols such as the up and down arrows signify where the talk immediately following that symbol is either significantly higher or lower in pitch than the surrounding talk. Slighter rises and falls in pitch are shown with an underlined colon and a colon with the immediately preceding letter underlined respectively.

1.1 CA transcription *in situ*

```
224  S     the sti:tches f↓ell ↓out
225        (0.4)
226  P1    yeah ho:w >did that< happe:n
227        (0.2)
228  S     I dunno
229        (0.6)
230  P1→   °you don't kno:w°
231        (1.4)
232  P1    isn't it true >that it was< Philip <that er> (0.4) assaulted Harry,
233        (0.6)
234  S     dunno:
235        (2.2)
236  P1    ri:ght >wh↑en you were< (.) taken to the police station this mo:rning, (0.5)
```

The transcription, however intricate, is not a substitute for the audio data; rather it is a visual representation of it (Hutchby and Wooffitt 1998; Have 2007; Liddicoat 2007) to be used alongside the audio. This addresses the impossibility of rendering every audio detail into transcript form (Hutchby and Wooffitt 1998; Liddicoat 2007). However, the transcript does remain the medium through which analyses are presented, and the method by which readers access the interaction and test the analyses. As conversation analytic convention dictates, the transcripts are shown in this book to accompany, and form part of, the detailed line-by-line analyses of the talk. This provides the reader with access to that interaction and the tools by which the analytic steps of the researcher can be tested, advancing the transparency and repeatability of the research. Where the inclusion of particular extracts referred to in the text is not practicable or necessary, they are provided in Appendix II.

The tapes were digitized and played through GoldWave, a digital audio editor computer programme that renders sounds on a spectrograph and provides a visual representation of the frequency and amplitude of speech in a waveform. Using digital copies of the tapes meant that the original data, held on tape reels, was not degraded by the continuous replaying required to transcribe and analyse the data. Using this software, sections of sound could also be looped on a continuous repeat, assisting the transcription process on a practical level. The software also enabled the sound playback speed to be manipulated, which proved useful when deciphering sections of quickly produced talk or places where the speech of several participants overlapped and individual utterances were difficult to extricate.

The following section illustrates how the visual representations of the interaction were applied in the practice of measuring pauses (also referred to as silences). In CA, pauses are timed in tenths of seconds, reflecting the serious attention given to the effect of silence – a 1-second pause for instance can signal a disagreement-to-come in the next turn (Jefferson 1989). Contrary to traditional methods of timing pauses such as listening and clicking a stopwatch when speech is heard to finish, or even counting its duration out loud (Jefferson 1989), I used the wavelength patterns produced in GoldWave[5] to locate the beginning and end of each episode of silence with high accuracy and consistency. This technique addresses problems encountered with the traditional methods, where 'one still has the problem of 'catching' the exact onset and finish 'points'' (Have 2007: 102) of the silence.

The figures that follow are used to illustrate points in the following discussion on the use of audio and mechanical means to capture points of silence in interaction. Each figure shows a visual representation of part of an interview in which an officer utters 'the date is the twentieth of May nineteen ninety four and the time is now seventeen fifteen. Tut- (silence) I must remind you darren'. The pertinent parts of the waveform are in a lighter shade. Figures 1.1 and 1.2 illustrate the location of the episode in the visual representation of the talk, Figures 1.3 and 1.4 identify the boundaries of the silence episode, the final selection of the episode for measurement is illustrated in Figure 1.5, and the effect of background disturbances is highlighted and discussed using Figure 1.6.

Figure 1.3 illustrates how the boundaries between silence and speech are not always clear cut, and are closely related to the type of word uttered before or after the silence. A plosive (such a 'p') yields a sharp contrast between it and silence; seen in the sharp increase in amplitude around 00:00:39.2 at the production of 'tut' after the silence. At the beginning of the silence, however, the voiced nasal consonant 'n' at the end of 'fifteen', is a sound produced at a lower amplitude than vowels or approximants and has a softer ending which makes it difficult to judge the end of the word and the beginning of the silence. The boundaries between silence and speech in this case are therefore determined by the subtle changes in the wavelength pattern (the wavelength becomes less regular and reduces in frequency) together with what is heard through the audio. This provides a

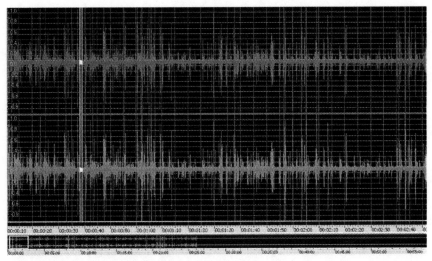

FIGURE 1.1　The silence episode in talk-in-interaction

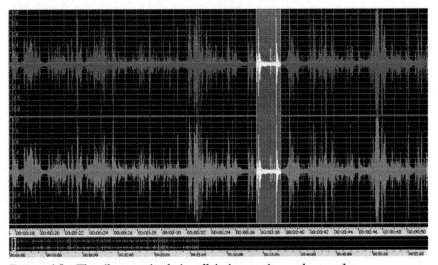

FIGURE 1.2　The silence episode in talk-in-interaction – close-up 1

clearer understanding of where the boundaries lie, which as the following figures will illustrate, is not always clear or advisable with the sole use of either method.

Figure 1.4 illustrates the difficulties in establishing the boundary between talk and silence in cases where a sharp contrast in amplitude is absent. The pale line at 00:00:38.1 illustrates the point at which speech ends and

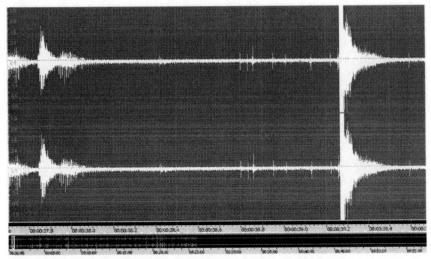

FIGURE 1.3 The silence episode in talk-in-interaction – close-up 2

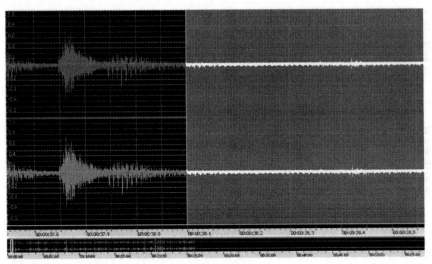

FIGURE 1.4 Establishing the start of the silence

silence begins, which I determined through merging the techniques of analysing the visual waveform and the traditional way of listening to the audio record of the talk and silence. The waveform shows subtle changes from the larger, more uniform, repetitive cyclic waveform patterns indicative of talk, to the smaller, less uniform peaks of silence. It is important to note that although the analysis of the waveform patterns affords the

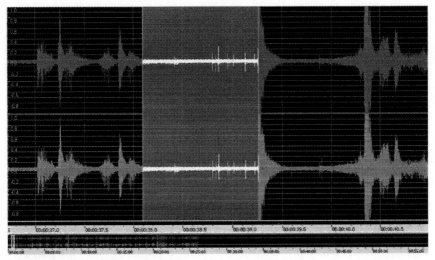

FIGURE 1.5   The silence captured

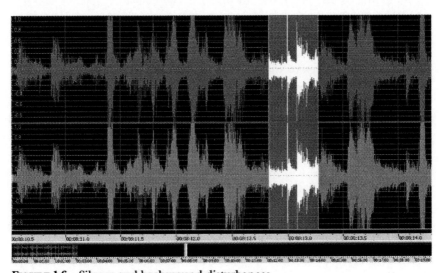

FIGURE 1.6   Silence and background disturbances

researcher greater accuracy in the exact timings of pauses, this level of accuracy often extends beyond what can be registered by ear. Situations where the vibration of the vocal cords remain after the sound appears to have diminished, mean the waveform represents 'talk' beyond what can be naturally heard in the course of interaction. Although providing an objective approach, this purely mechanical measurement of its boundaries also signifies a separation from what is naturally heard during interaction by the participants. Therefore, the pause measurement in this research does incorporate the analysis of the waveform to assist locating the cessation and commencement of talk, but is used alongside the analysis of the audio to ensure it's the diminishment of the sound to the ear that takes precedence over the relaxation of the vocal cord vibration reflected on the spectrograph. This balances the need to ensure rigorous and standardized timings with the need to attend to the reality of the silences as an interactional product of, and part of, real-time talk.

Figure 1.5 illustrates the silence captured using both mechanical and audio cues. The actual difference this type of pause timing makes may only correspond to an adjustment of hundredths of a second in real terms. However, the merging of mechanical and audio techniques in this book signals a turn towards a more consistent approach to timing pauses and comparability across research if adopted by the discipline. It addresses inconsistencies in the approach to pause timing, which can rely on often inaccurate techniques in practice, the analytic rigour of which is highlighted by Psathas and Anderson (1990) as worthy of caution: 'readers are cautioned not to interpret these timings in an overly precise fashion; not to attempt to compare, across different analyst's transcripts, the occurrence of timings of different length' (Psathas and Anderson 1990: 87). The technique developed here is also more aligned with the analytic importance attributed in CA to differences in pauses, and together with its consistency would maximize the replicability of this type of research.

Another advantage of this technique of using mechanical and audio means is that episodes of speech and silence can be extricated from background disturbances, instances of which in the corpus included the rustling of papers, long deep breaths or banging noises. These extra-interactional sounds also appear on the spectrograph and are impossible to distinguish from the output created by speech or silence. This is illustrated by the silence shown in the lighter shade in Figure 1.6.

The lighter section shows the silence in the suspect's utterance 'and the witness wasn't there then (*silence*) alright the witness was across' (from T18-16-06, line 230). The use of audio timing is necessary in this case, where the background noise of rustling of papers is indistinguishable from the utterance waveform, despite the utterance having ceased at this time.

CA in Practice: Problems and Solutions

Although CA provides an opportunity to explore police interview data on a detailed, interactionally focused level and to gain insights into its under-explored and unexplored areas, there are, as with any research, problems associated with both the methodology and the use of this type of data. These difficulties are in all probability factors that contribute to the gap in research using UK police interview tapes as data. Although the data was restricted to audio tapes of police interviews in the districts of only one police force, the ability of the reader to test the findings, and that the analyses are based on the principles of a basic, ordered, interactional structure means this research is repeatable and applicable to interaction in other forces and across other contexts.

A wealth of research into deception and false confessions suggests these are popular and well-visited areas of police interview research. The analyses presented in this book use a different approach which avoids moral or legal judgments, interpretations of the truth or guilt, or judgments on the deceptiveness or honesty of the participants. This is by virtue of both the conversation analytic framework and by the fact the police interview tapes hold no systematic written or audio record of the outcome of the cases, nor the participants' gender, class, ethnic origin, race, the presence of mental health or learning difficulties or any other extra-interactional or contextual information other than the names of those present, and the suspect's date of birth. Although the types of offences for which the suspects were interviewed are clear in the audio data, the interaction of the participants, rather than their suspected crimes, remain the primary analytic focus of this book. Tracing the use of particular communicative phenomena and mapping it to the suspects' alleged crime could be an interesting focus for future research.

Although the findings of this research have implications in police interviewing policy and practice, the analyses are not the product of debate-driven hypotheses. Rather, they are inductive and empirical explorations of the talk in action, the results of which are situated in the literature and in broader sociological and criminological debates. The analyses do not depend on the knowledge of the demographic details of the participants or other background, and the interaction is not considered more or less interesting or important in their absence. The communicative strategies in the police interview are ordered on a fundamental level beyond the 'individual variables such as personality, generation or career trajectory' (Reiner 1992: 109); factors that alter the application and interpretation of the rules of the institution (Reiner 1992). The basic 'rules' of communication are unchanged by such variables, and the use of a conversation analytic approach draws the focus to the composition, creation and maintenance of talk. The focus remains firmly on the mechanics of how the officer and suspect interact, and it is through their communicative processes and orientations that the participants' interactional identities are revealed. The impact of the absence of data beyond the talk itself is therefore limited.

The data does show how talk is shaped in accordance with the different roles created and maintained by the suspect and officer. This, however, is different from externally applied categories, such as social class, as the roles are created by and bound by the context in which they appear, and their shape is determined by, and determines, the interaction. This role-based shaping of interaction is explored throughout the analytic chapters, where the use of phenomena such as laughter can be directed towards different objectives in accordance with the differing obligations and rights of the suspect and the officer.

The data comprises audio recordings of police interviews conducted between 1993 and 1996. However, the age of the tapes and therefore their ability to address the current debates of police interviewing practices should not be a concern for two reasons. First, debates such as the conflicting interests of the officer to obtain information from the suspect and to protect the suspect's rights are still applicable. Second, as the police interview tapes are older than the current version of the PACE Act 1984, the interaction on those tapes cannot be expected to reflect or take into account legislatory changes (some of which were discussed earlier) introduced since their recording. In any case, these changes will not have, to any great extent, affected the treatment of the suspects in the specific cases in this book.

Analyses of the effect of legal requirements in this research, as a restrictive or shaping influence on the interaction, do not rely on the condition that those legal requirements are the most current legislatory mechanisms. The methodological techniques and analytic focus explore the patterns of communicative adherence to the then-current legislative requirements. The main foci of this book are the communicative characteristics of the participants and their production of phenomena such as laughter, uninitiated third turns and minimization (explored in detail later). Although it cannot provide a commentary on the tapes in relation to the current legislative requirements, this research does provide significant insights into the interactional structure of this highly constrained context. Where this research does explore the way officers deal with the (then) legislative requirements imposed upon that interaction, it investigates the relationship between the legislation and the talk of the participants. Although the research in this book was not specifically designed to evaluate factors related to current legislative requirements, it does provide a detailed and distinct analytic approach that will be applicable to research that explores current police interviewing practice alongside the current legislative requirements on that interaction. Similarly, there is also scope for comparative research that investigates the changes in these requirements through time alongside the corresponding interview interaction.

Although the use of police interview tapes provided access to the audio record of the police interview, interaction is not limited to verbal communication. Visual non-verbal communication has been anecdotally reported to constitute anywhere between 60% and 99% of all communication, and is not captured due to the audio format of the data. This discounts the possibility of analysing aspects of interaction involving body language, eye gaze, and the physical proximity of the speakers. However, non-verbal interaction is complementary to, rather than necessary for, CA analyses (Have 2007), and verbal 'leakages' such as shifts in intonation, tone, voice quality and pitch, in addition to other characteristics of talk such as slips of the tongue are available to analyse. These audio non-verbal cues can provide an insight into its interactional design (Goffman 1981). As Sacks (1984) states:

> [audio tapes] had a single virtue – that I could replay them. I could transcribe them somewhat and study them extendedly – however long it might take. The tape-recorded materials constituted a 'good enough' record of what had happened. Other things, to be sure, happened, *but at least what was on the tape had happened.*
>
> (Sacks 1984: 26, emphasis added).

CA in Practice: Turntaking

The organization of turntaking forms the basis of the construction of interaction, and that there is 'order at all points' (Sacks 1984: 22) in interaction is the bedrock of CA. The structure of the local, basic accomplishment of interaction can be a resource by which other, 'less ordinary' talk can be examined. So by identifying the structure of turntaking in ordinary conversation, the participants' business of constructing an institutionally oriented turn can be made visible:

The details of little, local sequences which at first seemed narrow, insignif-
icant and contextually uninteresting, turn out to be the crucial resources
by which larger institutionalized activity frameworks are evoked... It is
ultimately through such means that 'institutions' exist as accountable
organizations of social actions.

(Heritage 1984: 290)

This section briefly outlines the organization of turntaking as an essential
component of interaction in ordinary conversation, and introduces
turntaking in more institutional contexts. Chapters 6 and 7 will explore
this in more detail, in demonstrating how the manipulation of turntaking
can be used to accomplish specific tasks in interaction, before exposing
how it shows in the officers' orientation to the silent participant. The
'essential features of turntaking' (Boden 1994: 66, see also Sacks *et al.*
1974) in ordinary conversation are detailed in Table 3.1.

Table 3.1   Essential features of turntaking

1   One speaker speaks at a time.
2   Number and order of speakers vary freely.
3   Turn size varies.
4   Turns are not allocated in advance but also vary.
5   Turn transition is frequent and quick.
6   There are few gaps and few overlaps in turn transition

Boden (1994: 66)

Ordinary conversation is used as the 'benchmark against which other
more formal or "institutional" types are recognized and experienced'
(Drew and Heritage 1992: 19). As Sarangi and Roberts (1999: 229)
commented: 'Although Goffman developed his concepts in everyday
contexts, they apply superbly to institutional settings.' While turntaking
forms the bedrock of institutional interaction, as it does in ordinary
conversation, unlike ordinary conversation it is also heavily shaped and
constrained by the formality of the context. Modifications that the organization of ordinary conversational turntaking undergo when being used in
more formal or institutional situations include turn-type pre-allocation, as
seen in press conferences where members of the press are selected to ask
their question, and in the explicit mediation of turntaking by a chairperson
seen in debates. Greatbatch's (1988) analysis of news interviews found
that turntaking in institutional environments 'preallocates particular types
of turns to speakers with specific institutional identities' (Greatbatch
1988: 404), such as the allocation of questioning to the interviewer and

answering to the interviewee. Doctor-patient interaction (Heath 1981) also follows a prescribed format by which there is a summons, a greeting sequence, an identity check sequence, and then the initiation of the first topic. The doctor initiates each sequence, and the patient takes their cues from the doctor. Equally distinctive systems exist in courtroom interaction (Drew 1992, Atkinson 1992), where the defence counsel initiates the question-answer sequence by asking the questions, and the respondent (such as the victim or witness) is constrained to answering. Media interviews, in particular political and news interviews, are also usually highly structured in style. In the context of the police interview the turn-type pre-allocation of questioning to the officer and answering to the suspect (Watson 1990; Hester and Eglin 1992; Heydon 2005) is so important that is has been posited as a way in which power is displayed and accomplished (Watson 1990).

The central structure of the police interview shown in Table 3.2 and 3.3 illustrate the sequencing, content and structure of the opening and closing sequences, which is also echoed in Heydon's (2005) analysis of their institutionalized nature. Deviations from this general structure are attended to, as are the 'departures from the standard question-answer format ... as accountable and are characteristically repaired' (Greatbatch 1988: 404).

Table 3.2   The general structure of turntaking in the police interview opening

1   Self-introduction.
2   Interviewing officer elicits witness police officer's introduction.
3   Interviewing officer elicits suspect's introduction.
4   Temporal and spatial noting.
5   Suspects rights (1) – access to the tape (doesn't require response).
6   Suspects rights (2) – access to a legal representative (requires response).
7   Suspects rights (3) – police caution (requires response).
8   Reason for arrest.

(Carter 2003: 35)

Table 3.3   The general structure of turntaking in the police interview closing officer's actions

1   Note they have no more questions.
2   Ask if other officer has any questions.
3   Ask if suspect wants to say anything.
4   Confirming end of interview.
5   Temporal and spatial noting

(Carter 2003: 40)

Demonstrating how the rules of turntaking can be used to serve the agenda of the suspect, Johnson and Newbury (2006) analysed the police interview interaction between police officers and the suspect Harold Shipman, a doctor under arrest for the suspicious deaths of patients in his care. Using a discourse analytic approach Johnson and Newbury (2006) found Shipman used deliberate interactional strategies such as avoiding saying 'yes' and 'no', avoiding answering by retroactively labelling a question as a story, and using 'you' rather than 'I' in his answers. Shipman was then interactionally 'able' to display his power in the interview by resisting providing the officers with the confirmations or denials, responses and co-operation they required, while also deliberately avoiding the 'costs of resistance' (Johnson and Newbury 2006: 213) associated with violating the rules of turntaking, such as the dispreferred action[6] of challenging or disputing an officer's utterance.

The organization of turntaking and the sequential order of talk are vital for participants communicating understanding (Hutchby and Wooffitt 1998), and provide an insight into the intentions behind the production of utterances and how they are received. The next-turn proof procedure is an important conversation analytic technique that ensures that the analyses are accurate, repeatable and reproducible by the reader. It uses the sequential framework of talk to reveal the participants' understanding and interpretation of the previous turn. In other words, what is said by the recipient of the talk when it is their turn to speak shows their interpretation of what has just been said. This gives both participants the opportunity to monitor each other's understanding of the interaction, and to repair any misunderstanding, for instance by requesting a repeat of the previous utterance. It is through displaying understanding (or misunderstanding) in each turn that the conversation analyst can gain an insight into the participants' orientations to and their construction of talk, and can be used to reinforce the analyst's interpretation of the interaction, through using the participants' own interpretation of the other's turn. It is in this way that the investigations into laughter, confessions and the silent participant in this book use officers' and suspects' own real-time construction, interpretation and analysis of their own interaction as it happens turn by turn. The tools of CA and its in-built methodological transparency ensure the research is verifiable, repeatable and transferable across contexts, and give the reader access to the interaction as it unfolds, enabling them to go through the analyses step by step, repeat the analyses and test the conclusions reached.

Part One

Laughter

A laugh can be so much more than just a laugh. In conversational terms, it is not even a laugh; it is a serious part of conversational language.

(Billig 2005: 192).

Despite a wealth of research in other contexts, such as in ordinary conversation, in comedy venues and the interaction between doctors and patients, laughter remains under-explored in the context of the police interview. This section introduces Chapters 4 and 5 by exploring the range of research into laughter in ordinary conversation, humour in ordinary conversation and institutional interaction, and finally laughter in institutional settings. This research is then used in the following chapters to frame the investigation of the structure and uses of laughter in the police interview. These chapters present line-by-line analyses of the detail of the police interview in order to reveal how laughter in this setting is used as a tool which can be directed toward different objectives in line with the different positions, rights and obligations of the suspect and the officer. Specifically, Chapters 4 and 5 will illustrate how laughter can be used by suspects to help them in the difficult task of challenging an officer, and to reinforce the veracity of their statements. It will also indicate, in a show of salient symmetry, that laughter is used by officers to challenge the truthfulness of the suspect's version of events. Further analyses will then demonstrate how laughter is used by officers as a way in which they can circumvent the strictures of the PACE Act 1984 without being challenged. This research therefore has the potential to provide police officers and other practitioners with additional insights into interview techniques and the verbal and non-verbal interactional strategies available to them in the interview room.

Laughter punctuates interaction, but its production and maintenance in talk is a collaborative experience between participants that is 'distinguished from other non-speech sounds in that it has, for participants, the status of an official conversational activity' (Jefferson *et al.* 1987: 156). Despite 'no one seem[ing] to know quite what to do with laughter' (Provine 1997: 159), a significant body of literature focuses on what laughter is used to achieve. It is considered an important and recurrent part of conversational interaction, constrained and co-ordinated on a finely tuned level (Jefferson 1979, 1984; Jefferson *et al.* 1987) rather than simply an involuntary response to humour. Indeed, 'it does not occur in a simple and 'natural' way' (Billig 2005: 189), but it is co-ordinated and complex; the possible variety of prosodic characteristics alone, or the ways it can be produced, render the interpretation of laughter a complex and detailed undertaking. This is reflected in the changes in the ways laughter has been transcribed conversation analytically – from laughter being represented as ((laughs)), to increasingly detailed transcription practices in which laughter is represented in a more phonetic fashion which reflects different types of laughter such as bubbling-through and full laughter, and captures a wide variety of manners of articulation. Bubbling-through laughter is laughter that is produced during the articulation of an utterance, while full laughter is the production of laughter separate from the other utterances. Descriptions of the different types of laughter and their transcribed forms are shown in Appendix I.

Typically located after a laughable event in the prior turn (Sacks 1992), laughter reveals much about the participants, as does the organization of turntaking and other interactional phenomena such as the orientation to the silent participant, discussed in the introductory chapters and explored in detail in Chapters 6 and 7. As a 'coherent, shared achievement' (Glenn 1989: 146), laughter in ordinary conversation can be used to 'maintain group loyalty or to gain group acceptance' (Giles and Oxford 1970: 97ff), enable talk about troubles (Jefferson 1984), affirm or distance relationships (Glenn 1995), or used to create intimacy between participants (Sacks *et al.* 1974). Glenn (1991) and Critchley (2002) state that laughter is a way in which participants create, maintain and monitor their interaction, which in turn is what shapes the social world around them; for example it is used to show alignment with someone who is telling them about a complaint, or used to challenge that very complaint (Edwards 2005). There are specific laughing techniques, such as laughing after an utterance or laughing after a pause in which the addressee(s) failed to laugh, in order to elicit reciprocal laughter from the other participants (Jefferson 1979). Laughter in ordinary conversation can also provide an opportunity for a participant to take the floor in the next turn (Schenkein 1978), or be used to interrupt the current speaker without violating the rules of turntaking. It therefore helps maintain social order by identifying and 'smoothing over' complaints, disagreements or potentially offensive or embarrassing talk (Brown and Levinson 1987; Billig 2005). It can be used to alleviate difficulties such as those associated with the act of complaining; it helps the teller make light of complaints by showing that they are 'ok' and distances the teller from 'being a complainer' by presenting their talk as information rather than a personal difficulty (Edwards 2005).

Laughter can also be used to attend to drifting attention, something that is most obviously noticed in the wandering eye gaze of a listener during conversations, by extending the length of the utterance until the eye gaze is returned (Goodwin 1981). It can also be used as a response in itself (Jefferson *et al.* 1987); illustrated by the semantic similarity in the statements 'he laughed when I asked him out' and 'he said no when I asked him out'.

Laughter and humour are part of an implicit social understanding. This is evident, for instance, in the interaction between the teller and recipient of a joke (Critchley 2002). Analysing the interaction between the stand-up comedian and the audience, Rutter (1997) found audience laughter is part of a systematically and socially managed structure of interaction. This is not the sole reserve of comedy club interaction; in institutional settings such as doctor's surgeries, laughter has also been found to indicate humour (West 1984). Although not necessarily synonymous with laughter, humour is similar in that it can help people explore relationships by 'putting out feelers' (Goffman 1959: 191) and test the social climate and acceptability of a situation (Graham *et al.* 1992; Norrick 1993). Humour can help people display acceptance or rejection (Drew 1987; Glenn 1995), or help them to mitigate breaches of social etiquette or the production of dispreferred actions such as complaining (Morreal 1983). Davies (1982, 1988, 1991) shows that humour can be used as a way of recognizing and maintaining stereotypes of social groups, for example linking women from Essex with the brazen behaviour and vacuous nature of the 'Essex girl' in the jokes. This illustrates that even in these conversational or joke-telling settings, group laughter can be used to set, form and shape social boundaries by including (as a mark of social solidarity) or excluding others.

Similarly, humour in institutional contexts can also be applied to tasks associated with the demands of that context. Malone (1980) suggests humour can be used as a tool to increase the effectiveness of communication in the workplace and O'Quin and Aronoff (1981) cite humour as an influential tool which can be used in negotiations to increase financial gain. Speier (1998) posits that the use of humour in politics can more easily persuade the recipient of the argument in hand. The use of gallows humour or *l'humour noir* (Critchley 2002), such as humour among female sex workers (Sanders 2004) and police officers, can be a used as a coping mechanism; revealing much about the importance that laughter can hold, and the influence of the context in which it is produced. Critchley (2002: 88) describes this type of humour as the 'anaesthetization of death' which enables those in emotion work (Hochschild 1979) to cope with psychological trauma and moments of extreme stress (Alexander and Wells 1991).

The analysis of laughter in contexts in which it is not expected or sought, such as in institutional or morbid settings, as opposed to the 'expected' laughter of ordinary conversation or comedy club interaction discussed above, provides an insight into how it is used as an interactional device. It reveals much about the structure of that context and the rules and roles of the participants within it. Unlike ordinary conversation, which can quite ordinarily take place over the telephone, in the dark or shouted from a speaker in one room to a listener in another, many institutional interactions must occur face-to-face. It is the differences between conversational laughing practices and those that are produced as part of institutional talk that can reveal much about the constraints of the contexts and about the participants' roles. There have been recent advances in the exploration of laughter in police interviews through Stokoe and Edwards' (2007) work on complaints. Laughter is also discussed in Stokoe and Edwards' (2008) research into 'silly' questions and in Stokoe's (2009b) work on officers' self-disclosure to suspects. However, despite these advances, the treatment of laughter as the sole focus of research in this context remains relatively unexplored.

Similar to ordinary conversation discussed earlier in this section, laughter in institutional contexts can enable less dominant participants to produce utterances that reject some aspect of the dominant participant's turn, for example it can facilitate the production of dispreferred actions (Haakana 2001) in client-therapist interaction (Buttny 2001). It can also be used to 'soften socially improper utterances' (Gronnerod 2004: 36) and make communication easier in more difficult moments (Mulkay 1988). Similarly, Stokoe (2009b) found in police interviews laughter can mitigate the lack of affiliation associated with not responding adequately to a question. This suggests that laughter can be used as a communicative tool in institutional contexts, by enabling the participants to produce utterances that may otherwise be difficult or unacceptable due to their role in, or the constraints of, the context. Osvaldsson's (2004) research on laughter in youth detention homes has shown that laughter can draw frame certain aspects of the interaction as sensitive and this can be used to help avoid interactional difficulties between the workers and the youths. It is also used to focus the attention on the content of the complaint rather than the complainant (Stokoe and Edwards 2007).

According to West (1984) and Haakana (2001) it is the more subordinate of the participants that is typically the main and sole laugher; the more dominant participant reinforces their position of power by subordinating the laugher through not reciprocating their laughter. Such asymmetry of laughter is 'typical of institutional conversations' (Gronnerod 2004: 34); however, where there is joint laughter in the police interview, it can build and reinforce the relationship between officer and suspect (Stokoe and Edwards 2008) and be used by officers to align with the suspect's account (Stokoe 2009b).

By examining research into differing institutional contexts it is clear that, in addition to laughter reflecting the humour of a situation, there are also uses of laughter specific to, and defined by, the individual roles and requirements of the interaction in that context. The following two chapters examine where and how laughter manifests in police interviews, and will explore the presence of context and role-specific uses of laughter – for instance, by a suspect to facilitate a disagreement with an officer. Although certain elements of conversational interaction may be present in police interview interaction (as it is in other institutional settings), the chapters that follow will show that laughter in the police interview is used differently from laughter typical of ordinary conversation. For example, due to the strictures of the context laughter cannot be produced, as in ordinary conversation, as an acceptance of a laughter 'invitation' (Jefferson 1979) by the speaker. In the same way that the uses of third turns in institutional interaction discussed in Chapters 6 and 7 are shown to be specific to the police interview, Chapters 4 and 5 propose that uses of laughter in the police interview also differ from those traditionally associated with other types of institutional interaction. They will show that this laughter is produced and shaped in accordance with the differing orientations and roles of the participants, the objectives of the particular interaction, and the rules imposed upon that interaction by the criminal justice system. It is through establishing the use of laughter as a tool and by examining what it is being used to accomplish that this research can provide insights into both the context and into the objectives and constraints of the participants.

As the conversation analytic method involves studying sequential patterns of talk, it is intuitive for analyses to be managed and arranged in terms of action. However, the following two chapters are organized by examining the uses of laughter of suspects (Chapter 4) and officers (Chapter 5). They have been categorized by participant for several reasons, which it is important to detail here for clarity. Upon analysing the laughter present in the police interview tapes it became apparent that, with one exception, laughter is not reciprocated, meaning that in this work, the sequential study of laughter in police interviews does not mean the study of sequential laughter. Moreover, it became apparent that laughter formed distinct uses by officers and suspects, and presented a striking symmetry that lent itself to this grouping, where an action-based grouping simply did not. Finally, the uses of laughter of suspects and officers have separate implications for training and educational purposes, and the findings can be directed appropriately.

The chapters look at the general uses of laughter by the participants (such as to highlight or comment on some aspect of the immediately prior turn), as well as how each participant then employs that laughter as a tool to support their position and role in the interaction. Chapter 4 will show how laughter can provide the suspect with an additional method of expressing their innocence, truthfulness and other assertions that, when expressed lexically in this context, may not necessarily be believed. It is also used to mitigate dispreferred actions such as avoiding answering a question or producing a turn that contradicts the officer. Chapter 5 will show how laughter also affords officers an additional method of communication; it can be used to challenge the suspect or to mitigate the production of utterances that may otherwise be restricted or prohibited by the PACE Act 1984.

Chapter 4

Buttressing Innocence and Challenging the Officer: Suspect Laughter in the Interview

The suspect occupies a particular role in the police interview, and as an individual arrested and questioned on suspicion of committing a criminal offence, it is typically understood not to be a position of power. Although the suspect, unlike the officer, is not constrained by the codes of the PACE Act 1984, the suspect must still comply with certain requirements of the interview. For instance the suspect must, when questioned, account for incriminating evidence found upon their person (The PACE Act 1984 Code C, section 10c, paragraph 10.10) or risk their silence being used against them in court. They are also constrained by the nature of their role as a suspect; for example, protestations of innocence do not necessarily contribute towards an officer's understanding of events. Occupying this role also makes disagreeing with an officer, avoiding answering questions and other interactionally dispreferred acts such as not co-operating more difficult.

This chapter will show that, in addition to laughter being used to highlight some aspect of the immediately prior turn, the suspect also uses laughter to buttress their position of innocence in this setting. Extracts 1–6 illustrate the different ways in which this is accomplished; to reduce their culpability by distancing themselves from the crime (extract 1), to highlight an officer's statement as incorrect (extracts 2, 3, 4 and 6), and to avoid answering the question (extracts 5 and 6). The ambiguity of the laughter in extract 6 means there are two interpretations given for this extract (the alternative interpretation is labelled 6i).

Extract 1 is from an interview of a suspect who, after the police found drugs in his wardrobe, was arrested on suspicion of possessing amphetamines. The officer's question 'How long do you think it's been in your wardrobe?' (line 110) is significant as it is linked, by the suspect's admission in the prior turn (lines 107–108), to when he had last used the drugs, and therefore it has the potential to be used in further questioning to help identify their source. The suspect answers the question with 'months' (line 112). The officer does not respond to this, and after a pause the suspect makes a self-initiated self-repair (see 'Repair' in the glossary in Appendix III) of his first answer, by issuing a close repeat of it ('mo(hh)nths probably', line 114). The suspect's use of laughter during this repaired repeat, together with the addition of the word 'probably', retroactively reformulates his first response into a less precise answer.

Extract 1: Drugs in the wardrobe (i)

```
105   P1   why do you think it might be sp↓eed
106        (0.6)
107   S    cu:z (0.6) >over the par-< I've took it before and like it might just be: (0.3) from
108        when I've taken it and thro:wn it (0.5) >an like I↑eft it there< from ages *↓ago
109        (0.9)
110   P1   >ho:w long< do you think its been in your wardro:be
111        (0.8)
112   S    monthS:
113        (0.7)
114   S →  mo(hh)nths probably
115        (0.6)
116   S    coz I havent done it in about three months,
117        (1.6)
118   P1   wh↑o does it belong to:
119        (2.0)
```
(T22-20-06)

The use of laughter and 'probably' in the suspect's repaired answer emphasizes that the drugs had been there for a long time and creates a vagueness around the time that had elapsed since his last contact with them. This reduces the culpability associated with the suspect knowing the exact details of how long the drugs had been in his possession (and indeed that they still were), as well as distancing him from the possibility that they are still in use. This distancing is also performed verbally by the suspect in his previous utterance 'ages ago' (line 108); his laughter through this repaired answer is also a non-lexical enactment of the literally laughable period of time the drugs had been in his wardrobe. Although, in this case, the laughter is not used to disagree with the officer (as in the later extracts 2–4), it is used by the suspect to display his reaction to the charge as laughable, as if the drugs had been there for so long that even he had forgotten their presence. This is supported by the suspect's later statement that he had indeed forgotten the drugs were there.[7]

The pause on line 115 is indicative of the officer not responding to the suspect's reformulated answer. The suspect's provision of a more precise answer 'three months' on line 116 then suggests the suspect has interpreted the silence as an indication by the officer that his earlier, vaguer answers had not adequately answered his questions. Following another silence on line 117, the officer's turn to a different topic on line 118 signals a return to the questioning and indicates the conclusion of that episode. The officer does not directly respond to the suspect's answer by mentioning it or by requesting clarification, which suggests the suspect's answer is sufficient.

The following extract is from the interview of a suspect who has been arrested on suspicion of assaulting his wife. It opens with the officer reading a statement made by the suspect's wife in which she claimed she was hit on the head by the suspect. The suspect responds by claiming it was he who was hit on the head by his wife.

Extract 2: Hit on the head with a statue

```
420   P1   >but she can< hear the object breaking into smaller piece:s >I
421        think originally she said she thought it was a< bottle (0.8) but later on
422        she's found a small statue (0.2) which is broke:n
423        (0.5)
424   S    ↓hm[m
425   P1      [in the house and she's assumed its tha:t (0.3) i[s that ri:ght
426   S                                                        [↓yeah
427   S →  n(hh)o I-I I've had the statue over my: head
428        (0.9)
429   P1   have you got any ↑injuries to your head
430   S    yes (0.5) your doctor (0.6) °pointed them out°
(T29-31-06)
```

The suspect's laughter (line 427) follows the statement read by the officer in which the wife alleges the suspect had hit her over the head. The suspect uses the laughter to signal the mistaken, indeed laughable nature of the content of this statement in the prior turn. This is supported by the suspect's production of the contrasting account 'I've had the statue over my head' (line 427). This use of laughter echoes Haakana (2001) and Buttny (2001) who show patients using laughter to reject doctors' turns.

The laughter is also used to deflect the dissafiliative consequences of contradicting an officer, similar to Morreal (1983), Jefferson (1984),

Brown and Levinson (1987) and Billig (2005). This is shown in the suspect's bubbling-though laughter physically breaking up the word 'no' and softening and distorting its output. The stuttering, self-repaired start to this production of the suspect's alternative account 'I-I-I've' similarly suggests, in its delay of the statement-to-come, the dispreferred nature of his answer. As described by Hutchby and Wooffitt (1998: 45), 'preferred actions are characteristically performed straightforwardly and without delay, dispreferred actions are delayed, qualified and accounted for'. The suspect's laughter buttresses his innocence by framing the officer's account of his guilt as physically laughable. In doing this, the suspect also uses laughter to mitigate the production of an alternative account that differs from the ones provided by the officers.[8]

The silence of line 428 shows that the officer does not immediately respond to the suspect's laughing answer. Unlike extracts 5 and 6, the officer does not then go on to request a further explanation from the suspect, and therefore the silence does not appear to indicate the suspect needed to expand on his answer. In his turn (line 429), the officer asks a question based on the suspect's statement. He does not attend to the suspect's laugh or laugh in response, which suggests the laughter was not taken to be reciprocal by the officer, but as part of the suspect's turn.

Although not accompanied by the production of an alternative account as seen in extract 2, the suspect in extract 3 also uses laughter to support his position of innocence while mitigating the dispreferred action associated with contradicting an officer. The extract is from an interview with a suspect who is being questioned on suspicion of assaulting two men the night before, first inside and then outside a public house. In the interaction prior to this extract, the suspect has denied striking the man inside the pub, and the officer has established that the suspect was deemed by a doctor to be too drunk to be interviewed at the time of his arrest. In the extract, the officer suggests the suspect's consumption of alcohol prior to the offence may have compromised his memory of the events of that night.

Extract 3: Nah

```
329   P1    >i:sn't it< the case tha:t (0.5) <perha:ps e:rm> (.) >you've had so much
330          to drink that you< can't remember what's happene:d
331          (0.6)
332   S     n(hh)ah >..hh<
333          (0.7)
334   P1    why no:t
```

335   (0.4)
336   S   coz I we̱:ren't that dru̱:nk
(T11-80-06)

The suspect laughs on line 332 in response to the officer's suggestion that the suspect's excessive drinking has led to a loss of memory of what happened on the night of the assault (lines 329–330). The officer's question is significant as the suspect must either remain consistent with his earlier accounts of his relative sobriety and disagree with the officer's comment, or risk implicating himself by providing a response that contradicts his earlier assertions. What the suspect does is draw attention to the laughable nature of the officer's question, using laughter supported by his denial 'nah' (line 332). The suspect's laughter, similar to the laughter in extract 2, facilitates his disagreement with the officer; the use of laughter during his utterance 'nah' literally breaks up the word and softens its production. The laughter could also be indicative of the repetitive nature of the officer's question as the suspect has, during the course of the interview, denied being drunk that night on several occasions.[9] That the laughter was produced at this point and not during the suspect's earlier denials suggests it may have been used to strengthen the veracity of the denial as a retroactive measure to address the fact that his earlier assertions of sobriety were disregarded.

In common with the other extracts, the officer does not take his turn following the suspect's laughing response, shown in the pause on line 333. This absent turn suggests the officer requires or expects a further response or explanation from the suspect. This is supported by the officer's explicit initiation of one ('why not', line 334), when that further response or explanation is not automatically provided. The officer does not topicalize the suspect's laughter by referring to it explicitly, but does attend to the answer in that turn by initiating a clarification of it, which shows it is not responded to as an invitation to laugh (as in ordinary conversation, Jefferson 1979), but is received as part of the suspect's turn.

The use of laughter to facilitate the production of an alternative account is also shown in the following extract (extract 4), where the suspect, arrested on suspicion of breaking and entering a shop, is being questioned about how close to the scene of the crime he had been. The laughter is produced during the account that follows the utterance 'no' ('not anywhere at all near there', line 149), rather than through the word itself as seen in extracts 2 and 3.

Extract 4: Anywhere near there

```
138  P1   ..hh as you've come out there you've turned left o;nto Tyne so you've
139       started walking u;p Turne:r (.) and (.) >you've got the shops on your right
140       hand side< (.) the (.) LowPrice store:s dry cleaners: newsagents on your
141       right hand side haven't you
142       (0.2)
143  S    yeah
144       (0.9)
145  P1   did you go anywhere near there
146       (0.2)
147  S →  no
148       (0.4)
149  S    not anyw(h)here at all near there
150       (0.2)
151  P1   not anywhere at all
152  S    no (0.5) jus- (0.8) out of the subway and round the co;rner
```
(T2-111-06)

The officer asks the suspect if he had been 'anywhere near' (line 145) the parade of shops where the crime had taken place. This, the first of the officer's questions of the interview directly related to the suspect's opportunity to commit the crime, is significant as it has the potential for the suspect to implicate himself in his response. The suspect's first response 'no' (line 147) is followed by a pause, which is indicative of the officer's turn not being taken. Similar to extract 1, the suspect's provision of a supplementary turn on line 149 suggests that the suspect has interpreted the officer's silence as a signal that more explicit information is required from him. The suspect's subsequent provision of a more comprehensive answer on line 149 then explicitly incorporates the officer's question in its production. The laughter is produced as part of the suspect's second, upgraded response, where he partially repeats the officer's question 'anywhere near there' with an insertion that strengthens his denial; not only was he not 'anywhere near there', but he was 'not anywhere *at all* near there' (line 149). This draws attention to the potentially implicatory nature of the officer's question, similar to the suspects' use of laughter in extracts 2 and 3, 5 and 6. It is used by the suspect to buttress his position of innocence by highlighting the suggestion of having been near the scene of the crime as physically laughable. The laughter, on a further level, and similar to extracts 2, 3, 5 and 6, is also used to support and reinforce the suspect's denial, but is also used to ease its dispreferred turn shape, as described by Jefferson (1984), Brown and Levinson (1987) and Billig (2005).

The officer's response to the suspect's laughing turn does not attend to or reciprocate the laughter, rather, as in the above extracts, he responds to the content of the suspect's turn by producing a third turn repeat ('not anywhere at all', line 151) which elicits the more specific answer from the suspect from line 152 onwards.

While extracts 2, 3 and 4 have shown the suspect using laughter to mitigate the dispreferred action of contradicting an officer, the following extracts (extracts 5 and 6) show the suspect using laughter to mitigate the dispreferred action of avoiding answering the officer's question, and the lack of co-operation associated with this. The interaction shown in extract 5 is from later on in the interview from which extract 1 was taken. The officer attempts to elicit details, such as what the drugs are and where the suspect bought them. First the officer states the drug they found 'looks like speed or amphetamine' (lines 126–127) and then asks what else it could be. This is a significant question, as it requires the suspect to respond by either declaring or denying knowledge of the drug. Instead the suspect responds by producing bubbling-through laughter through his answer 'gluc(hh)ose' (line 129). This laughter is used by the suspect to highlight the leading nature of the officer's question.

Extract 5: Drugs in the wardrobe (ii)

```
122   P1    can you remember where you got °it fr↓om°
123         (0.4)
124   S     n*ah
125         (4.5)
126   P1    >you say< >I mean it< >its ce:rtainly< (.) it's a white powder< and it looks like (.)
127         speed or amphe:tamine to me: (0.9) is there anything else >that it< could be:
128         (1.5)
129   S →   gluc(hh)o:se
130         (1.6)
131   P1    °right° but you tell me you think its spe:ed
132   S     yeah its not (0.2) >nothing more than speed or<
(T22-20-06)
```

The suspect's provision of a literal answer to the officer's question (line 129) shows the suspect's lack of co-operation in answering that question. The suspect's initial unwillingness to respond is seen in the pause on line 128, and when he does respond, his laughter is used as a way to avoid answering and incriminating himself in response to the officer's leading question. This is supported by the content of the suspect's answer, 'glucose';

a facetiously literal answer, which shows the suspect is unwilling to provide the answer the officer is seeking. The suspect's laughter is used to allay this deliberate mismatch between the intent of the officer's question and the response that he, the suspect, provides. The laughter presents his turn as a joking episode (laughter to indicate humour has been discussed by West, 1984) rather than as a serious answer to the question in the serious framework of the interview. In doing so, the suspect mitigates the dispreferred action of avoiding providing a serious answer to the officer's question.

The silence after the suspect's turn (line 130), in which the officer does not take a turn, suggests the suspect has not answered her question sufficiently, and highlights the suspect's answer 'glu(hh)cose' (line 129) was not interpreted by the officer as a serious answer. This is seen in the officer's next turn on line 131, where, after the suspect fails to take another turn, she then asks a direct question in order to elicit the information she required. That the suspect did not fill that pause (line 130) with a further explanation or a serious answer supports that he had used the non-serious talk as a method of avoiding answering and self-incrimination. The officer then continues without topicalizing the laughter; however, the fact that she reformulates her prior leading question into a direct question (line 131) suggests the suspect's use of laughter, which highlighted its leading nature, has been understood as such and has been subsequently repaired by the officer.

The use of laughter to mitigate avoiding answering an officer's question is also shown in extract 6, which is from an interview of a suspect arrested in the street earlier that evening for the possession of cannabis. There was a scuffle at the scene and, after causing a tear to the arresting officer's coat, the suspect was also arrested for inflicting criminal damage. In the extract the officer attempts to establish if it was the suspect's intention to give the drugs to anybody (line 152). This is a significant question, as it can determine whether the suspect is guilty of the far more serious crime of possession of the drugs with intent to supply. The following analysis of the interaction poses two possible interpretations of the laughter that ensues: the single paragraph which contains the second, alternative account is labelled and referred to as '6i' for ease of reference. In the first account, detailed below, the laughter is interpreted as being used to highlight the officer's potentially implicatory question (of line 152) as laughable, whereas in the alternative explanation, the laughter is interpreted as being framed as a joking response by the suspect as a way to avoid answering the question.

Similar to extract 5, the suspect's laughter highlights the potential for self-implication in answering the officer's question of the previous turn (line 152). The laughter in the suspect's response to the officer's question of whether she was using these drugs to supply others draws attention to that question as laughable. The laughter is used to indicate the humour (West 1984) of the officer's suggestion, and highlights it as ludicrous enough to provoke a bout of laughter – used to support the suspect's position of innocence of this suggested additional crime. The laughter accompanies her denial, which, interestingly, appears to be based on the logical premise of there being an insufficient quantity of drugs to sell, rather than on the basis that she would not commit that crime (line 153).

Extract 6: No deal

```
147   P1    so BASICALLY >I MEAN IVE< (.) >arrested you for being in possession
148         of cannabis< which you admit to hↄaving (0.2) >and you're saying that
149         you-< (0.4) had- (.) that- (.) to smoke for yourself is that corre:ct
150   S     mmh↑mm
151         (0.5)
152   P1    rↄight did you intend on (1.1) >giving it< to anybody e:lSe
153   S →   kh-he th(h)ere's no:t enough (.) °°sorry°°
154         (0.4)
155   S     nah
156         (0.3)
157   P1    no:
158         (1.2)
159   P1    >what d'you mean< there's not enough
160         (0.4)
161   P1    well how much >would you say< was the:re
162         (1.4)
163   S     °I°-dunno
(T31-27-06)
```

After the laughing episode the suspect, very quietly utters 'sorry' (line 153), pauses and then takes another turn in which she directly answers the officer's question with 'nah' (line 155). That the suspect apologizes suggests she has assessed her laughing episode as inappropriate or wrong in some way. The pause following that turn (line 154) is indicative of the next turn not taken by the officer and suggests, as discussed earlier, that the suspect has not responded to the officer's satisfaction. That this is interpreted as such by the suspect is supported by her subsequent provision of the direct response 'nah' on line 155. This retroactively attends to her earlier answer by providing the 'real' answer to the officer's question, although this does not alter the suspect's original answer (line 153) as a response to the negative.

This production of another (in this case serious) answer after the officer's silence is similar to extracts 1 and 4. The officer does not topicalize the laughter of the suspect's initial response; however, the suspect's turns are responded to as separate turns by the officer. This is shown in the officer's responses to the suspect's first and second answers on line 159 and line 157 respectively. The officer responds first to the suspect's second answer by repeating her answer 'no'. She then, in her next turn, attends to the suspect's first answer by reformulating that answer into a further question (lines 159 and 161); avoiding mentioning the laughter but drawing on the suspect's apparent knowledge of drug quantities. The officer rejects the suspect's laughter and non-serious response by displaying her interpretation of the suspect's laughing account as part of serious talk, achieved through both her lack of topicalization of the laughter and through her requests for clarification.

6i

Alternatively, the 'sorry' issued by the suspect on line 153 may be indicative of the suspect continuing the humour of her answer by retroactively framing the officer's question on line 152 as a personal request for some of the cannabis, and then apologizing to the officer for not having enough drugs to share with her. Despite the possibility of this alternative explanation, it does remain in either case that the suspect's laughter is used to draw attention to the potentially incriminating nature of the immediately prior turn of the officer. In this alternative case, however, the laughter is interpreted as being used by the suspect to situate her answer in a non-serious framework, through which, similar to extract 5, she avoids seriously answering the question and mitigates her lack of co-operation with the officer. The pause after the suspect's turn remains, as in the above account, indicative of the officer pausing for the suspect to produce a further answer. Additionally, despite the possible ambiguity of the 'sorry' on line 153, the suspect's next turn (line 155) retains the negativity of her original, laughing response.

The ambiguity about which interpretation is most accurate remains, as the next-turn proof procedure of CA (the method of clarifying the intent and receipt of utterances, see Chapter 3) is unavailable due to the officer's response not providing sufficient enough an insight to exclude one or other of the above accounts.

Discussion: Suspect Laughter

These analyses show that laughter is used by the suspect to highlight and respond to some aspect or combination of aspects of the immediately prior turn – for example, their mistaken (extracts 2 and 3), leading or implicatory (extracts 3, 4, 5 and 6), obvious or repetitive (extract 3) nature. This reflects how laughter in ordinary conversations is 'tied in a most powerful way to the immediately prior utterance' (Schenkein 1972: 365), and is also reminiscent of Sacks' (1992, Vol. I, Lecture 14) discussion of laughter being positioned after a 'laughable' event. Although this illustrates similarities of police interview laughter to characteristics of laughter in ordinary conversation, differences such as the lack of reciprocal laughter are also evident. In ordinary conversation, laughter is usually reciprocated to display social solidarity (Jefferson 1979). However, as illustrated by Stokoe and Edwards (2008) and Stokoe (2009b), joint or reciprocated laughter is not the sole preserve of ordinary conversation. They found that where joint laughter is present in police interviews, it demonstrates and creates affiliation between the officer and suspect. Reciprocal laughter is almost wholly absent from the data, but the analyses illustrate how laughter is drawn as a communicative resource; in the case of the suspect, it is used to support their account.

On a further level, suspects use laughter to buttress their position. One way in which this is accomplished is by suspects using laughter to help them produce dispreferred actions such as challenging the officer's prior turn (extracts 2, 3, 4 and 6). This is seen in Haakana (2001), who identifies laughter as a way in which patients can produce rejections of doctors' turns, and Buttny (2001), who cites laughter as one of the tools available to the client to enable their production of a contrasting account to that of the therapist. Extracts 2, 3, 4 and 6 also show the suspect using laughter to strengthen the veracity of their denials, while extract 1 reveals laughter being used by the suspect to reduce his culpability by distancing himself from the crime. This buttressing is also shown in extracts 5 and 6, where the suspects use laughter to avoid producing an incriminating or dissafiliative answer that could damage their position of innocence. It is see alson in extracts 2, 3, 5 and 6, where the suspects frame the officer's prior utterance as 'silly' or a joke, which then accounts for their own lack of a serious response to it. This is reminiscent of Stokoe and Edwards (2008), who discussed laughter as a way in which speakers acknowledge that the question they are about to ask is obvious or 'silly' (although this chapter shows the suspects using laughter to assign that label of 'silliness' to the officer's question, rather than it being used to do so on one's own question). The use of laughter to deflect the production of a dissafiliative response is similar to the findings of Morreal (1983), who identified humour in ordinary conversation as a way to mitigate dispreferred actions or breaches of social etiquette, and Jefferson (1984), Brown and Levinson (1987) and Billig (2005), who discussed laughter as a tool to 'smooth over' disagreements. Similarly, Gronnerod (2004) found that laughter can be used to facilitate problematic moments in institutional interaction such as in disagreeing with a higher status participant. This shows that, despite the differences in the interactional basis, design, obligations and participants, there are also commonalities in the uses of laughter in police interviews to those in other contexts.

This chapter has shown there is a variety of uses of laughter which are suggestive of uses traditionally associated with both conversational and institutional interaction, which, similar to the analysis of the officers' orientation to the silent participant in Chapters 4 and 5, reflect the mixture of conversational and institutional aspects in police interview interaction. However, it has also revealed that the interactional makeup of this setting differs from both ordinary conversation and other types of institutional talk. In those differences, the rules of the context, the obligations and understandings of this setting, and the roles of the suspect and the officer are revealed. The differences in the uses of laughter in the police interview from laughter in other contexts reveals the distinctiveness of the police interview as a type of institutional talk. However, the similarities also reveal the interaction in this setting to be more akin to ordinary conversation than common understandings of the police interview might dictate. This research can provide officers with further insights into the potential range of uses of laughter as a non-lexical tool. Laughter can be used by suspects to create a particular representation – for example, to support their position, and as part of a useful, ordered and systematic part of the suspects' interactional toolkit. This can be used in training to help understand the presence of, and potential uses for, further interactional cues in communicating with suspects. Although this book does not claim to provide a blueprint of the uses of laughter, it does examine the ways in which laughter can be used by suspects, and can provide officers with information on interactional strategies they can use that could widen the scope and capability of their interviewing practices. In exploring the uses of officer laughter, the following chapter could provide officers with a wider understanding of how they can use and expand their *own* interactional design on a further level to broaden their own communicative capabilities in the police interview.

Chapter 5

Officer Laughter: Challenging the Suspect and Breaking the Rules

Police officers operate under different constraints from the suspect in the interview, as they are subject to the legal as well as institutional constraints of the setting. The main legal constraint the officer must adhere to is the PACE Act 1984. As discussed in Chapter 2, this is a legislative framework that governs the conduct of the officer, a breach of which may result in the interview, or part of it, being ruled inadmissible as evidence. It is the officer's responsibility to ensure that the interview is conducted in accordance with its codes of practice – for example, by stating the suspect's right to legal advice and giving the suspect an opportunity to clarify or add anything prior to closing the interview. This chapter examines laughter produced by officers in the police interview and shows how officers laugh in a similar way to suspects – that is, as a way to highlight some aspect of the immediately prior turn. It will also show how laughter is used by the officer to navigate the legal and interactional constraints of the context and the objectives of their role. This is shown in officers' use of laughter to mitigate the production of utterances that may breach the codes of conduct (extracts 7–10) or to support a challenge of the truthfulness of suspects' versions of events (extracts 11–13).

Laughter to Mitigate Potential Breaches of Protocol

It is one of the suspect's rights to decline to comment in response to any question in the interview, and as such the officer must not attempt to dissuade the suspect from exercising that right. The extracts in this first half of the chapter show how officers can use laughter as a mitigating tool to facilitate utterances that may potentially breach the PACE Act 1984 codes of conduct in their responses to suspects' uses of 'no comment'. The first of these (7 and 8) are from an interview of a suspect arrested for the theft of petrol from a petrol station forecourt and for being in possession of a stolen car, following a long distance high-speed police chase. At this point the interview has been running for almost 10 minutes, during which the suspect has made no comment to all of the questions put to him. In the following exchange, the officer (P1) attempts to ascertain whether the suspect will respond in the same way to all future questions. The suspect responds with 'no comment' (line 60).

The position of the laughter (line 61) suggests it is used by the officer to draw attention to the immediately prior turn (as in ordinary conversation, Sacks 1992, and as found in Chapter 2). The officer's laughter is used to highlight this turn as an unusual response to a question to which 'no comment' would be nonsensical. Indeed, the suspect's turn is one in which he answers 'no comment' to a question about whether he is going to answer 'no comment' to further questions. The suspect's 'no comment' is not produced in response to a potentially implicatory question, or even one pertaining to the crime, to which this answer may then be usefully, or more usually, employed. The officer's use of laughter is supported lexically by his statements 'he can't even say yes to that' (line 61), and later 'it's not quite a catch question you know' (line 66, extract 8).

Extract 7: No comment to that

```
58    P1    okay is it your intention (0.5) to: (0.3) offer no comment to (1.8) any further
59          questions ..hh I should put to you (0.4) with regard to this matt⌊er
60    S     °no comment°
61    P2 →  tk- he can't even say yes t⌈o that eh hu hu hu he he ha ha
62    So                               ⌊>mr. gou<- mr. gould will be exercising his right to
63          silence obviously yes
64    P2    okay
65    P1    okay
(T19-26-06)
```

The officer's utterance on line 61 is significant as issuing a comment on the suspect's use of 'no comment' could constitute a breach of the codes of conduct. While on one level the laughter highlights an aspect of the prior turn, on a further level, the laughter that accompanies his utterance (line 61) is also used to mitigate the potential breach of PACE (1984) associated with that utterance. The laughter, having not begun until after the solicitor's interruption, may therefore be being used by the officer, after the onset of the solicitor's utterance, as a reparative measure to attempt to absolve his production of the (then reprimanded) utterance. Laughing after the potentially breaching utterance has been produced illustrates the officer's attempt to retroactively situate that utterance as a time out from the institutional rigours of the interview. In other words, the laughter is used by the officer to facilitate his production of that utterance by situating it as a conversational aside separate from the interview interaction and its rules rather than as a direct challenge of the suspect's talk. This is supported by the officer's use of the third person singular 'he' to refer to the suspect at this point, rather than the second person 'you' which the officer uses for the remainder of the interview, and which identifies the suspect as the addressee.

The officer's use of the interactional properties of laughter to mitigate utterances is further illustrated when we consider the interruption in the above extract occurs *prior* to the officer's laughter and therefore the utterance was produced without laughter being present to account for it. In the following extract from the same interview, the officer's comment (line 66) on the suspect's use of 'no comment' *after* laughter is successfully produced and unchallenged by the solicitor. This suggests that laughter can successfully mitigate an utterance that potentially breaches PACE (1984) when produced prior to the utterance, or before sanctions are articulated.

Extract 8: What's the catch?

```
65    P1    okay
66    P2→  hhha its (.) not quite a ca- (0.2) catch question you know >yeah go on< (0.4) so:rry
67          (1.0)
68    P1    I've got nothing else in that case as you've er (.) declined to comment to far, (0.5)
69          and your solicitor has said that you will be exercising your right of silence
70          throughout, I've got nothing else ...hh (1.2) .hh >that I consider it's worth asking<
71          you at this stage, unless my colleague's got anything that he'd like to say
72          (2.5)
73    P2    °no°
(T19-26-06)
```

The officer's laughter (line 66) revisits the topic of the suspect's earlier 'no comment' and is again used to highlight this use of 'no comment' as an unnecessary response to his administrative rather than crime-related question. This is explicitly supported by the officer's statement 'not quite a catch question'. This use of laughter defends its prior and reprimanded use on line 61 by retroactively accounting for its production by highlighting it and making its use explicit. The laughter is not reciprocated by the other participants; the pause after the laughter on line 67 shows this opportunity to reciprocate remaining untaken.

The interaction in extracts 7 and 8 shows laughter being used to attempt to situate utterances as conversational or separate from the normal rigidity of this institutional talk. This suggests that laughter can be used to mitigate, and perhaps therefore facilitate, the production of utterances that may otherwise be potentially prohibited in the police interview. The following extract shows the officer using laughter *itself* as the response to the suspect's use of 'no comment'.

In extract 9 the suspect is being interviewed following her arrest on suspicion of theft and deception after she had been caught using stolen cheques to purchase goods. In the extract the officer, after opening the interview by reading the suspect her rights and confirming her identity, goes on to attempt to establish terms of address. The officer laughs after the suspect refuses to answer and produces a 'no comment' response to his polite aside on how she would like to be addressed (lines 31–32). As with the laughter in extracts 7 and 8, the position of the laughter (line 35) immediately after the suspect's turn suggests it is produced by the officer in response to the content of that turn (of line 34). Another similarity to extracts 7 and 8 is the laughter highlights that turn as an unexpected and nonsensical response – in this case, to a 'housekeeping' question unnassociated with the crime and devoid of the potentially implicatory connotations that may ordinarily compel a suspect to state 'no comment'. However, the officer's laughter is not accompanied by an explicit comment on the suspect's use of 'no comment' – unlike extracts 7 and 8. Rather, as seen in Jefferson *et al.* (1987), the laughter is used *as* the comment in itself, thus avoiding the production of an utterance that potentially breaches PACE (1984). Indeed, although the officer is laughing in response to the suspect's prior turn, he is not questioning it; in fact, he deems it 'okay' (line 35). This is similar to Osvaldsson's (2004: 517) work on the use of laughter in network conferences in youth detention homes, where 'laughter ... provided both lay and professional participants opportunities to participate meaningfully in the flow of talk without actually expressing much through words'. Despite the power of this non-verbal phenomenon, if this part of the interview were to be used as evidence in court, it would most likely be in transcript rather than audio form, and the transcript would strip such interactional information from the exchange. This would mask the officer's challenge to the suspect's use of 'no comment'; in fact, with the officer's use of 'ok, ok' (line 35), it would suggest the officer supports it.

Extract 9: What shall I call you?

```
26   P1   you do not have to say anything unless you wish to< do so (0.[.h]3) but anything
27        you say (.) may be given in ↓evidence (0.2) do you understand tha:t
28        (0.2)
29   S    °yes°
30        (0.3)
31   P1   °okay° tha:nks (1.2) no::w (.) you were ori:ginally arrested (0.5) ker >is it
32        alright if I call you< kerry: o:r (.) what >d'you prefer< to be ca:lled
33        (1.5)
34   S    no c↑omme:nt
35   P1→  ↑h::::: ((wheezy laugh)) h(h)o(h)k(h)ay (0.2) o(h)k(h)ay, (0.4) E:RR (1.7) you were
36        ori:ginally arrested on the sixth of a:pril this ye:ar (0.3) errm (.) fo:r (.) on suspicion of
37        two offences of decept↓ion (0.[.h]3) and that is that yo:u (0.4) <on that date> went into
     (T30-25-06)
```

On a further level, the suspect's 'no comment' (line 34) represents a rejection of the officer's attempt at a friendly aside and marks her response firmly within the serious framework of the police interview, and not in line with the more conversational framework of the officer's question. The officer manages that rejection by responding to it as laughable in some way and then explicitly situates his response to the suspect as part of non-serious interaction to indicate the humour of the situation (West 1984). This is perhaps as a retroactive reparative measure as a result of his earlier attempt at a friendly aside unexpectedly being received in a serious, institutional way, and deals with the mismatch between his politeness (lines 31–32) and the 'no comment' offered by the suspect. It also highlights the episode as an aside from the interview, as after its production the officer signals the return to the serious business of the interview by repeating the utterance he had made immediately prior to the aside ('you were originally arrested', line 31), again on lines 35 and 36.

In extracts 7, 8 and 9 the officers' use of laughter to mitigate an utterance that potentially breaches PACE (1984) has been made transparent through the officer responding to the suspects' 'no comment'. However, the laughter in extract 10 is used to mitigate a more subtle potential breach of PACE (1984) in the officer pressuring the suspect to confess. Extract 10 is from an interview of a suspect arrested on suspicion of the theft of a video and computer games from a video rental store. The items were reported stolen after they had not been returned to the store several weeks after they were due. The interview has been going for about 30 minutes, and the suspect has continuously denied having anything to do with the crime. Prior to this extract the officer had offered the suspect some reasons why he may have kept the items and suggests that, for whatever reason they were taken, the suspect should admit it so they can 'get this all cleared up'.[10] The officer's statement on line 616 continues this theme by implying that he believes the suspect knows more than he is claiming to know.

Extract 10: Very annoying

```
616   P1   I th↑ink you know what it's ab↓out
617        (1.5)
618   S    no:, [I (.) <I find it> very ann↓oying that I've been dragged out of b↓ed
619   P1        [>it's g<
620   P1   ↓mmm
621   S    you kn↓ow
622        (0.3)
623   P1→  I mean I: find it very °ann-° h..h..y- anno(hh)ying as we:ll >yo:u kno:w<
624        (0.6)
625   S    h..u:r...
626        (0.3)
627   P1   >co:uple of< video games and (0.3) vide:os, >or whatever,<=
628   S    =°wha:te:ver ye:ah°
629        (0.6)
630   P1   °I° just wa:nna get this matter cleared u:p and I th↑ink you know a bit
631        more abo:ut i:t tha:n what you're >letting o:n<
(T18-23-06)
```

The suspect responds by stating his annoyance at being 'dragged out of bed' (line 618). The officer's laugh on line 623 is in response to this, shown through his close repeat of the suspect's turn 'I find it very annoying'. His laughter is used to highlight the unexpected nature of the suspect's earlier turn, in which the suspect chooses to express annoyance about being questioned rather than submit a defence to the officer's turn.

On line 627 the officer states his own annoyance, possibly as a result of the lack of success of his repeated requests for the suspect to admit his role in the incident, such as 'you've hired the computer game and for some reason ... you just haven't bothered returning them' (lines 593–594) and 'I just wanna get this matter cleared up and I think you know a bit more about it than what you're letting on' (lines 630–631).[11] It is also used to highlight the discrepancy between the suspect's repeated, strenuous denials and the minor level of the crime, which is supported by the officer's accompanying statement 'couple of video games and videos, *or whatever*' (line 627). It is also used to challenge the suspect's complaint (Edwards 2005), but also, displaying similarities to the suspects' use of laughter to soften dispreferred actions, the officer's laughter produced during his utterance literally breaks up and softens the officer's expression of annoyance. It mitigates an utterance that could be seen as annoyance at the suspect not confessing, and therefore could be seen as an attempt to pressurize the suspect to confess.

So far, this chapter has shown that laughter is used by the officer to navigate the legal constraints imposed on him/her in the police interview, by facilitating or mitigating his/her production of utterances that potentially breach PACE (1984). The extracts that follow will also show the officer using laughter as a facilitative tool. However, rather than being used to negotiate the *institutional* constraints of the codes of conduct, as seen above, the laughter in the following extracts is used in the navigation of the *interactional* constraints associated with the role of police officer. It will show how officers can use laughter to support their position in a manner reminiscent of the suspects' use of laughter to support their innocence in Chapter 4.

Laughter to Challenge the Veracity of the Suspects' Version of Events

The suspect in extract 11 has been arrested on suspicion of possessing a stolen car. The extract opens with the officer summing up the suspect's version of events.

Extract 11: You're not a garage

```
575   P1    dave (1.2) never met before (1.3) turned up at your derelict (0.8)
576          workshop (0.9) with no (.) car equipment in it at all (1.5) with fifteen
577          grand car (0.8) and says to you (0.5) >°I want the plate< I want the car
578          sprayed° (1.7) he then leaves a fifteen grand car with a total stranger (.)
579          with the keys (0.6) not at a proper garage (0.5) yeah=
580   S     =well tha- (.) they are pretty well kno↓wn like
581          (0.5)
582   P1    yea:h
583          (0.7)
584   P1→  well y↑ou're not hh.. (0.2) y(hh) ou're not a g(h)ara:ge ( ) are yo:u
585          (0.2)
586   S     ..hh (.) no well the sprayers were in my yard you see >they the[y've<=
587   P1                                                                    [but
```

588 S   =moved out (0.4) I can <u>prove it alright</u> if y[ou need me to
589 P1   [yeah (0.4) but you're not a
590   garage: y[ou've got no signs so he's left a fifteen (0.4) grand car with a=
591 S   [°no: no no no°
592 P1 = total stranger (0.4) yeah (1.3) an asked you to do some work on it (1.0)
(T1-67-06)

On lines 575–579 the officer juxtaposes the suspect's version of events – the man who owned the car drove it to the suspect's garage and left it with him to spray paint it – with the fact that the suspect's garage was derelict and had no signs identifying it as a garage. In his next turn, the suspect attempts to dispute this challenge to the veracity of his story. He does this by using 'well' to signal his disagreement with the prior turn (see Pomerantz 1984 and Holtgraves 1997, 2000) and then offering an explanation that the garages near his building 'are pretty well known' (line 580). The officer then responds to this by using bubbling-through laughter to draw attention to the laughable nature of the suspect's explanation.

The officer's laughter is also used as a retroactive measure to reinforce his earlier challenge of the suspect's story (lines 575–579), which is perhaps symptomatic of the suspect, on line 580, not resolving the officer's concerns. The laughter displays the officer's doubt of the truthfulness of the suspect's account; this is supported by both the officer's raised intonation 'you're' (line 584), which shows the officer emphasizing his challenge of the suspect's account, and by the content of this challenge, which makes it more explicit. This content 'you're not a garage are you' (line 584) shows the officer issuing another strengthened challenge to the suspect's explanation following his earlier one (lines 575–579) not eliciting the required or expected response from the suspect. It makes the officer's argument more explicit by stating although there are other garages in that street, the *suspect's* premises do not constitute a garage. The suspect then continues to dispute the officer's challenge by responding to the content of the officer's turn ('no well ...' line 586), without mentioning the laughter. The officer uses laughter in a similar way later on in the same interview (extract 12), when he questions the suspect about his claim that he had driven in the (stolen) car to Pottington, a seaside town, the previous afternoon in order to try and find the man who had left the car at the garage.

Extract 12: Offshore boating

```
694   P2                    [first of all you didn't get permission to drive it down to
695         Pottington (0.4) you went there looking for him and spent ten minutes
696         looking for him
697         (1.1)
698   S     well we- once he's not there there's no point in staying there w[en-
699   P2                                                           [>well he
700         could've been out and about couldn't h↑e<
701         (0.7)
702   S     >yeah but no but the boats< you can see em like you know they're there
703         (0.2)
704   P2 →offsh(hh)o;re how are you going to see him if he's out and about
705         (1.3)
706   S     no that's what I'm saying I was waiting f- (.) bout ten fifteen minutes there
707         an there was (.) all the boats were in (.)[there was no
708   P2                                       [if you'd been serious about
709         looking for the geezer you would've been there in the morning and you'd
710         stayed there all da;y
(T1-67-06)
```

In his first two statements (lines 694—696 and lines 699–700), the officer challenges the suspect's story that, after arriving in Pottington and looking for the man for ten minutes, he decided to leave. Both of these challenges are responded to by the suspect who issues explanations in response (on lines 698 and then 702). On line 704, the officer then laughs following the suspect's response to the second of his challenges; the response being that he (the suspect) could tell that the man was not there by looking at the boats. The officer uses laughter to highlight this response as mistaken or laughable and on a further level it is used to facilitate the officer's production of this direct challenge to the suspect's utterance. Although the officer has previously issued challenges of the suspect's story throughout this interview, it is only during a similar repeat of the challenge issued earlier on lines 699–700 that the officer laughs. This suggests that the officer's laughter is used in part to facilitate his production of a repeated and strengthened challenge in response to the suspect's explanation. This is supported by the officer's accompanying statement 'offshore? How are you going to see him if he's out and about' (line 704), which explicitly challenges the suspect's prior answer that he could see all the boats (and as such could tell whether the man was there or not). The content of the suspect's response 'no that's what I'm saying' (line 706) suggests the suspect has also perceived the officer's turn as a repeated challenge to his version of events, although, as in all of the extracts in this part of the chapter, he does not topicalize the laughter.

Later in the same interview (extract 13), the officer implicitly calls the veracity of the suspect's version of events into question by again summarising some of the suspect's earlier responses (lines 804–806).

Extract 13: Complete idiot

```
804  P1    ..hhh your statement of story is that some geezer's turned up (1.7) left a
805        fifteen grand car (0.4) at a place that's not a garage (1.4) without any
806        contact number and says (0.4) do some work on it
807        (1.5) ((pen click))
808  S     I can only tell you what's happened can't I (.) I can't (0.2) make stories u:p
809        (1.5)
810  P →   hh. hh.. as f(h)ar as I'm concerned you're probably saying we're almost
811        a complete idiot (0.2) inni (0.3) in a fifteen >gra- I< certainly wo[uldn't=
812  S                                                                        [oh no no
813  P1    =leave a fifteen grand ca:r
(T1-67-06)
```

That the officer's turn is an implicit challenge to the suspect's version of events is illustrated by the suspect's response, in which he stands by his story (line 808). The suspect does not dispute the officer's concerns of the incongruities of the story, but asserts the events as true. This shows the suspect's interpretation of the officer's turn (of lines 804–806) as a challenge to his version of events rather than as a request for further information. The officer then responds to that turn by explicitly calling the suspect's story into question (lines 810–811 and 813), which suggests the suspect's answer has not sufficiently addressed the officer's concerns.

The officer uses laughter to draw attention to the immediately prior turn, in which the suspect maintains his version of events, as literally laughable. It is used as part of a challenge of the truthfulness of the suspect's turn, supported by the officer's statement that believing the suspect's story would make him and the other officer present 'complete idiot[s]' (line 811). The suspect's repeated and overlapping denial in response to the officer's laughing turn (line 812) shows his strenuous refutation of the assertion that he is lying or making an idiot of the officer. His lack of topicalization of the laughter suggests he does not interpret the laughter as reciprocal, but as part of the officer's utterance.

Discussion: Officer Laughter

The analyses have shown that the officer, similar to the suspect, uses laughter to highlight some aspect of the immediately prior turn, such as it being incorrect (extracts 11, 12 and 13), unexpected or nonsensical (extracts 7, 9, and 10) or laughable in some way (extracts 7, 9, 10, 11, 12 and 13). The exception, extract 8, is a continuation of the laughter of extract 7, and its presence is in part related to that first laughter (line 61, extract 7) having not accomplished the intended action of mitigating the officer's utterance. As found with suspect laughter in the previous chapter, there is no reciprocal laughter present in the above cases. This means the laughter is not used in this way to create a relationship between the participants, as discussed in Stokoe (2009b). However, it is used in the performance of particular objectives by officers, enabling them to mitigate possible breaches of PACE (1984) by situating the utterance as a 'time out' from the serious business of interviewing, suspending the prescribed rules of the interaction and deferring them to a conversational framework. That is, officers use laughter to situate the utterance in a non-serious framework, which enables them to produce implicit (extract 9) or explicit (extracts 7 and 8) comments on the suspect's use of 'no comment', or to produce a comment without rebuke (extract 10) that may otherwise constitute a breach of protocol. It can be used as a retroactive reparative measure to mitigate that possible breach after it has occurred (extracts 7 and 8), or used as communication in itself which performs that breach (extract 9). In striking similarity to suspects' laughter in the previous chapter, the laughter in the extracts in this chapter demonstrates how officers also use laughter to frame the immediately prior turn as 'silly'. This has similarities to the work of Stokoe and Edwards (2008), although they discussed laughter as a way of acknowledging one's own question about to be asked as obvious or silly, whereas here laughter is used to identify the other participant's turn as such.

Conclusion to Part One

Part One has shown how both the suspect and the officer use laughter as an additional communicative tool in the police interview. Although it may appear tautological to claim laughter is used by the participants to demonstrate the laughable properties of the prior turn, it reflects Sacks' (1992) and Schenkein's (1972) findings on laughter in ordinary conversation (as discussed in Chapter 2), and it is simply identified here as a primary use of laughter through which secondary tasks can then be accomplished and masked. Although similar to laughter in ordinary conversation, there are also key differences present in police interview laughter. The context of the police interview renders uses of laughter such as to affirm relationships (Glenn 1995) or to create intimacy between participants in conversation (Sacks *et al.* 1974) less accessible than in ordinary conversation. Laughter is also not used as an invitation to laugh (Jefferson 1979); all of the extracts show laughter is not topicalized or responded to in that way by the recipient. When laughter is met with a pause, this behaviour further suggests the recipients' lack of alignment with the laughter. The lack of reciprocal laughter suggests, similar to Haakana (2001), and unlike Jefferson (1979) and West (1984), that the laughter was not intended for reciprocation, but to perform a specific action in the interaction. The lack of reciprocal laughter in the data means that it is not used to create affiliation between the participants as illustrated by Stokoe and Edwards (2008) and Stokoe (2009b), but both chapters have shown that laughter is employed to perform particular interactional tasks, and that these tasks are participant-specific.

Although both suspects and officers use laughter to draw attention to some aspect of the immediately prior turn, it can be used to perform secondary tasks beyond this. It can be employed to facilitate the production of utterances that might otherwise be problematic. This reflects Schenkein's (1978) findings that laughter can be used to interrupt a speaker without the customary breaches of turntaking this ordinarily entails, and Gronnerod's (2004: 36) claim that laughter can 'soften socially improper utterances'. While these 'improper utterances' for both suspect and officer are those that violate the interactional rules, for the officer they can also be ones that violate the legal rules of this setting. This suggests police interview participants direct their laughter towards different objectives in accordance with the differing positions, rights and obligations associated with their respective roles. However, in addition to the different objectives to which laughter is directed, both the suspect and the officer are also shown to use laughter to accomplish *similar* tasks, which suggests their objectives as officer and suspect are more alike than perhaps traditionally expected. This is illustrated by the uses of laughter in extracts 2, 3 and 4, where it is used by the suspect as a way to strengthen their position of innocence, and used in extracts 11, 12 and 13 by the officer to strengthen their challenge to the suspects' version of events.

The participant-specificness of the further uses of laughter uncovers the personal, interactional and institutional requirements of the participants and of the context. The projection of innocence or the avoidance of self-incrimination reflects the inclinations and requirements that may be usefully attributed to the role of the suspect, as a person arrested and being interviewed on suspicion of committing a criminal act. Their subsequent use of laughter to present, enhance, or to avoid damaging their version of events reflects the requirements of that role. Similarly, the suspect may defend themselves from potentially incriminatory utterances or accusations by the officer in the interview, and such defences, despite their dispreferred turn shape, can usefully be described as part of the suspects' interactional repertoire. The suspects' use of laughter to aid the rejection of the officers' turns is similar to their management in ordinary conversation (Jefferson 1979, Jefferson *et al.* 1987), and echoes Haakana's (2001) finding that laughter is used by patients in the rejection of doctors' turns in doctor-patient interaction. Laughter being used to signal a time out from the rigours of the interview echoes Mulkay's (1988) humour which signals a type of 'unreality' in which the participants can draw attention to difficulties encountered in the talk and communicate more freely in difficult moments. The act of laughing by interviewers in telephone surveys (Lavin *et al.* 2001) is comparably orientated; a departure from the serious business of interviewing. It also reflects the suspect managing their personal need to defend their (image of, or actual) innocence, and their interactional need to mitigate the dispreferred act that the defence entails. The officers' role in the interview, however, comprises their establishment of the facts of the crime and the suspects' part in it, which traditionally entails the officer challenging the suspect's version of events.

Lee (1997) suggests that differences in status between the interviewer and interviewee lead to the participant with the lower status laughing less frequently. For West (1984) and Haakana (2001), it is the participant with the institutional affiliation (the interviewer) who holds that higher status and the interviewer's refusal to laugh may be a result of their reinforcement of subordination of the other participant, or a tool to avoid the rapport that shared laughter brings. The extracts in previous chapters also show this asymmetry, as all but one extract involve unreciprocated laughter; however, the interviewee is not predominantly the main and sole laugher. Although officer laughter does appear to be less frequent than suspect laughter in the corpus (out of 67 instances of laughter, 25 were produced by the officer – 37% of cases), this does not reflect a profound bias. This shows that despite similarities, there are also key differences between the uses of laughter in the police interview and other institutional contexts, which suggests that both the frequency and uses of laughter are modified in accordance with the context.

The differences in officer and suspect laughter, while perhaps not particularly surprising considering the contrasting roles they hold in this context, do illustrate that laughter has many applications, which can be modified or directed to accomplish different actions. The examination of what the laughter is used to achieve in the police interview provides an insight into the objectives of the speaker, and the rules imposed upon participants in this context.

Chapters 4 and 5 challenge traditional understandings of laughter by illustrating its use as a tool which can be applied in different ways from laughter in other contexts, and in different ways by the officer and the suspect. Displaying similarities to O'Quin and Aronoff (1981) and Speier's (1998) laughter as a tool to influence others, and Malone's (1980) analysis of workplace humour increasing communicative effectiveness, laughter in the police interview has been revealed to be a useful part of the communicative toolbox of both the suspect and the officer. It has implications in the suspect's presentation of innocence and also in the officer's circumvention of the suspect's rights. These findings could inform police training and raise the serious issue of how they can be used effectively to avoid sanctions in a breach of the spirit of the PACE Act 1984 codes of practice.

The current lack of empirical analyses that focus on laughter in police interviews could be indicative of a perception that this particular aspect of interaction does not occur in this context, or where it is understood to be present, it might be deemed unimportant or unable to provide insights into the interaction or the phenomenon. The gaps in evidence-based research and police interview training also preserve the perception of laughter in this setting of interviewing officers (if considered at all) as solely a natural, unintentional, conversational phenomena, rather than as a tool with huge potential and an equally huge warning sign attached to it. This chapter has illustrated its application as a tool by the suspect and the officer, and it has provided an insight into, not only the structure of police interview interaction and its legal and institutional constraints, but also the communicative and personal responsibilities and requirements that accompany the roles of suspect and officer. Perhaps most seriously, the research has revealed that laughter can be used, without immediate detection, by officers in the circumvention of the PACE Act 1984 codes of practice. This less explicit or non-verbal challenge that laughter can mount on the suspects' rights remains hidden beyond the interview room and can continue into the courtroom. This is the result of a combination of the rarity of playing tapes as evidence in court, and the transcription processes subsequently used to represent the taped interaction, which usually strip the non-lexical parts from the interaction. This highlights the potential for such phenomena to compromise the protection of the suspect and their rights, without detection or challenge within the police interview and beyond.

Part Two

The Silent Participant

While the previous two chapters revealed how laughter can be used by officers and suspects to accomplish particular tasks in their interaction with each other, the following two chapters look at the phenomena used by officers to accommodate the wider audience which is not physically present. Chapters 6 and 7 investigate how the presence of the tape recorder in the police interview affects the interaction it is used to record. In the police interview, the tape recorder represents the future listeners of the tape: an audience (also referred to as the silent participant and the overhearing audience) comprising members of the criminal justice system such as legal advisers, members of the court and the jury, as well as supervisory officers. As Reiner (1993: 13) states, 'police officers are accountable to internal supervisory officers for their conduct with respect to the rules of law and the police disciplinary code'. These chapters examine how the production and design of officers' talk is shaped to recognize and accommodate these future silent participants. They also explore what effect the officers' accommodation of the wider audience has on the dynamics of the local interaction between the officer and the suspect.

From the design of the opening sequences of counsellor–client and doctor–patient interaction (Heath 1981), to the design of news interview talk for an overhearing audience (Heritage and Greatbatch 1991), institutional talk is orderly. The use of specific language in institutional environments affects the participants' orientation to the talk (Drew 1992; Shuy 1993; Butters 1993). Atkinson *et al.* (1978: 113) describe the type of talk by participants in meetings as a method to 'achieve and sustain the meeting as a social setting'. It is this orientation to talk that shapes and is shaped by the institutional nature of the context, and is 'centrally and actively involved in the accomplishment of the "institutional" nature of institutions themselves' (Hutchby and Wooffitt 1998: 145). Although the effect of the silent participant on police interview talk is under-explored, it is possible to gain insights into this phenomenon and frame the exploration of how it manifests in the police interview by drawing on the fundamental communicative structures of interaction, and the effect of the silent participant in other institutional contexts. This principle is echoed by Maynard (1989: 130), who states of his findings that 'if these points are true about the ethnography of plea bargaining, they may also apply to studies of other kinds of institutional interaction'.

While the talk in police interviews is essentially a private exchange (albeit one that may be heard later in court) conducted 'behind closed doors', in other institutional contexts such as the news interview, the audience is considered the primary addressee (Greatbatch 1992). The talk is 'overheard' by parties that do not necessarily contribute verbally to the interaction, but who are integral to its outcome in various ways. This is seen in courtroom interaction (overheard by the jury) and in interviews on television and radio (overheard by the studio audience and those receiving the broadcast). In police interviews, the tape recorder both represents and facilitates the later listeners of the interaction.

Drew (1992: 495) states 'the structural feature that talk in (cross-)examination is designed for multiparty recipiency by nonspeaking overhearers can immediately be seen to have certain consequences for sequential patterns and activities in the talk'. This study of cross-examinations between the prosecuting attorney and a witness identified the attorney's use of a third turn in the interaction as a way of communicating to the silent participant (the jury) through the turntaking structure. The uninitiated third turn, constructed by repeating pertinent facts and explicitly questioning responses (see extract 1.2), addresses the fact that the jury does not, unlike ordinary conversational interaction, display understanding and ask questions (Drew 1992). Members of the jury 'have a legal right ... which they almost never exercise – to ask questions during a witness's examination' (Drew 1992: 517, footnote 3). In effect, the third turn is a reflection of the presence and behaviour of the silent participant. The different ways in which the silent participant is oriented to and accounted for in the speakers' talk highlights the differences between institutional interaction and ordinary conversation, as well as the differences between institutional settings themselves.

Extract 1.2. The uninitiated third turn in a courtroom question-answer sequence

1	Attorney:	Uh now, Sergeant ((name)), was the print put on these before the
2		shotgun shell was fired or after?
3	Witness:	Before it
4	Attorney: →	Before?
5	Witness:	Yes sir

(Drew 1992: 476)

However, the pre-allocated structure in institutional environments can also be manipulated; for instance, a prosecutor can present an unfavourable impression of a witness or victim in court and then disable their ability to correct it by using the fact they cannot challenge that impression as they are restricted in terms of what turns they have available (Drew 1992).

Uninitiated third turns (also referred to as third turns) are extra turns taken by the interviewer after the interviewee has responded, in which the interviewee's response is repeated. In the courtroom, the uninitiated third turn represents an attorney's only opportunity to highlight the prior turn of a witness, as repeats of questions are disallowed in courtroom questioning (Drew 1992). The design of the talk is tailored to the third (overhearing) party by the participants and reveals the interactional orientation of the speakers. This is seen in interviewers omitting tokens characteristic of ordinary conversation, such as news receipts and assessments (like 'oh' and 'good' respectively), from their responses to the interviewee's answers in news interviews (Heritage 1985; Greatbatch 1988). This actively distinguishes the interviewer's role as elicitor, rather than recipient of, the interviewee's 'news' and the silent participants (the audience) as the primary recipients. That this is also present in courtroom (Atkinson 1992) and police interview interaction (Heydon 2005), illustrates the modifications phenomena can undergo across contexts, and the participants' ability to shape and structure their orientations to a particular phenomenon in accordance with the contextual requirements.

The police interview, similar to courtroom interaction, is characterized by question and answer turns, pre-allocated to the officer (or attorney) and suspect (or witness) respectively (Heydon 2005). Although differing in their level of formality, institutional constraints similarly prevent the officer from highlighting certain responses from the suspect in the police interview. For example, officers cannot produce a comment or question which can be seen to dissuade the suspect from making no comment, as it is one of the rights of the suspect contained within the PACE Act 1984. However, unlike courtroom interaction, the uninitiated third turn in the police interview does not represent the only opportunity for the officer to highlight some aspect of the prior turn. Aside from non-verbal or non-lexical means the officer in the police interview can legitimately repeat questions, comment on the content of suspects' answers and directly challenge the veracity of their statements. The legal representative (if retained) and/or the later listeners of the interview tape can, however, call for the interview to be made inadmissible as evidence if harassment or a violation of rights are deemed to be exhibited by the officer. The use of non-lexical means was explored in the analysis of laughter in Chapters 4 and 5.

The importance of the silent participant understanding the pertinent points of interaction in courtrooms and police interviews is illustrated by their responsibility to ensure the admissibility of that interaction as evidence, and, more specifically, in the jury's charge to ultimately decide the guilt or innocence of the accused. The ability to communicate effectively to the silent participant in such settings where the very liberty of the suspect may rely on the facts, information and the way the character of the interviewee is presented, compounds the importance of that courtroom or interview room interaction being correctly understood. Despite exploration in other institutional contexts and the high stakes associated with effective communication to the silent participant, there is little research that provides a detailed, conversation analytic examination of the effect of this silent participant on the construction of talk in the police interview. Two notable exceptions are Heydon (2005: 39), who states that in 'both police interviews and news interviews, the talk is knowingly produced for a third party', and Stokoe (2009a), who explores this third party production in detail. Stokoe's (2009a) work looks at the presence of officers' orientations to the silent participant, with specific reference to the phrase 'for the benefit of the tape' and 'for the tape', their use and position in the sentence (e.g. before or after the subject of the turn). It also explores how officers use the first names of suspects to try and reconcile the semantic redundancy[12] of their utterance and show the information they seek is for legal rather than their own investigative requirements. This is also found in the research presented in the following two chapters, which also explore less explicit references to the silent participant and how these too are reconciled by the officer. The chapters will explore how the requirements of the silent participant actually impact on the suspect by drawing the officers' attention away from them. They also explore the way that orienting to the silent participant can create interactional difficulties that the officer then has to try and reconcile, and suggests such orientation away from the suspect could compromise the communicative relationship between the suspect and the officer if the delicate reconciliatory behaviour is not performed or achieved.

In examining the ways in which officers accommodate the future audience of the police interview, Chapter 6 will show how they can be compelled to produce different types of redundant utterances, and Chapter 7 explains how officers manage this by producing additional turns in the interview. Both also demonstrate how the demands of the silent participant and the officers' need to maximize the admissibility of the interview can override the officer's need to attend to the local interaction of the interview and the needs of the suspect. Although police officers are trained in interviewing suspects and are knowledgeable of the entailing protocols and constraints, there can be no assumption that suspects are similarly equipped. It will be argued that officers display a dual orientation to both the conversational aspects of the talk (represented by the suspect) and the institutional constraints and protocol (epitomized by the silent participant). This dual orientation is made transparent in two ways: one is in the officers' orientation to the suspect by accounting for their semantically or legally redundant utterances, and the other is in the presence of two different (conversationally and institutionally oriented) types of third turns. As such, in Chapter 6 the officers' adherence to the silent participant is reflected in the semantic and legal redundancy of their adherence to protocol (extracts 14–19), both unequivocally (extracts 14–16) and in more subtle ways (extracts 17–19), to counteract future questions of the admissibility of the interview. Chapter 7 then investigates how the silent participant affects the interactional design in ways both similar to and different from courtroom interaction. It first analyses the local, conversational use of uninitiated third turns to communicate with the suspect (extracts 20–22). It then demonstrates how the officer can direct third turns towards the institutional orientation of the silent participant, to highlight significant and specific parts of the interview for the benefit of, and to address the lack of communication afforded to, the overhearing audience (extracts 23–26).

Chapter 6

The Silent Participant: Institutional Constraints, Semantic and Legal Redundancy

In addition to creating a copy of the interview, the recording device also represents the legislative mechanisms that are in place to ensure appropriate behaviour is maintained by the officer(s) conducting that interview. This ensures the rights of the suspect are protected, and seen to be protected, with the record of the interaction being created and the recording device itself constituting a physical reminder in the interview of possible future listeners. For the interview to remain admissible as evidence it must satisfy a court that it was conducted according to Codes C and E of the PACE Act 1984. The interviewing officer is responsible for the interview remaining within protocol, and as such must account for any breaches. Non-conformance to the Act (1984) can result in the interview being ruled inadmissible as evidence, disciplinary procedures for the officer, including potential liability for obstructing the course of justice, or causing distress to the suspect.

The officers' responsibility to adhere to the legislative constraints despite the circumstances of the interview is shown in the following three extracts, where the officers produce semantically redundant utterances in order to adhere to the institutional constraints of protocol. The physical presence of the solicitor in these extracts compounds the transparency of this orientation to the silent participant, rather than to the suspect. The analyses explore the organization and production of these redundant turns and examine how they are accounted for by the officers in their interaction with the suspects.

Extract 14 is from an interview of a man who has been arrested on suspicion of committing grievous bodily harm. It opens with the officer's explanation of the suspect's rights, which, as discussed in Chapter 3, is part of the standard opening sequence of the police interview. On lines 29 and 30 the officer informs the suspect of his right to legal advice, a right the suspect has evidently already taken, as his solicitor is demonstrably present in the interview room. This reminder highlights the officer's orientation to the institutional constraints of the Act (1984) and the requirement to state particular phrases in order to remain within protocol, despite the particularities of the interview rendering such phrases unnecessary. Its production is shown to satisfy the legal requirements of the interaction, and therefore the requirements of the silent participant, rather than offering the informative or protective value for the suspect that is intended in the spirit of the Act (1984). In effect, the officer's attention to the suspect is usurped by his attendance to the requirements of the silent participant.

Extract 14: Free legal advice

```
25   P1    >we:n e:n< (.) >↑interview room at< (.) mosedon police stati:on->at the<
26         ...<enD> (.) of the interview (.) I'll give you a notiCE of how you can have
27         a: (.) copy (.) <of the> ta:pe (0.2) <do you> understa:nd that yea:h
28         (0.6)
29   P1→  >you're a:lso< entitled to (0.4) free (.) legal advi:ce which (.) obviously
30    →   you've taken because your solicitor's h↓ere
31         (1.7)
32   P1    your father's also here, (.) if he: thinks (.) >thayen< (.) i:nterview is going
33         wrong in any wa:y he can er (0.5) say so: (0.6) during (0.2) the interv↓iew
34         (0.4)
35         okay do you under<u>stand</u> that yea:h
36   F     yeah sure
(T6-119-06)
```

The officer first informs the suspect of his right to free legal advice and then uses the word 'obviously' (line 29). This accounts for his utterance through framing it as something he has no choice but to perform, by acknowledging its semantically redundant properties while performing it regardless. The officer's use of 'obviously' not only explicitly identifies the prior statement as obvious, but also introduces the next utterance 'you've taken because your solicitor's here' (line 30), which then explicitly identifies the redundancy of the original statement (of line 29). The officer then continues (linked to the prior turn by the use of 'also', line 32) by mentioning the presence of the father, which further justifies the production of his earlier utterance (of line 29), by characterizing it as one part of a list of required statements.

The officer is shown to orient to the frameworks of both conversational and institutional interaction in his frequent attendance to the suspect throughout his production of these legally required, yet semantically redundant, utterances. This overlap between the officer's attendance to the suspect and the institutionally prescribed performance of duty is shown in the officer's monitoring of the suspect's understanding. This is seen in the officer's use of 'yeah' (lines 27 and 35), and his fuller requests for confirmation that the suspect has understood: 'do you understand that' (line 27) and 'okay do you understand that' (line 35).

A similar deferment to protocol is shown in extract 15, which is taken from an interview of a suspect who has been arrested on suspicion of demanding money with menaces. The extract begins during the opening sequence of the interview, in which the officer establishes the time, explains the suspect's rights and notes the people present. Similar to extract 14, the officer explains the suspect's right to legal representation (lines 20–21), despite the presence of the solicitor. At the beginning of this turn (line 20), the officer explicitly informs the suspect that the information about to be given is a repeat of prior information by stating 'as has been explained to you'. It is in this way that the officer attends to his repeated administration of this right; he acknowledges and accounts for it prior to its production by framing it as a repeat-to-come. This display of recognition also accounts for its production by identifying it as a statement required by protocol and produced for the silent participant rather than as an informative utterance produced for the suspect.

Extract 15: As has been explained

```
16    P1    ((clears throat – (0.6) )) da:te toda:y (0.3) is (0.2) >the tw<e:nty fir<st>
17           (0.3) of- may (.) nineteen ninety two, >and the< time by the clo:ck on the
18           wall is (.) two thirty one (.) pee e:m
19           (2.1)
20    P1→  I'v:e err (0.8) a:s (.) >as has been< explained to you (.) you are entitled to
21      →  (.) legal representation, (0.5) erm you have a solicitor here with you, (.)
22           >co:uld I< ask you to introduce yourse[lf please
23    So                                          [dominic woodson, °an°
24           authorised representative for hart and hart solicitors °in mono:lo°
(T13-84-06)
```

The officer repairs his start to the pre-account (the account prior to the redundant information, line 20) by altering his utterance 'I've' to 'as has been explained'. His fleetingly conversational, more personal opening 'I've' is repaired to one of a more impersonal, institutional framework with 'as'. This modification shows the officer alternating between the conversational and institutional frameworks. It also changes the focus from a first person perspective to a passive voice, which frames the officer and the present interview as separate from an earlier discussion, in which the suspect's rights had already been explained. This enables the officer to distance himself from the production of the original explanation, and therefore from the responsibility of his next utterance being a repeat. It also manages the fact that during their time in custody, suspects are informed of their rights on several occasions[13] prior to their administration in the interview. This highlights the officer's need to balance the requirements of the Act (1984) and those of the suspect in the individual circumstances of their interview. It also reveals that those requirements, traditionally understood to be one and the same, can actually conflict.

On lines 20 and 21 the officer then performs the protocol of announcing the suspect's right to legal advice, followed by stating the presence of the solicitor. This statement, as in extract 14, is used to perform some implicit reparative work in itself as, by stating the solicitor's presence, the officer displays his knowledge of the incongruity between this statement and his statement of the suspect's rights. Unlike extract 14, however, the officer's turn is also used to complete a separate requirement; that of eliciting the solicitor's self-introduction. This enables the officer to ease the semantic redundancy of the repeat he has produced for the silent participant by also framing it as part of a request for information that is also required by protocol. This request that the solicitor introduce himself (line 22) signals the closure of the semantically superfluous part of the interview.

The final extract of this section (extract 16) is from an interview of a suspect arrested on suspicion of theft. In the opening part of this interview, in a similar pattern to the above two extracts, the officer advises the suspect of his right to legal representation despite the solicitor's presence rendering that advice redundant to the suspect.

Extract 16: Your representative

```
16   P1   ...that will explain how (.) you can have access to the ta:pe (1.8) ..hh at this
17        stage (0.3) >I should also remind you that you< are entitled to free le:gal
18        advice, that is now or at any ti:me (.) ..h you have your representative with
19        you toda:y (0.3) if I could ask you to introduce yours[elf please si:r
20   So                                            [>pa:ul davis< of polte:rs
(T9-76-06)
```

The officer signals his attendance to the institutional framework with the utterance 'at this stage' (lines 16–17), which implies that particular statements are required at prescribed stages of this interaction. He then follows this with 'should' (line 17), which is an important indicator of announcing a protocol, as it highlights the utterance-to-follow as something he is required to, or 'should' do. Both of these distance the officer from the authorship of the statement by framing it as required to be produced, at that particular point by protocol, and to be heard by the silent participant. This distancing behaviour is see alson in extract 15 and later in extracts 18 and 19.

The officer then informs the suspect of his right to legal advice (lines 17–18). The officer's remark 'you have your representative with you' (lines 18–19) shows the officer displaying awareness of the tension between the institutional requirement to produce that utterance for the benefit of the future silent participant, and his interactional need to attend to the current situation in the interview. Following this, the officer then focuses on the conversational aspect of the talk; tailoring it to the current interview by the use of 'today' (line 19). This enables the officer to resolve the problem of having to produce an otherwise semantically redundant utterance. He does so by individualizing his performance of protocol to the current interview and to that particular suspect's situation. Similar to extract 15, the officer's statement of the suspect's right to legal advice is also utilized in the initiation of another non-redundant performance of protocol – namely the request for the solicitor to identify himself. This shows how the officer, although required to produce these utterances, counteracts their redundancy by distancing himself from the ownership of their production, accounts for their production, and also directs them towards non-redundant and interview-relevant objectives.

Orientation by Linguistic and More Subtle Means

Unlike the extracts of the above section, the semantic redundancy of the officers' utterances in the following extracts is not made visible through the presence of the solicitor. Although extracts 17–19 show officers accounting for their semantically or legally redundant utterances in order to orientate to the silent participant, they do so through more subtle means.

Extract 17 has been taken from an interview of a man arrested on suspicion of the possession of amphetamines. In the extract the primary interviewing officer (P1) asks the suspect to read the notes she had made in the lead up to, and during, the suspect's arrest earlier that evening. The lengthy pause in which the suspect silently reads the statement (line 206) is interrupted by the officer drawing attention to 'grumbling sounds' by attributing them to her colleague's stomach (lines 207–208).

Extract 17: The benefit of the tape

```
205   P1    >if you< cant (.) read my writing just let me know
206         (51.8)
207   P1→   for the benefit of the tape (0.2) the err (.) <grumbling so:unds-
208         >are< petes stomach
209   S     .fhh ↑huhh↓urrr >.hhh<
210         (0.7)
211   P2    .hh ↑I(°h°)t's st(hh)o:pped
212   S     ...fhh
213         (22.9)
214         ((shuffling papers, cough, writing noises))
215   S     no its no:t ..[hh
216   P2                  [.hh [h↑uh
217   P1→                      [for the benefit of the t(h)ape huh °hu↑[hh:°
218   P2                                                              [..hh
219         (29.7)
220   S     (e:rnt) (0.5) >did you hand me a ro:rrant tho< (.) >I d-< haven't got a copy
221         of the warrant though,
```
(T22-20-06)

Without identification, noises in the taped police interview may be questioned by later listeners, and therefore have the potential to cause harm to the admissibility of the tape as evidence if left unaccounted for. Stokoe (2009a) also found 'for the benefit of the tape' formulations are used to make explicit some inaudible action that is or has occurred in the interview room. The officer's utterance (lines 207–208), although legally superfluous, demonstrates her orientation to the silent participant by identifying it, in her own words, for 'the benefit of the tape', thus removing the potential ambiguity of the noise. Her production of this statement immediately prior to her explanation of the noise allows the officer to switch from a more casual, conversational framework (seen on line 205) to one of a more institutional nature. The phrase itself makes it explicit that the utterance-to-come is for the benefit of the tape, and to satisfy the silent participant and institutional requirements of the interview, rather than to satisfy the needs of the suspect. Following this statement the officer once again attends to the conversational aspect of the talk; illustrated by her casual use of first-name terms when referring to 'Pete', the other officer present (line 208).

However, the mismatch or tension between the officer's statement of protocol and her attendance to the suspect has not been resolved, and it is this that is highlighted by the laughter that follows the sequence. As the officer has not made it explicit why, or accounted in some way for her deferment to the institutional framework (saying 'for the benefit of the tape'), the suspect has interpreted the officer's reference to the 'grumbling' as a joke rather than an attempt to ensure transparency of the interaction and protect its admissibility as evidence. The suspect's laughter (line 209) demonstrates how the mismatch between the two constraints has not yet been resolved by the officer. This laughter and, after a pause, the laughter of the second officer (lines 209/212) also highlights the amusing nature of the first officer's identification of the grumbling noise and her deference to protocol in accounting for it. This mutual laugher shows the second officer aligning himself to the suspect (Stokoe 2009b) and the suspect's reaction to the first officer's deferment to protocol.

After a long pause the laughing episode is followed by a second bout (lines 215–218), in which the first officer herself also laughs (line 217). This laughter displays her attendance to the earlier mismatch by retroactively attending to the conversational aspect of the talk. The laughter, bubbling through the partial repeat of her earlier statement 'for the benefit of the tape' (lines 207/217) is significant as it shows her recognition of the laughable properties of her earlier deferment to protocol, and the placement of the laughter among laughter that is already occurring, shows her attempt to display joint affiliation (Stokoe and Edwards 2008) with the second officer and the suspect. Despite this use of laughter to retroactively repair her earlier utterance, the officer's lack of reciprocal laughter earlier on lines 210/213 reveals the seriousness of her original statement. It reveals its original intention as a comment for the silent participant rather than the joke she later frames it as. This illustrates the delicate interactional work required of the officer to match the requirements of both the silent participant and the suspect through balancing her attendance to institutional and conversational aspects of the talk. It highlights the difficulties that can occur, and the retroactive repairs that may be needed, when these two aspects are not promptly consolidated.

In the following extract (extract 18) the suspect is interviewed following his arrest on suspicion of committing assault in a pub earlier that evening. The extract shows the opening exchanges of that interview, in which the officer successfully navigates one semantically and one legally redundant statement of protocol by attending to the conversational aspect of the talk, both following (18i) and prior to (18ii) their production. The officer administers the standard police caution as part of the opening sequence of the interview (lines 45/56). As in extract 16, he then accounts for its production by distancing himself from the authorship of the utterance and explicitly framing it as something he has '*got to* tell' (line 50) the suspect. This enables the officer to account for what may be a repeat of what the suspect already knows, ('I'm sure you know all this', line 50), by highlighting it as an utterance required by protocol, rather than a mistaken repeat. Indeed, in accordance with the PACE Act 1984, it is the officer's responsibility to ensure the suspect's rights have been fully administered in the interview[14] and that the caution is understood.[15] Here the officer makes it fully explicit that he is cautioning the suspect in order to satisfy the legislatory requirements of the interview, rather than for the benefit of the suspect.

Extract 18: Heard it all before

```
45 P1→       and the la:st thing >which is very important is that you don't have to say anything
46           unless you wish to but anything you do say may be given in evide̲:nce do you
47           understand th↓at<=
48 S         =yeah
49           (0.2)
50 P1 (18i)→ r↓ight (.) > °>I'm sure you know all this but<° >°°ive°°< (.) >got to tell
51           you it anyway,<
52           (0.7)
53 P1        right
54           (0.6)
55 P1        >do you understand why you've been arre:ste̲:d<
56           (0.2)
57 S         v↓eah
58           (0.6)
59 P1 (18ii)→ I'll go: <through it> anyway (1.0) an ↑allegations been made, that on ...
(T11-80-06)
```

The officer's accounting behaviour and the quickened pace under which the caution is administered (lines 45–46) are both quite at odds with his stating of its importance (line 45). The officer's hurried production of the caution is reminiscent of Baldwin (1992b: 12) who describes these opening statements as 'regarded by officers as minor preliminaries to be dealt with in a perfunctory manner', that 'tend to be delivered hurriedly' (Baldwin 1993: 336). As he explains, 'many cautions [are] delivered in a sloppy manner, often so garbled as to be devoid of all meaning' (Baldwin 1992b:

15; see also Baldwin 1993: 337). Bridges and Sanders (1990) found that one of the main reasons that detainees declined their right to legal advice was because their rights were read too quickly and incomprehensibly. If this part of the interview were to be presented in court as evidence, it would most likely be in the form of a transcript rather than the audio record, and the transcript would be stripped of extra-interactional detail such as the pace and tone of the delivery of the caution. Therefore the question of whether the suspect has indeed understood the caution, or whether it was produced in a manner in accordance with the spirit of the PACE Act 1984, would also disappear.

The quickened pace, together with the officer's explanation 'I'm sure you know all this ...' (extract 18, line 50) suggests the officer is reacting to the fact that the suspect may have been cautioned several times by the time he had come to be interviewed and therefore has a pre-existing under-standing of the police caution (see endnote 13). This is perhaps reflected in the immediacy of the suspect's response (line 48), latched onto the officer's turn, with less than one-tenth of a second pause before affirming he understands the caution.

The officer therefore attends to the suspect by accounting for the production of the police caution in a retroactive manner (lines 50 and 51), and then returns to the questioning in his next turn (on line 55), where he asks 'do you understand why you've been arrested'. Despite the suspect's answer 'yeah' (line 57) indicating that he *does* understand the reason for his arrest, the officer's ensuing explanation of the arrest (line 59) again reveals the conflict between the officer's attendance to both the suspect and the requirements of protocol. Attending to the silent participant in this way overrides the rules of interaction and causes the officer to engage in reparative work. Although not acting on the content of the suspect's response, the officer does attend to its production by saying 'I'll go through it *anyway*' (line 59, emphasis added) prior to his explanation of the arrest. This enables the officer to show he knows that he is about to explain the reasons for the suspect's arrest despite the suspect stating he already understands them. The interactional work seen here demonstrates the officer's 'need' to make his disregard of the suspect's answer explicit – by doing so, he implicitly frames it as somehow required or unavoidable, rather than it being rudeness or a mishearing on his part.

However, the officer's utterance, so delicately accounted for and framed as required by the silent participant, is not so required. According to the PACE Act 1984, the suspect is shown documentation of the circumstances of his or her arrest upon detention[16] and the officer does not have to ensure that the suspect understands the circumstances of their arrest in the course of the interview. The officer's 'I'll go through it anyway' (line 59), and repeat of the reasons for the arrest despite the suspect's answer, demonstrates the officer's deferment to protocol over and above the stipulated requirements of the Act (1984). That the officer still frames this legally redundant statement as required by protocol suggests he is using the Act to account for its production and ensure the integrity of the interview is safeguarded beyond doubt, despite this very act creating a conflict with his need to attend to the suspect.

At both points 18i and 18ii the officer alternates between attending to the conversational and institutional constraints of the talk. The tensions of these are made transparent by the officer in his utterances 'I've got to tell you it anyway' (lines 50–51) and 'I'll go through it anyway' (line 59). These highlight the officer's deferment to protocol despite information from the suspect rendering such deferment semantically redundant, and in the case of 18ii, legally redundant. The officer's monitoring behaviour 'right' (lines 50 and 53) during this extract illustrates, as in extracts 14 and 19, his attendance to the suspect throughout the episode.

Extract 19 has been taken from an interview of a suspect who has been arrested for the possession of amphetamines. The extract starts 25 minutes into the interview, in which the suspect has declined to comment in response to all the questions put to him so far. The officer refers to the tape on lines 99–101, where she explains that the tape recorder is making a record of the interview. This is a semantically redundant statement; it has no informative value for the suspect, as the presence of the tape recorder is clear (akin to the presence of the solicitor in extracts 14, 15 and 16). Accordingly, the officer frames her statement as semantically redundant – as a legal requirement of the silent participant. She does so both before and after the utterance, using the same accounting behaviour that is shown in the other similarly redundant extracts of this chapter. However, the officer's statement is also legally redundant. The officer has already stated[17] during the opening sequence of the interview that it is being tape recorded, and this second explanation is not required. Officers are required to state at the commencement of the interview that the interview is being audibly recorded, (the PACE Act 1984, Code E, section 4 (b), paragraph 4.4 (a)), but no further mention, expansion of this or need to 'remind' (extract 19, line 99) the suspect is necessary. Unlike the examples of legal redundancy seen in extracts 17 and 18ii, it is not an example of the officer going over and above the requirements in an attempt to avoid damaging the admissibility of the tape.

Extract 19: Presence of the tape

```
94    P1    ... remind you that- (0.7) as the caution expla:ins a court may draw inference
95          (0.8) if you <don't now> (.) answer any of the questions that are put to
96          yo:u (0.9) do you understand [all of tha:t
97    S                                    [yeah
98          (1.0)
99    P1 →>I know it< sounds daft but ive gotto <remind you> that (0.4) a record of
100      →this interview is being made (0.6) >and its< being made by the t(h)ape
101        recorde:r (1[.0) okay (0.2) that could be used in co:urt (1[.1) as=
102   ?              [((coughing))                              [((coughing))
103   P1    =evidence °if require:d° (0.2) do you understand all of that
104   S     mm↑hmm
(T22-20-06)
```

The officer acknowledges the semantic redundancy of her utterance and frames it as required by the silent participant by characterizing what she is about to say as 'daft' (line 99); this is a recognition of the superfluity of what she is about to say, and displays her alignment with the suspect. The officer then qualifies this by stating that she is required to issue the reminder – 'I've *gotto* remind you' (line 99, emphasis added), which also accounts for the utterance that follows, as something that she has no choice but to perform, despite its 'daftness'. Both her use of 'I know it sounds daft but' and 'I've gotto remind you' are part of the officer's conversational framework, used to prepare the suspect for the semantic redundancy of her next utterance. The officer's use of 'but' on line 99 is used to contrast her characterization of the 'daftness' of the utterance-to-come with the necessity of her saying it. This demonstrates the officer, as with extracts 15, 16 and 18, acknowledging the semantic redundancy, distancing herself from the authorship of the statement and accounting for its production as externally required for the benefit of the silent participant. She then performs the announcement of the interview being taped; her laugh token during this statement (through the word 'tape' itself, line 100) is perhaps an additional, non-verbal enactment of the daftness of what she is currently saying. As in extracts 14 and 18, the officer explicitly displays her orientation to the suspect by slipping into the conversational framework to monitor his understanding throughout ('do you understand all of that', line 96; 'okay', line 101; 'do you understand all of that', line 103).

It is interesting that, despite the legally redundant nature of the officer's turn, this extract demonstrates her framing it as legally required, in order to account for the semantic redundancy and successfully navigate its production. Taking into consideration the skilled accounting behaviour involved in orientations to the silent participant in general, and the fact that there is no semantic or legal basis for the officer's utterance, it appears that the officer's turn is using the same means, but is performing quite a separate function from the redundant utterances seen in the other extracts in this chapter.

Examining the context of the officer's turn, it occurs midway through an interview in which the suspect has repeatedly offered no comment, and follows the officer's reference to the negative consequences that could befall a suspect who remains silent (in a legally redundant repeat of the caution, lines 94–96). The tape is framed as both the record of the suspect's lack of co-operation and the means by which those negative consequences of his silence could be enacted (used in court as evidence). By doing so the officer positions herself as encouraging the suspect to start responding to her questions, and her statement appears less of a threat and more of a directive from the silent participant that the officer reluctantly produces. This enables the officer to produce an adversarial statement without taking an adversarial stance against the suspect; indeed, the conversational tone and laughter used suggest this is also an attempt to establish rapport. Taking these elements into account, it appears that here, the orientation to the silent participant is being used by the officer as a technique to draw information from the suspect.

Discussion: The Silent Participant – Institutional Constraints, Semantic and Legal Redundancy

The extracts in this chapter have revealed the officers' dual orientation to the suspect and to the protocol. They illustrate how the officers' orientation to the silent participant is observable through their production of semantically and legally redundant utterances in the interview. The presence of the solicitor (and in the case of extract 19, the presence of the tape recorder) makes the redundancy of this adherence to protocol immediately visible. Indeed, concerning the phrase 'this interview is being tape recorded', Stokoe (2009a: 1890–1891) states: 'the status of this phrase as a legal requirement overrides its hearability as "stating the obvious", despite the fact that those present in the interview room can presumably see the recorder, hear the "bleep", and know they are being recorded.' However, where the redundancy of the officers' utterance is less visible, the officer must rely on more subtle means such as linguistically framing the utterance as one required by protocol in order to account for the discrepancy between it and the local interaction.

This chapter has shown that officers signal some aspect of the utterance as repeated (extracts 15 and 18i), obvious (extract 14) or daft (extract 19), either before (extracts 15, 16, 17, 18ii and 19) or after the utterance (extracts 14 and 18i). They also distance themselves from authorship of the utterance (extracts 15, 16, 18i and 19). The chapter has shown that officers adhere to protocol despite the semantic redundancy that that adherence entails, or despite no explicit legal requirement to do so. While officers produce semantically redundant utterances in their enactment of protocol, the production of legally redundant utterances demonstrates that they going beyond these requirements. This can be used to minimize the possibility of the interview being ruled inadmissible or account for utterances by framing them as legally required. These forms can also be directed toward the function of information elicitation.

The structure of the officers' production of both types of redundant utterances is tailored to reflect their orientation to both the local structure of the interview, as well as the broader audience, which includes the silent participant. Specifically, the findings have shown that officers display their orientation to the local context of the interview when accounting for utterances which appear to disregard the circumstances present in the interview (extracts 14, 15 and 16), be semantically superfluous (extracts 14, 15, 16, 17 and 18i) or legally so (extracts 18ii and 19), or disregard the suspect's response (extract 18ii). Officers account for these utterances by framing them as unavoidable or pre-defined by some other authority and, in all cases, the officer first adheres to the institutional constraints, and therefore the requirements of the silent participant, and then attempts to account for that adherence through more conversational means. The analyses have shown that officers account for the semantically redundant utterances by framing them, in a conversational framework, as institutionally required. Even the interaction in extract 19 where, rather than engaging in the reparative and accounting work to satisfy the requirements of the silent participant and the interactional requirements of the suspect, the officer directs this work to a different objective: attempting to draw information from the suspect. The production of these utterances is also systematically managed, which, failed or otherwise, for the objective of orientating to the silent participant or for a secondary purpose, shows how officers, in addition to the institutional rules, are also bound by the ordinary rules of conversation. The presence of these conversational rules in this institutional setting provides evidence of the wider, general interactional order to which all participants adhere, as first claimed by Sacks (1984) in his analyses of ordinary conversation. That elements of this general and conversationally originated order are visible in this highly constrained context of the police interview reinforces the replicability of conversation analytic research, which was formed on the basis of this 'order at all points' (Sacks 1984: 22), and indicates that interaction can be generalized across contexts. The differences that are present in transposing this basic order from ordinary conversation to its application in this particular context also reveal the rules and roles that are particular to this context and its participants.

The officers' accounting behaviour demonstrates the constraints imposed upon the officer to orientate to these institutional aspects of the talk and shows they understand that their production violates interactional rules. Their very presence despite this demonstrates the officers' inability to circumvent their need to be produced and reveals, contrary to traditional understandings of the police interview, the officer in a position of power-lessness. However, through orientating to the conversational constraints, the tension between the institutional and conversational can be managed without the officer having to engage in reparative work. This management of the interactional requirements is reminiscent of Harold Shipman's delicate avoidance of producing dispreferred actions as a suspect (Johnson and Newbury 2006).

The officers' orientation to suspects is shown in the fleetingly conversational aspects of their talk, which explicitly attend to the suspects' understanding (extracts 14, 18 and 19), and to the conversational aspect of the talk more generally (extracts 15, 16 and 17). However, tension is apparent in the officers' negotiation of their adherence to both the protocol and to the interaction with the suspect. This reveals the silent participant and the suspect are both constraints to which the officer must attend, on legal or interactional levels respectively. The troubles associated with the adherence to one and not the other are shown in extracts 17 and 18ii, where the officer attends to the institutional constraints and the future listeners of the tape, and not to the conversational aspect of the immediate interaction. This mismatch leads to the semantic redundancy not being resolved, which is important because if the officer attends to the conversational aspect to frame an institutional constraint, it avoids the difficulties and the need to engage in the reparative work seen in extract 17. This tension of the dual constraints on the officer both shapes and is shaped by the context of the police interview; the officer is constrained by the codes of conduct, but then is see alson to define those boundaries by deferring to a self-imposed, more restrictive and legally superfluous additional set of constraints. This is used by officers to ensure they remain well within the guidelines, which minimizes the possibility of damaging the admissibility of the interview as evidence. It has also been shown that this orientation to an external party can also be used as a tool; it can mitigate the adversarial nature of an utterance by framing it as authored by that other party, can maintain, build or avoid damaging rapport with the suspect, or be used in an attempt to elicit information.

With the exception of extracts 17 and 19, each of the extracts concerns the opening stages of the police interview. This is one of the most heavily constrained parts of the interview, governed by strict and specific rules that are absent in the main body of the interview.[18] Analysing officers' talk in this part of the interview, where the institutional requirements on the officer are most prevalent and standardized, offers a clear picture of their management. Although typically holding no evidentiary value regarding the criminal act under investigation, the opening sequences are present to ensure the suspects' rights are safeguarded. As such, if the officers' performance of the opening sequence satisfies the silent participants in accordance with the PACE Act 1984, it will be of little interest to future audiences such as the court or members of the jury. However, the importance of these sequences is clear if a potential breach of the codes of conduct *is* present in its administration. In these cases the opening sequence would be of interest to the court and could be used to argue the interview to be inadmissible as evidence. Interestingly, despite extract 18 demonstrating a breach of the spirit of the Act (1984), the common practice of using simple (non-conversation analytic) transcripts to represent police interviews as evidence in court would mask the very interactional intricacies that posed the breach in the first place.

The analyses have demonstrated that the opening sequence can be produced to fulfil the legal requirements of the interview, rather than to inform the suspect, and officers are compelled to satisfy the requirements of the silent participant over and above the requirements of the interaction with the suspect. This is illustrated by the reparative and accounting work performed by the officers, which shows the difficulties present in tailoring their adherence to attend to the individual requirements of the suspect. It also suggests that in some cases the officers' perception of the requirements of the silent participant is broader or wider reaching than the legislation actually dictates; which could be symptomatic of the officer being ultimately responsible for that interview adhering to the legislation. The analyses highlight how the pressures on the officer to ensure the admissibility of the interview can impact on their communicative capabilities in that interview. They also provide an insight into the composition of police interview interaction and reveal the difficulties faced by officers in the execution of their institutional duties to the law and to the suspect. This chapter exposes the reality of the demands of the silent participant, and by proxy the PACE Act 1984, as a competitor for the attentions of the officer with the suspect, as well as acting, as traditionally understood, as their protector.

These insights could inform the training practices of police and other authorized officers insofar as the potential for specific interviewing practices to impact on their communicative abilities in the interview. Knowledge of the potential impact of the silent participant, and training in the management of the difficulties of the conflicting needs of the suspect and the legal requirements can prepare and provide officers with the interactional mechanisms they require to combat problems in the management of these difficulties, such as failing to account for redundant utterances. Training officers in the use of those mechanisms, such as using the constraints of the context to frame the semantically or legally redundant utterances as indexical, would empower officers to adapt their talk to incorporate the requirements of both the silent participant and the suspect, without compromising the codes of conduct. This would ultimately bring the suspect to the forefront, together with ascertaining information they may hold, and their individual interactional needs during that particular interview; and signal a step away from the silent participant (Heritage 1985, Greatbatch 1988, 1992, Drew 1992) being the primary addressee.

Chapter 7

The Silent Participant: Uninitiated Third Turns

In Chapter 6 it was argued that officers' orientation to conversational aspects of the interaction facilitates their navigation of the (real or perceived) institutional requirements. Officers ensure they adhere to the requirements of the silent participant by producing semantically or legally redundant utterances, and manage the often conflicting reality of the talk-in-progress by attending to the interactional requirements of the suspect. This dual orientation to the local and wider aspects of the interaction is also reflected in the differing forms of uninitiated third turns. As outlined earlier, uninitiated third turns are extra turns in interaction, seen, for example, in the exchange of a prosecution barrister in a courtroom cross-examination, who uses this additional turn in the question-answer sequence to repeat the answer of the witness to highlight some aspect of that turn to the jury as silent participants to the interaction (Drew 1992). This chapter explores the presence of third turns. In the first half it explores the third turns that display characteristics typical of ordinary conversation, such as an invitation for clarification, a request for repair, or to attend to the answer in the immediately prior turn in some way (Drew 1992; Hutchby and Wooffitt 1998). These extracts will be used to argue that this conversational third turn structure is used by officers to elicit clarifications or repaired responses from the suspect, in addition to being used to comment on some aspect of the prior turn, such as its mistaken or unexpected nature. The extracts in the second half of the chapter will then explore third turns that have a structure similar to those typical of courtroom or newsroom use; structured to highlight pertinent facts for the benefit of the silent participants or designed to take into account the overhearing audience as the primary addressees (Drew 1992). It will be argued that these different appearances of third turns reveal the differences in the constraints imposed upon the interaction and on the participants in courtrooms and police interviews.

Uninitiated Third Turns and the Local Interaction

Extract 20 is from an interview of a suspect arrested, along with several other men, on suspicion of inflicting grievous bodily harm on his neighbour. Up until this point in the interview, in which the officer attempts to establish who did what in the assault, the suspect has provided vague or 'don't know' answers, or has responded with 'no comment'. In this particular extract the officer asks the suspect about his relationship with the victim.

On line 69 the officer's close repeat of the suspect's immediately prior utterance 'he's my neighbour' (line 67) is an uninitiated third turn designed to draw further information from the suspect. However, this is unsuccessful, shown in the pause of line 70, where the suspect does not subsequently provide that information. That the third turn was intended to elicit further information from the suspect is supported by the officer's production of a more explicit attempt on lines 71–72. The officer's turn makes the original objective of his third turn, as a question about the specifics of the relationship, more transparent.

The officer's difficulties in eliciting more detailed information from the suspect are continued on line 74, where the suspect responds to the officer's question with 'neighbour'. This one-word partial repeat of his earlier (line 67) answer is uttered by the suspect despite the officer's explicit attempt to get a descriptive answer by requesting the suspect to '*describe* your relationship' (line 71, emphasis added). It is only after the officer attempts to elicit the information for a third time on line 76 that the suspect provides the officer with further details of the relationship.

Extract 20: Describe it to me

```
65   P1    ho:w d'you know h↓arry
66         (1.0)
67   S     because he's my °ne:igh°°bour°°
68         (0.5)
69   P1→   he's your neighbo:ur
70         (0.2)
71   P1    >is he a< (0.3) ..hh (.) >what would you describe yourl< (.) relationship, a
72         fri:end, or (.) >just a< neigh°bour°
73         (0.2)
74   S     neighbour
75         (0.5)
76   P1    you don't (0.4) go out with him o[r
77   S                                      [I used to be °good friends with hi:m,°
```

78   (0.6)
79   P1   >but not any< m↓ore
80   S   no
81   (0.7)
82   P1   r↑I::ght (0.4) well >can you< >TELL US< (.)<u>what happened last night</u>
(T6-119-06)

The continued elicitation attempts by the officer highlight how the third turn can be used, although unsuccessfully in this case, to attempt to draw information from a suspect. It is upon the failure of this implicit tool that the officer issues more explicit requests for the information he requires. The conclusion of the episode is signalled by the officer moving to a different line of questioning on line 82; his use of 'right' at this point indicates that either he is finally satisfied with the suspect's response, or will cease pursuing an alternative response to his original question (of line 65).

Later in the same interview the officer attempts to place the suspect's friend Philip at the scene of the crime as the attacker, shown below in extract 21. He introduces this line of enquiry by asking how Philip's stitches, from an earlier injury to his hand, had come to fall out on the night of the attack.

Extract 21: Don't know

224   S   the sti:tches f↓ell ↓out
225   (0.4)
226   P1   yeah ho:w >did that< happe:n
227   (0.2)
228   S   I dunno
229   (0.6)
230   P1→   °you don't kno:w°
231   (1.4)
232   P1   isn't it true >that it was< Philip <that er> (0.4) assaulted Harry,
233   (0.6)
234   S   dunno:
235   (2.2)
236   P1   ri:ght >wh↑en you were< (.) <u>taken</u> to the police station this mo:rning, (0.5)
(T6-119-06)

The officer's close repeat of the suspect's answer 'I dunno' on line 230 draws attention to, and attempts an other-initiated self-repair of, the suspect's answer. That is, the officer uses this third turn in an implicit attempt to elicit a different answer (one other than 'I dunno') from the suspect and gain information about Philip's involvement in the attack. (Definitions of types of repair are detailed in Appendix III.) When this is unsuccessful (signalled in the silence in the suspect's next turn, line 231), the officer makes his intentions clear. He, in a more explicit attempt to secure the information, refers to the attack and suggests that Philip was responsible (line 232).

The officer's (failed) third turn on line 230, similar to extract 20, is subsequently followed with an explicit question from the officer as a second elicitory attempt, which reveals the intention of his original utterance. This provides evidence for the uninitiated third turn being used as an implicit method of elicitation that, if unsuccessful, can be 'upgraded' to more explicit (although failed on this occasion) questioning. The officer's repeat of 'don't know' rather than a pertinent, ambiguous or incriminating answer is a further indication that the officer uses the repeat to attempt to draw information from the suspect, rather than to highlight the answer as a pertinent point in attendance to, or for the benefit of, the silent participant, as seen in courtroom interaction and demonstrated later in this chapter.

Extract 22 shows the officer using an extra turn in the question-answer sequence to repeat the suspect's answer, in his own expanded account on behalf of the suspect. The suspect is being interviewed on suspicion of assaulting two men outside a pub. In the turns prior to extract 22 the officer has attempted to establish the identity of the 'black guy',[19] a man seen outside the pub at the time of the crime. In the extract, the officer asks the suspect about 'another black guy' (lines 413–414), who was armed with a bottle at the scene.

Extract 22: Didn't see

```
413   P1    and there was another (0.2) black guy >next to him you didn't< (0.3)
414   →     >armed with a bottle as we:ll< you didn't see him
415         (0.2)
416   S →   nah
417         (0.2)
418   P1→   no (.) you didn't >see hi:m<
419   S →   no:
420         (1.2)
421   P2    what were you dri:nking that (°lassa:-°) (0.2) °tha:t ni:ght°
(T11-80-06)
```

On line 414 the officer asks the suspect to confirm he had not seen the man, to which the suspect responds that he hadn't ('nah', line 416). The officer, after a pause, utters a close repeat of this answer ('no', line 418), followed by a partial repeat of his previous question 'you didn't see him' (line 414, repeated on line 418). The officer uses these close and partial repeats to perform an other-initiated other-repair of the suspect's answer (line 416). In other words, the officer identifies the suspect's response 'nah' as insufficient, and then corrects it himself to a fuller, more specific answer. This close repeat of the suspect's prior turn ('no', line 418) and partial repeat of his own prior turn ('you didn't see him', line 418) also invites the suspect to agree, clarify or repair the officer's interpretation of his answer. The suspect responds on line 419 by issuing a close repeat of his earlier answer; his response 'no' implying that, by not objecting to the officer's reformulation, the officer's statement is correct. The resulting close repeat of the question-answer sequence first seen on lines 414 and 416 and again on lines 418 and 419 demonstrates that the third turn is used by the officer to disambiguate the suspect's answer by making it more explicit, and to achieve confirmation that his interpretation was accurate.

The extracts in this section have shown officers using the uninitiated third turn as a resource by which they can draw on the conversational aspect of the interaction by initiating a repair of some part of the suspects' prior turn. This third turn repeat is used as a tool to recycle a source of trouble in the suspects' previous turn and bring it to their attention (as seen in Hutchby and Wooffitt 1998). In extracts 20 and 21 the officers attempt to elicit other-initiated self-repairs of the suspects' turns; these turns are used by the officers to identify and attempt to elicit further, repaired or expanded answers from the suspects. However, extract 22 shows the officer performing an other-initiated other-repair on the suspect's utterance himself, in which he identifies the trouble source (the ambiguity of the suspect's answer) and carries out the repair (by restating the answer). The officer then invites and receives confirmation of its accuracy from the suspect. The third turn repeats also enable the officer to comment on a particular answer without explicitly issuing a remark about it, although, as illustrated in extract 20 in particular, these implicit utterances are superseded by their more explicit counterparts when they fail to perform the intended action. The failure of the third turns in their use as elicitory attempts, such as in extracts 20 and 21, may be indicative of the context in which they were uttered. That is, the institutional nature of the police interview may lead to the suspect automatically and indexically interpreting the officer's third turns as institutionally, rather than conversationally, oriented. The difficulties present in interviewing suspects in this environment, and the way traditional perceptions of the interaction actually shape its structure, highlights the importance of research that explores its reality. Awareness of the use of third turns as potential tools in the interview, and the difficulties in the use of third turns and the potential for their misuse, could add another dimension to the communicative capabilities of investigative interviewers.

The extracts in this section have shown the officer using uninitiated third turns to attend to the local interaction with the suspect in ways that are characteristic of ordinary conversation, such as to identify sources of trouble (such as ambiguity and non-cooperation) and to initiate a particular response from the other participant. This illustrates that third turns in the police interview are not limited to being the interactional equivalent of third turns in other institutional contexts, but are also produced and used as a separate tool to facilitate interaction with the suspect.

Uninitiated Third Turns and Institutional Constraints

While the uninitiated third turns in the above section have exhibited similarities to those typical of ordinary conversation, the following extracts illustrate the officers' use of uninitiated third turns as institutionally structured orientations to, and negotiations of, the presence of the silent participant.

Extract 23 has been taken from an interview in which the suspect is being questioned on suspicion of assaulting his wife. In the extract the officer establishes how long the suspect had been living in the house with his wife prior to the alleged assault. This timeframe is particularly relevant as the officer later uses this information to establish contradictions between the stories of the suspect and his wife,[20] as the wife had claimed the suspect had not been living there at the time of the offence. On line 81 the officer utters a partial repeat of the suspect's answer, creating a third turn in the interaction. The suspect's answer, made vague by the use of the hedging 'errm' and the adverb 'maybe' (line 80) is repeated by the officer in his turn on line 81. This repeat ('six months ago') is rendered more precise by the officer as it is produced without the hedgings of the original utterance. The officer also uses the repeat to provide the suspect with an (in this case unused) opportunity to correct or comment on his partially repeated and clarified statement in the next turn. The pause on line 82 is symptomatic of that opportunity not being taken by the suspect. This suggests the suspect does not disagree with the officer's repaired, partially repeated utterance.

Extract 23: Time away

```
78    P1    how long ago did you move back in
79          (1.1)
80    S     °e:rrm° maybe six months ago
81    P1→   six months ago:
82          (0.3)
83    P1    how long were you away fo:r
84          (0.9)
```
(T29-31-06)

Following the suspect's silence, the officer does not then explicitly request
a response in the next turn (line 83), as seen in the conversational use of
the third turns in the previous section, but instead he continues the line
of questioning. This suggests that the repeat was not specifically designed
to attend to the conversational aspect of the interaction, that is, to elicit
information from the suspect. It suggests the third turn was used instead to
orient to the institutional concerns of the silent participant by highlighting
and clarifying a pertinent fact in the exchange, similar to the prosecution
highlighting a pertinent answer of the victim for the benefit of the jury
(Drew 1992). The officer's use of the third turn in this case (on line 81)
is two-fold: to draw attention to the answer as a pertinent point in the
exchange; and to highlight and correct the suspect's ambiguity in the prior
turn.

This use of the third turn to highlight aspects of the interaction for the
attention of the silent participant is also shown in extract 24, taken from an
interview of a suspect who has been arrested on suspicion of possessing a
stolen car. The suspect claims that he was in possession of the car because it
was left at his garage by a man who had wanted him to fix it. In the extract
the officer establishes the location of the garage and the length of time the
suspect has been in business. As discussed below, the significance of the
location is highlighted later in the interview, when the officer constructs a
challenge to the veracity of the suspect's story by juxtaposing these answers
with the fact that other, more established garages exist on that road.[21]

The officer repeats the suspect's answers to two consecutive questions.
The officer's first repetition (line 61) differs slightly from the other extracts
in this section, as it is followed by the receipt token 'right'. The officer uses
this third turn repeat to highlight the suspect's answer, while the quietly
uttered 'right' also signals his receipt of that utterance. This frames the
officer's repeat as a statement not requiring a response (and none is forthcoming). It also suggests the officer's repeat is used to orient to both the

conversational aspects of the interaction (as a display of understanding) and the institutional (the officer does not use the repeat to repair or elicit a response from the suspect, but to draw attention to a potentially implicatory utterance).

Extract 24: Green lane

```
58   P1    ri:ght where abouts is tha:t
59   S     in green lane
60         (0.5)
61   P1→  in green lane °r:igh:t°
62         (0.6)
63   P1    and how long have you had that ya:rd
64   S     two weeks >huhuh<
65   P1→  two we:eks
66         (1.0)
67   P1    so when did this geezer turn up
(T1-67-06)
```

The officer's second repetition, on line 65, is of the suspect's answer 'two weeks'. Similar to his earlier repetition on line 61, the officer uses this third turn to draw attention to the suspect's answer, which is one that identifies his business as recently established, and therefore potentially less likely to attract 'walk in' business than the other more established garages in the street. The suspect's laughter on line 64 prior to the repeat is perhaps a non-verbal acknowledgement of this. Drew (1992) has shown courtroom interaction follows a similar structure, where the attorney uses a series of questions, designed through their juxtaposition to the witness' answers, to call into question their moral standing or the validity of their testimony.

Similar to extract 23, both of the officer's repeats draw attention to pertinent points in the interview. The significance attached to the answers 'green lane' and 'two weeks' are made clear in the officer's repeated references[22] to these pertinent points throughout the interview to challenge the suspect's version of events. The officer uses the suspect's own account of his machineless and signless garage[23] which had been in his possession for two weeks, and located at the very end of a road of other garages, to challenge the suspect's version of what had happened.[24] When given the opportunity, the suspect does not comment on or contend with either of the officer's repeats of his answers. This is shown in the suspect not taking his turns on lines 62 and 66 respectively. This suggests the suspect either complies with (in the act of not objecting to) the content of the officer's repeats, or interprets them as not requesting a response. That the officer does not go on to request a response from the suspect (as is done in the conversational uses of third turns seen in the above section), suggests that none is required. This provides evidence for this type of third turn not being used as, or interpreted as, a tool to elicit a response.

The use of the third turn by the officer to highlight the suspect's answer for the benefit of the silent participant is shown again in extract 25, which is taken from an interview with a suspect arrested on suspicion of assault. In the extract below, the officer focuses the questioning on the suspect's possession of illegal drugs they had found when searching him at the police station. The officer asks the suspect to name the 'herbal substance' found in his possession, to which, after a pause, the suspect replies 'cannabis' (line 242). After another pause the officer repeats this answer (line 244), one that is significant as it explicitly confirms the suspect's knowledge of the drug. The officer uses a third turn to emphasize the presence of the drugs and to highlight the suspect's answer, therefore drawing attention to the suspect's knowledge of the substance.

Extract 25: Herbal substance

```
236   P1    ri:ght >wh↑en you were< (.) taken the police station this mo:rning, (0.5)
237         <you we:re> (0.5) found in possession of (0.9) >I'll sho:w< you this it's
238         wrapped up in a (0.7) a drugs ba:g, (1.3) S:ealed (1.1) with a number <ay>
239         ↑one two three four five s↓ix (1.0) °it's like a° (0.3) herbal subst↓ance
240         >can you< tell us what tha:t is
241         (0.5)
242   S     ca:nnab↓is
243         (0.4)
244   P1→   cannabi:s
245         (0.3)
246   P1    whose >is i:t<
247         (0.4)
248   S     mi:ne
(T6-119-06)
```

The officer requests the name of the 'herbal substance' despite this information already being known to the officer as the suspect has been arrested for possession of cannabis.[25] Therefore, the officer's repeat of the elicited information cannot constitute a request for clarification or be employed to initiate a repair from the suspect, simply because the officer already knows the information to be true. As a consequence, the repeat must be being used, similar to Drew (1992), by the officer to draw attention to the suspect's self-implicatory answer 'cannabis' for the benefit of the silent participant.

The suspect does not respond to the officer's repeat, shown through the pause on line 245, and accordingly does not draw any further attention to his answer. In the same way as the other extracts in this section, the officer does not request an answer from the suspect when none is forthcoming, but continues the line of questioning following his third turn repeat. This is indicative of the institutional, rather than conversational intention of the repeat, and highlights that the interactional orientation is to the silent participant rather than to the suspect.

The final extract is from later in the same interview. In extract 26 the officer attempts to establish how the suspect came to have the drugs in his possession. After receiving an unclear answer from the suspect in response to this question (line 266), the officer asks the suspect how much he paid for the drugs. Interestingly, the repeat made by the officer on line 271 is an exact repeat of the suspect's answer 'ten pound' (line 269), and not a grammatically repaired repeat to include the plural 's'. This suggests that the uninitiated third turn in this extract is not partly designed, as in extract 23, to repair an aspect of the suspect's utterance, nor to attend to the suspect or to elicit information as seen above, but is designed to draw attention to the suspect's answer, as seen in courtroom interaction (Drew 1992).

Extract 26: Ten pound

```
264   P1    >can you< tell me where you got it from
265         (0.2)
266   S     (°y↓ur°)
267         (0.8)
268   P1    how much you paid for i:t
269   S     ten °p↓ound°
270         (0.3)
271   P1→   ten po:und
272         (0.2)
273   P1    >but you< do:n't wanna tell me:
274         (0.4)
275   P1    you know <that's> illegal t'have cannabis
276         (0.2)
277   S     y↓eah
```
(T6-119-06)

The suspect's utterance on line 269 is important as, in stating the cost of the drugs, the suspect (knowingly or unknowingly) implicates himself as having bought them, and by virtue of the nature of that transaction, that he has done so from a drug dealer. Therefore in this case it is the substance of the officer's repeat, and that the officer does not go on to explicitly request a response from the suspect, that indicates the repeat is used to draw attention to this incriminating answer for the later listeners of the interview rather than attend to the suspect and the conversational aspect of the interview. Like the other extracts in this section, the suspect does not respond to the officer's repeat, shown in the silence of line 272. The officer, in his next turn, continues the questioning and contrasts the suspect's willingness to reveal implicatory information (by putting himself at the scene, buying drugs from a dealer), with his earlier reluctance to identify and implicate that dealer: 'but you don't wanna tell me' (line 273).

The third turns in this section exhibit similarities to third turns found in courtroom interaction in that they are used by officers to orientate to the silent participant rather than solely to attend to the local interaction with the suspect. This is made clear for example in extract 25, where the officer's knowledge of the suspect's answer renders a third turn repeat as a reparative measure unnecessary. None of the suspects repaired their answers or responded to an officer's third turn repeat, and none of the officers went on to explicitly request a response from the suspect. This suggests, unlike the extracts of the previous section, that the turns were not designed to initiate one. Rather, the structure of the third turns appear similar to courtroom interaction, where they can be used to emphasize the prior turn for the benefit of the silent participant (Drew 1992), who is framed, as described by Greatbatch (1992) and Drew (1992), as the addressee of the repeat.

This difference from the use of third turns typical of ordinary conversation, seen in the earlier section, highlights that these turns are being used for the benefit of the silent participant rather than to attend to some aspect of the local interaction-in-progress. Additionally, the presence of conversationally oriented third turns reveals how it is the interactional work achieved through the use of third turns, rather than simply their very existence in the police interview, that defines their presence as part of the structural orientation to the silent participant. Uninitiated third turns, although they are constructed to, and can be used in similar ways to courtroom interaction, are also used in the accomplishment of different tasks. This highlights that although these tools are used across contexts, it is the context-specific elements of the interaction and the particularities of the participants in that setting that ultimately governs their construction and use.

Discussion: The Silent Participant – Uninitiated Third Turns

While the third turns shown in extracts 20–22 follow the characteristics typical of ordinary conversation, the third turns of extracts 23–26 exhibit characteristics more typical of courtroom interaction (Drew 1992) and news interview interaction (Greatbatch 1992). These more conversational third turns can be used to emphasize or draw attention to some aspect of the answer given by the suspect in the prior turn. They can also be used to elicit a disagreement or confirmation of that repeat (Hutchby and Wooffitt 1998), or minimize the scope for potential misunderstanding by initiating a repair to ensure the meaning of the utterance. Institutional third turns, however, are used to highlight a suspect's pertinent or significant answer for the primary recipiency of the silent participant (Heritage 1985, Greatbatch 1988; Greatbatch 1992; Drew 1992). They are also used to resolve potential future ambiguities in an utterance's comprehension for an audience that does not request clarification (Drew 1992), or to form the basis of a juxtaposing argument in order to challenge the veracity of the suspect's version of events (Drew 1992).

In conversational third turns, silence from the suspect after the officer's repeat was responded to by officers with an explicit request for a response, whereas institutional third turns were characterized by their continuance of the question-answer sequence without topicalizing the silence or requesting a response. This suggests that officers' third turns are institutionally constructed to repeat the facts to the silent participant as the main addressee (Greatbatch 1992), or are conversationally constructed to initiate interaction with the suspect, for example to initiate a repair of the prior utterance from the recipient or to highlight that answer as troublesome in some way (Hutchby and Wooffitt 1998). Although extract 21 shows the use of third turns failing to elicit information from a suspect, it is made clear through the subsequent turns in the interaction that it was designed and employed to extract that information. It is interesting that third turns are not present in the successful elicitation of confessionary turns explored in the following two chapters; this is perhaps indicative of a low success rate of third turns as elicitory tools.

This chapter has explored third turns in the police interview, revealed the different types of third turns, their varied applications and success.

It has explored the structure of police interview third turns through their similarities to and differences from third turns in other institutional interaction. These findings demonstrate the officers' orientation to the structural constraints of institutional interviewing and to a future audience, who, similar to the silent participants in courtroom interaction (Drew 1992), are unable to or do not interject with requests for repeats. These findings also highlight the effect of the silent participant on police interview interaction, and could be useful in advancing the use of third turns by officers as a tool in the interview.

Conclusion to Part Two

Part Two has highlighted the importance of the officer's orientation to both the suspect and to the silent participant, and has revealed the difficulties of the officer in managing the often conflicting demands of the suspect and the silent participant, despite the purpose of the silent participant to ensure the protection of suspects' rights. The chapters illustrate officers directing the third turn as an interactional tool towards two different, and often competing, uses – attending to the silent participant and attending to the suspect; skilfully managing their attendance to the silent participant by orienting to the conversational aspect of the talk. Similar orientation is shown in Chapter 5 where officer laughter is used to avoid sanctions by framing potential breaches of protocol as conversationally oriented.

In accordance with legislation officers inform suspects of their rights. However, the rigidity of these legal strictures is made apparent through the officers' inability to tailor those utterances to the individual circumstances of the interview. This is illustrated by the performance of the officers as they are compelled to disregard their local talk with the suspect to defer (redundantly or otherwise) to the requirements of the PACE Act 1984. This heavily routinized approach to the adherence to the legislative requirements may result in the individual needs and rights of the suspect being overlooked – although interestingly, it is this routinized nature of the interview that can also be used as a tool to account for the production of semantically redundant talk or more adversarial techniques.

The presence of the silent participant could detract from the interactional requirements of the suspect as the officers' attendance to the legal requirements takes precedence over the suspects' interactional ones. These findings draw attention to a problematic area of the current scope and administration of the codes of conduct as they reveal that, despite being introduced in part to protect the suspect, the mechanical adherence to these requirements and the inability of officers to tailor them to the individual suspect can in fact leave the suspect under-protected. Although the scope of this research does not reach to surveying suspects' reasons for declining legal advice, the extracts do show officers hurriedly administering the suspects' rights which could leave suspects under-informed. These results, if used in interviews to actively orient to each suspect in every interview from the outset, rather than the opening sequence being viewed as merely a formality, could pose a real benefit to the protection of the suspect. This deeper focus on the suspects' interaction at all stages of the interview has the potential to provide officers with an enhanced communicative understanding and rapport with suspects.

Part Two provides empirical evidence that the silent participant affects the interaction of the officer. As Moston and Engelberg (1993) state, the introduction of tape recording made the interaction more transparent, rendering any flaws of the officer audible and therefore accountable. This research has itself revealed flaws, although they are a product of the communicative mechanisms to which officers are accountable. The overarching presence of the silent participant and the consequences of the officer failing to satisfy their requirements can leave the suspect legally protected but interactionally neglected. This may compromise the suspects' opportunity to put across their side of the story. This research challenges the claim (Law Reform Commission of Canada 1988) that by tape recording the interview the suspects' rights are increased. It is in fact the officers' *adherence* to those mechanisms, created to protect the suspects' rights, that has increased. The transparency of the officers' adherence to the Act (1984) has led to officers self-imposing stricter requirements on their own talk than legislatively required in order to ensure the admissibility of the interview, often to the detraction of their attendance to the suspect.

The research reveals the points at which there can be a misalignment of these legislative requirements and the interactional requirements of the suspect, and highlights officers' difficulties in maintaining an orientation to these often conflicting aspects of the interview. The findings provide empirical evidence of successful and unsuccessful uses of third turns, offer practical insights into avoiding communicative difficulties in the orientation to the silent participant, and highlight potential difficulties with the practicality and scope of the officers' adherence to the codes of conduct. It has highlighted the tension between the officers' interactional requirement to attend to the conversational aspect, and their legal requirement to attend to the institutional aspect of the interaction. It has illustrated how the talk in the police interview is designed to accommodate the silent participant, who is at points identified, in common with the findings of Heritage (1985) and Greatbatch (1988), as the main addressee. This research could be used to advance officers' interviewing and elicitation techniques as it shows the difficulties in managing the conflicting demands of the PACE Act 1984 and the suspect, and could be used in training officers in how to minimize those difficulties.

The police interview is the exposition of facts from a suspect arrested on suspicion of committing a criminal offence, in order to gather information about that offence. Although the primary objective of the interaction in the police interview is to obtain the facts in a dialogue with the suspect, and not to attend to an overhearing audience, the institutional requirements reinforced through the presence of the tape, both shape and are shaped by the officers' overriding orientation to the wider interaction of the silent participant.

Part Three

Confessions

The final two analytic chapters examine the interviews in which suspects either produce confessions or information they have been withholding during the course of the interview (which, for ease of reference, will be referred to as confessions). The officers' role in the police interview is to draw the facts from the suspect in order to establish the events that took place; the suspect may, however, withhold the information they have from the officer. Chapters 8 and 9 examine how officers successfully draw information from previously non-responsive suspects through line-by-line analyses of the interactional turns that precede the suspects' eventual production of a confession.

Under the PACE Act 1984 a confession is defined as 'any statement wholly or partly adverse to the person who made it, whether made to a person in authority or not, and whether made in words or otherwise' (the PACE Act 1984 part viii, supplementary section 82; McAlhone and Stockdale 1999: 66). Baldwin (1992b: 17) defines a confession as where 'suspects completely changed their story during the course of an interview and admitted the offence'. For the purpose of this book, a successful elicitation of a confession is defined as where officers procure previously withheld information from a suspect; information that had been withheld in that interview by the suspect through omission, deception, or in exercising their right to silence. This is broader than the definitions used in PACE (1984) and by Baldwin (1992b), as it includes the production of previously withheld information that is *perceived* by the suspect to be potentially detrimental to their case or that of their associates.[26] This definition indicates the confession may not necessarily be (and is not required to be) a direct confession of the crime for which the suspect is under arrest as it recognizes the production of elicited information, procured by the officer despite prior resistance from the suspect, as confessed material. It also includes admissions of small parts of a crime, described by Shuy (1998) as 'part-confessions' (see Chapter 2).

As discussed in Chapter 3, the nine extracts used in this analysis are drawn from a total of seven police interview tapes from the original corpus of 150. These were selected on the basis that they constituted the entire body of tapes in which confessions by the suspect were present, illustrating the rarity of confessions in the data (present in 4.6% of cases). Despite using a broader definition, this is similar to the findings of Baldwin (1992b), where confessions were present in only 20 out of 600 police interviews (3.3%).

The importance of the police interview confession is reflected in the quantity of literature devoted to techniques for its elicitation. Despite a large body of literature in the area of confessions, very little empirical exploration of this phenomenon exists, and there are only a handful of studies that examine the interactional construction of the turns prior to a confession on a conversation analytic level. Considerable research explores American rather than British police interviews. In the USA the restrictions imposed upon police officers are different from those in the UK, which are governed by the PACE Act 1984. Despite the differences, an overarching interest in a 'formula' for extracting confessions remains constant. The two concerns of confession evidence in court are whether it was made by the suspect – 'the confession issue', and whether it was gained inappropriately – 'the exclusion issue' (Mirfield 1985). The conflicting interests of the officer to ascertain guilt and protect the suspect's rights are compounded, as the officer must demonstrate the integrity of the interview through their conduct. However, the lengths to which an officer can go to in the interview are certainly unclear, as the Act (1984) does not provide straightforward definitions of what is acceptable and unacceptable behaviour. The literature on this topic is varied, spans different countries, criminal justice systems, and tactics, techniques and procedures. The following chapters analyse the elicitation of confessions without particular distinction or attribution of behaviours to a specific country unless dictated by relevance, such as in the case of a flout of UK law.

The sections below outline specific techniques employed by officers, given in training manuals, reviews and research on their efficacy, and outline suspects' techniques and the potential for false confessions. Interestingly, many of the elements described in Chapter 2 as indicative of a good interviewing technique are either absent from or contrary to many of the techniques described here that are purported to aid the elicitation of confessions from suspects. Due to the nature of the data as interaction drawn from one element in the criminal justice system process, neither the eventual outcome of the confession in court, or judgements on the validity of the confessions are accessible. This exploration therefore represents a different approach to the confession by discounting the psychological background of, or the veracity of, the production of the confession. While acknowledging the importance of the interview as a whole, reflected in systematically referring throughout the analyses to points prior to and after the confession sequence, Chapters 8 and 9 also challenge the common-sense understandings of the police interview by empirically examining its jointly negotiated nature on a line-by-line level. 'Because ... confessions are dialogically constructed, they bear the imprint of not only the suspect but also the interrogator, and the end product must be analysed in that light' (Shuy 1998: 9).

Confessions and the Officer: Techniques and Tactics

It is commonly accepted by juries that obtaining involuntary confessions requires some kind of coercion, and although the physical type and verbal tactics such as repeated questioning are prohibited by the PACE Act 1984, psychological techniques are also highly effective and persuasive (Zimbardo 1967b; Inbau *et al.* 1986). Some, despite often being discounted by juries as too coercive (Kassin and McNall 1991), do remain admissible as evidence, including silence, emotional appeal such as flattery (Field Manual 1987, hereafter FM 1987; Shuy 1998) and the minimization and maximization of the offence (Kassin and Wrightsman 1985; Inbau *et al.* 1986, Kassin and McNall 1991; Pearce and Gudjonsson 1999; Napier and Adams 2002). Indeed, as described by Baldwin (1993: 333), 'It is extremely difficult to induce suspects to confess by methods that would nowadays be regarded as acceptable.'

A confession can be elicited through a series of 'truth-finding activities' (Komter 2003), such as offering rationalizations for the crime, which are bound to the sequential nature of interaction and borne from lengthy repetition. Watson (1990) posits that the suspect must first be encouraged to talk; through a combination of asking questions, initiating storytelling, using minimal responses or continuers (such as 'mmhm' and 'go on'), and then persuaded to confess. Preference organization in this context, that is, the suspects' preference for a particular turn shape (see 'dispreferred action/turn' in the glossary of technical terms in Appendix III), can be used by officers to make it interactionally difficult for suspects to avoid answering a question, or dispute an officer's knowledge claim (Watson 1990). Other tactics include the use of silence, which can draw attention to, and signal, the officer's disbelief of the suspect's versions of events (Komter 2003). Interruptions, or the 'rapid fire approach' (FM 1987), can confuse the suspect into uttering contradictory answers, although the permissibility of such techniques in UK police interviews is questionable. Using 182 police interrogations from three American police departments, Leo's (1996) results indicate that, unlike Baldwin's (1992b) finding that they have little effect, interrogation tactics do have a significant effect on a suspect's likelihood of producing incriminating information. The most successful tactics were identifying contradictions in the suspect's story (91% success rate), flattery (91% success rate) and providing justifications for the crime (90% success rate). This reflects the findings (Moston *et al.* 1993; Sigurdsson and Gudjonsson 1996; Gudjonsson and Sigurdsson 1999) that suspects are most likely to confess when they perceive that there is evidence against them. Although the analytic approach of this book is not conducive to similar quantification, further research could explore the type and frequency of successful confessions in relation to officers' techniques and the type of crime alleged.

Pearce and Gudjonsson (1999) analysed the framework of tactics outlined by Inbau *et al.* (1986) by which officers can overcome suspects and compel them to confess, identifying the 'Intimidation factor' as the most used of the 39 tactics. This is 'a hard sell technique in which the interrogator tries to scare and intimidate the suspect into confessing by making false claims about evidence and exaggerating the seriousness and magnitude of the charges' (Kassin and McNall 1991: 234). Extract 19 (see Part Two) showed how an officer drew out and repeated the negative consequences of remaining silent to the suspect but also counterbalanced this by invoking a conversational stance and framing her utterance as institutionally required and for the benefit of the suspect. Inbau *et al.* (1986) also recommend playing down or minimizing, a tactic which involves behaviour such as officers not wearing a police uniform and avoiding 'realistic' words to describe the crime in question (for instance referring to arson as fire). Minimization can also include downplaying the seriousness of the crime and severity of the situation (Kassin and Wrightsman 1985; Kassin and McNall 1991; Pearce and Gudjonsson 1999), providing justifications for the offence or apportioning blame to another party (Napier and Adams 2002; Inbau *et al.* 2004).

Irving (1980) and Irving and Hilgendorf (1980) suggest that by increasing the disadvantages of denial and advantages of confessing, and reducing factors that may deter the suspect from confessing (for example the fear of reprisal), the suspect can be enticed to confess. Referred to by Komter (2003) as a 'hypothetical situation', justification and minimization are illustrated by officers providing rationalizations and logical outcomes of suspected criminal activity, which enables suspects to rationalize their own acts of criminality. In experiments designed to determine lay opinions of different elicitation techniques, Kassin and McNall (1991) found those who observed interviews in which minimization took place were more likely to estimate that suspects received leaner sentences than in the interviews where maximization[27] was used. The minimization technique was also shown to be as effective in implicitly *inferring* leniency as actual, explicit promises of leniency (Kassin and McNall 1991). Napier and Adams (2002) claim the success of this technique lies in its similarity to the suspects' own techniques employed to downplay or account for their criminal behaviour. These defences not only rationalize their activities after the event but also make the committal of the crime easier or even possible, as an 'episodic release from moral constraint' (Matza 1964: 69). Sykes and Matza (1957) categorize the sub-types of denial as the denial of responsibility, injury and victim, the condemnation of the condemners and the appeal to higher authorities. Officers can use these justifications to appear to identify with the suspect's perspective, lessen the moral and social culpability of the deviant (Mills 1940) and appeal to the suspect's need to account for their actions as a product of reasoned rather than perverse behaviour. That justifications and minimizations are used by the officer as an elicitory technique suggests crime can be viewed by the officer as part of, and therefore responsive to, societal reasoning, rather than a product of an undefendable and separate criminal subculture of values.

In his analysis of the interaction prior to a confession, Watson (1990) reveals knowledge claims are a significant elicitory factor; the stronger an officer's claim to knowledge, the more likely the suspect will confess. Also known as the 'file and dossier' and the 'we know all' approach (FM 1987), knowledge claims are an effective technique for controlling information and power (Hodgson 1994) and eliciting confessions from naïve or scared suspects. Knowledge claims feature heavily in the literature on police interrogation tactics – for example, being used to signal disbelief and challenge the suspect's story (Komter 2003), constructing or upgrading information to the status of factual evidence (Underwager and Wakefield 1990, Watson 1990), or controlling information and intimidating suspects (Hodgson 1994). Other examples include constructing evidence to convince a victim to reveal more information (Underwager and Wakefield 1990), such as producing claims of a witness to compel a suspect to confess (Inbau *et al.* 1986).

Investigating favoured elicitory techniques, Kassin *et al.* (2007) found officers frequently isolated suspects from family and friends (66% reported always using this technique); used a 'small private room' for the interrogation (42%); and identified contradictions in the suspect's story (41%). Despite claims of its effectiveness (discussed earlier), only 13% of officers stated they always offered justifications to the suspect. This highlights the often-conflicting findings of theoretical and practical research on police interviewing and confession elicitation. This is also reflected by Kassin *et al.*'s (2007: 382) statement that 'one cannot determine [from interrogation manuals and programs] what constitutes common police practices'. The prevalence of police interviewing myths must compound the difficulties of the officer in their selection of elicitory techniques and subsequently impact on their interviewing ability. The following two chapters explore these discrepancies between research and training manuals, as well as the role of the PACE Act 1984 in influencing the exchanges that take place. In doing so, this work challenges the myths of police interviewing by empirically investigating the officers' interviewing techniques. In examining the interview data for the presence of elicitory techniques outlined in this section, the chapters that follow reveal and investigate the use of knowledge claims and minimization respectively in drawing confessions from suspects.

The next section focuses on the anticipated result of these techniques – the suspects' confession. The tactics of the officer are not necessarily the sole factor in procuring a confession; Gudjonsson's (1996) 'suggestibility scales', created to test and measure a person's suggestibility, indicate the suspects' suggestibility is also a contributory factor. The effect of interviewer tactics and the suspects' likelihood of confessing (Gudjonsson 1996), the production of false confessions (Kassin and Kiechel 1996; Horselenberg *et al.* 2006), suspects' deception cues (Inbau *et al.* 2004) and their validity (Vrij *et al.* 2001; Caso *et al.* 2005) are also explored.

Confessions and the Suspect: Deception Detection, Behavioural Cues and False Confessions

A discussion of the truthfulness or deceptiveness of the suspect is salient in any dialogue of confessions. Kassin *et al.* (2007) found officers rated themselves on average 77% accurate at detecting truth or lies of a suspect. Walsh's (2006) paper revealed 71% of Fraud Investigation Service investigators questioned believed they could 'read' guilt through suspects' body language, and Inbau *et al.* (2001) claim their technique is 85% accurate in determining truth and deception. According to Inbau *et al.* (2004), identifying deception cues such as nervousness, gaze aversion and self-grooming are a major part of the interrogators' toolbox in establishing guilt or innocence. The 'information recovery and credibility assessment method' (Walters 2005b) claims deception can be detected by combining a number of factors including stress cues, hand and body movements and voice pitch, tone and quality (Walters 2005a, 2005c). Similarly, microexpressions, that are involuntary facial expressions that can reveal underlying emotions (Ekman *et al.* 1971, Shuy 1998), could be used to expose falseness or can signal an imminent confession (Walters 2005a: 1).

However, deception detection has been widely criticized (for an overview, see Miller and Stiff 1993; and Robinson 1996) as inaccurate and inconsistent (see also Ekman and O'Sullivan 1991, Shuy 1998), with both amateurs' and experts' ability to detect deception falling at or around the level of chance (Miller and Stiff 1993; Kassin and Fong 1999; Meissner and Kassin 2002). Vrij *et al.* (2001: 186) claim 'professional lie catchers are no better in detecting deception than college students', and Vrij (2000), Memon *et al.* (2003) and Grenhag and Stromwall (2004) provide comprehensive reviews on the accuracy of deception detection. Deception cues also are often confused with truthful utterances skewed by stress or in response to an incriminating question (or a question with a high 'Incriminating Potential Rating', Davis *et al.* 2005). Caso *et al.* (2005) found that those behaviours documented as deceptive by Inbau *et al.* (2004) were actually more likely to be found in the utterances of those telling the truth. Tellingly, many deception cues, such as pauses, silence (Inbau *et al.* 1986, FM 1987) and rushed speech and laughter (Inbau *et al.* 1986), are also known to be characteristics indicative of ordinary interactional behaviour. Silence, for example, is also known as a method of signalling disagreement without causing offence to the speaker (Pomerantz 1984), and is arguably a particularly relevant tool for a suspect in the police interview as the suspect may encounter communicative difficulties in directly challenging the officer. Laughter also has particular interactional properties potentially useful to the suspect in the police interview, such as to facilitate the production of dispreferred actions (Jefferson 1984, Brown and Levinson 1987, Billig 2005) and enable talk about troubles (Jefferson 1984). Pausing is widely understood to be part of the interactional design of turntaking

(Sacks *et al.* 1974; Drew 1992) and rushed speech is widely used as a tool to hold the floor in interaction (Drew and Heritage 1992).

Whether an accurate measure of truthfulness or deception, or a futile measurement of ordinary verbal leakages, any standardized interpretation of suspects' behaviour as a signal of deceptiveness could lead to the insistence of an innocent suspect's guilt. As highlighted in Chapter 2, this conflicts with the premise of the police interview as a means to establish information, and furthermore, interpreting a suggestible suspect's interaction as deceptive could result in their production of a false confession. The second most common cause of wrongful imprisonment after mistaken eyewitness evidence (Brandon and Davies 1973), false confessions are structurally similar to confessions (Inbau *et al.* 1986). Confession evidence cannot reliably be distinguished from its false counterpart, and, 'once regarded as the 'queen of evidence', its reliability is now in considerable doubt' (Greer 1994: 113). The level of success of manipulative or coercive techniques in eliciting a confession depends in part on the degree to which the suspect is suggestible to these approaches. Mansfield (1993: 2) posits 'false confessions are readily and regularly forthcoming', stating that less articulate, less educated, scared or emotional suspects regularly produce false confessions.

Confession evidence features in 68% of criminal trials (Kassin and Wrightsman 1985), carries more weight with juries than other evidence such as eye witness accounts and character testimony (Kassin and Neumann 1997; Kassin 2005) and makes 'the other aspects of a trial in court superfluous' (McCormick 1972: 316). Trowbridge (2003) and Zimbardo (1967a) claim confessions contribute to solving criminal cases by as much as 80%. However, the United States Supreme Court (1967) have stated that: '[A] system of criminal law enforcement which comes to depend on the "confession" will, in the long run, be less reliable and more subject to abuses than a system which depends on extrinsic evidence independently secured through skilful investigation'. Additionally, the ease by which confessions can be coerced, threatened or otherwise falsely obtained from suspects in the police interview that has led Mansfield (1993: 2) to describe them as 'the worst and most unreliable form of evidence you can find and should be considered as no evidence at all'.

In complete contrast, the Report of the Royal Commission on Criminal Justice (1993) states its willingness to sacrifice the liberty of false confessors in order to safeguard the punishment of the guilty:

Against the risk that defendants may be tempted to plead guilty to charges of which they are not guilty must be weighed the benefits to the system and to defendants of encouraging those who are in fact guilty to plead guilty.

(Royal Commission on Criminal Justice 1993: 111, para. 45)

Scheck et. al's (2000) study revealed false confessions led to the wrongful conviction of 15 out of 62 exonerated suspects, with police misconduct featuring in 31 cases. Kassin (1997), Gudjonsson (2002, 2003) and Kassin *et al.* (2003) suggest false confessions can be elicited through police techniques, although this is disputed by Inbau *et al.* (2001) and Buckley (2003). Other contributors to false confessions include mental health problems or language difficulties of the suspect[28] (Kassin and Kiechel 1996; Gudjonsson 2003), the interrogation (Leo and Ofshe 1998), and the presentation of false evidence (Kassin and Kiechel 1996). The results also indicate the likelihood of false confessions increase with the presence of a 'corroborating witness' or increased pressure to confess. Although analysing false confessions to non-criminal activity under laboratory conditions (in this case, the act of striking the F12 button during a simulated computer test), Kassin and Kiechel (1996) demonstrate an interviewer's ability to dramatically alter the likelihood of false confessions and lead the subject to internalize, that is believe, their confession. Horselenberg *et al.* (2006) replicated this research to test the effect of plausibility and consequences on false confessions. The results revealed, similar to Kassin and Kiechel (1996), the more plausible the crime, the higher the rate of internalized false confessions, while the higher the consequences of confessing, the less likely false confessions become. Kassin and Gudjonsson (2004) also manipulated the conditions to include punishments for confessing. The results indicate the strength of the factors compelling the subject to confess override the negative implications for confessing.

Isolation and inexperience in the police interview can contribute to the stress of the suspect, which can lead them to lose contact with reality (Gudjonsson and MacKeith 1982), and enter a 'trance-like state of heightened suggestibility' where 'truth and falsehood become hopelessly confused in the suspect's mind' (Foster 1969: 690–691). Combined with a presumption of guilt, the officers' ability to coerce and manipulate suspects into producing confessions and the real possibility of those confessions proving false, must raise serious concerns in the protection of suspects' rights. Despite the availability of research detailing elements of a good interview technique, such as open-ended questions (see Chapter 2), a considerable amount of police interview guidance in eliciting confessions involves some kind of deception, force, trickery or exploitation of a suspect's suggestibility. These factors, for the protection of the suspect and the reputation of the confession as evidence should surely be absent from the officers' interviewing toolbox.

Chapters 8 and 9 juxtapose common understandings of the confession with a real-time, line by line analysis of the techniques used by the officer, exposing much of what has been written and understood about confessions as misconceptions, myth and mystique. They use the analysis of audio police interview tapes to focus on the construction and negotiation of the interaction of the suspect and officer prior to, and culminating in, the suspect's eventual production of a confession (or production of withheld information). Chapter 8 explores the officers' elicitation of confessions through their production of utterances that refer to sources of knowledge, and Chapter 9 looks at confessions that result from the officers' minimization of the negative connotations of confessing.

Chapter 8

Confessions: Knowledge Claims

This chapter explores the officers' use of knowledge claims in the elici-tation of confessionary turns from the suspect. This technique is seen in the data as the officer's production of evidence that contradicts the suspect's account (extracts 27, 28 and 29), as an invitation for the suspect to implicate another suspect (extract 30), or to vindicate their own involvement (extract 31). Knowledge claims are used to draw responses from the suspect to repair the officer's knowledge claim (extracts 30 and 31), or compel the suspect to alter their version to take that claim into account (extracts 27, 28 and 29).

The following extract is from an interview of a suspect arrested on suspicion of assault. The suspect has been accused of striking the victim in an altercation that occurred between the two men after their vehicles were involved in a road traffic collision. Prior to this point, the suspect has repeatedly denied striking the victim.[29]

Extract 27: I'll tell you what I did do

```
239   P1→ >so we got an< i:ndependent witness that says you hit him,
240   S    no=
241   P1→ =obviously (.) [m↑ister de:an said that you hit hi:[m
242   S                  [no                              [no, and I >di:dn't hit
243      → hi:m< (0.4) I'll tell you what I did do, (0.5) I at ↑one stage, >not at< tha:t
244        stage, [I did actually throw a punch at him and m↑issed him
245   P1         [°mhm°
246        (0.3)
247   P1   °r:↓ight°
248   S    I missed h↓im I didn't even to[uch h↓im NEVER come into contact with=
249   P1                                [was this
250   S    =him <at ↓all>=
(T33-22-06)
```

On line 239 the officer produces a knowledge claim by referring to a statement of an independent witness, whose account, in stating the suspect did strike the victim, contradicts the one given by the suspect. In the next turn, the suspect denies this account (line 240), and the officer, in his immediate latched response then issues a partial repeat of his earlier turn ('says you hit him', lines 239 and 241). In this second turn, the officer refers to the account given by the victim rather than the witness. The officer uses the turn shape 'says you hit him' when presenting this evidence, which is almost an exact replication of his earlier turn, drawing attention to the similarities between the statements of the witness and the victim. This is significant as the accounts from these two sources both dispute the version provided by the suspect. The suspect responds during the officer's turn, by denying the statement again ('no', 'no and I didn't hit him', lines 242–243), and then producing an augmented account of his actions ('I'll tell you what I did do ...', lines 243–244). The suspect's increased response from a straight denial (line 240) to a denial together with an explanatory account (lines 242–244) mirrors the officer's increased challenge from stating an alternate account exists (line 239) to aligning the witnesses and the victim's accounts (line 241).

The suspect responds to the officer by producing new information about his involvement in the assault (lines 243–244) and although the suspect does not confess to striking the victim, he does produce previously withheld information by stating that he had thrown a punch at the victim and missed. This new account enables both the suspect's earlier assertions that he did not strike the victim, and the witness's statement to coexist without the suspect implicating himself in the offence or contradicting his own earlier statements. This assertion, that he threw a punch and missed, could then account for what the witness claims he saw (the suspect throwing a punch) without the suspect admitting that he struck the victim. The suspect had not until this point provided this relevant and potentially exonerating account of his actions, despite having had opportunities to do so, for example in response to the officer's prior references to the witness and his statement.[30] This suggests that this account has been elicited from the suspect by the officer's challenge of the suspect's story through referring to, and juxtaposing, the statements given by the witness and the victim.

This extract has shown the suspect being compelled to give additional information that had until that point been withheld. It has shown the suspect revealing this information in response to the officer aligning the victim and witness statements, which were both contrary to the information provided by the suspect. The suspect produces the previously withheld information as a way to manage the contradicting information presented to him by the officer while avoiding incriminating himself. The suspect's 'I'll tell you what I did do' (line 243) is reminiscent of a part-confession (Shuy 1998), in which suspects minimize their part in the crime by admitting to a less serious offence.[31]

Extract 28 is from an interview of a suspect arrested on suspicion of causing criminal damage earlier that night to a car in a car park I have named Drewer Mead. Prior to this extract the officer had asked the suspect to give his version of events and an account of his movements that evening. The suspect claimed that he drove to the car park so that he and a friend could urinate, stating that they drove directly to the car park after leaving a pub. Extract 28 begins with the officer informing the suspect of a statement, made by the owner of that pub, Mr French, in which he states the men had left an hour earlier than the suspect had claimed. This information, if correct, means there was an hour unaccounted for between the times the suspect claimed the men left the pub and their arrival at the car park. The officer produces Mr French's statement on lines 187–188 as evidence that the men had left earlier than the suspect's claimed 11:15pm. The suspect does not respond; his turn not being taken is shown in the pause on line 189. In the absence of a turn by the suspect, the officer then makes the explicit connection that this time is earlier than the suspect had stated 'so you left quite early' (line 190).

In another absence of a response from the suspect in the following turn (line 191), the officer then draws on the account of Mr Smith, one of the men who had been in the car with the suspect, who had also declared they had left the pub at an earlier time than the one claimed by the suspect. The officer's use of 'also' on line 192 draws attention to the corroborating nature of Mr Smith's statement with that of the landlord, which he then juxtaposes, together with the time of the arrest, to the suspect's claim that they had left the pub and gone straight to the car park (lines 192–195).

Extract 28: Got anything to say about that?

187   P1   the place is closed up by >sort of< half past (0.2) according to: (0.7) er
188   → mister french (0.4) that you left you weren't the last to leave
189   (0.5)
190   P1   so you left quite early
191   (0.8)
192   P1→ he's (.) he: also said quarter past ten (0.4) miste:r (0.6) e:rm smith also

193		said quarter past ten (0.8) a:nd (0.5) having heard what you just said you
194		came out turned left turned left (0.4) and you've gone straight to drewer
195		mea:d (0.3) yet you were arrested at °five to er five to twelve:° (0.8)
196		you're missing (0.2) >sort of< quite a long time
197		(1.0)
198	S	°hm°
199		(3.2)
200	P1	an hour
201		(4.9)
202	P1	got anything to say about that?
203		(1.0)
204	S →	we did have something to eat as well
205		(0.6)
206	P1	I'd <u>asked</u> you before
207	S	yeah but it wasn't sort of (0.3) the only reason I didn't sort of say it
208		because if I's said it it would've looked sort of more suspicious

(T7-120-06)

The officer's implicit request for an explanation in his statement 'you're missing ... quite a long time' (line 196) is minimally responded to in the next turn by the suspect (line 198). However, this response does not provide an explanation for the discrepancy in the accounts highlighted by the officer. The officer then uses his next turn ('an hour', line 200) to make explicit this 'long time' he had alluded to in his previous turn. This repair of his prior turn to a more explicit one indicates the officer has perceived the lack of a satisfactory response to be a result of his temporal vagueness in his own prior turn (line 196). The pause on line 201 is again indicative of the suspect's turn not being taken, and the suspect not responding to this repaired turn by the officer. That the officer's prior turns were designed to elicit an explanatory account from the suspect is shown, upon their failure to do so, by the officer's production of an explicit request for a response when none has been forthcoming (line 202), to which the suspect finally responds. That the suspect provides new, previously withheld information in that turn (line 204) is highlighted in the officer's response 'I'd asked you before' (line 206), and that this information was hidden[32] by the suspect as a deliberate act is also explicitly verbalized by the suspect in his next turn – 'I didn't ... say it because ... it would've looked ... more suspicious' (lines 207–208).

The suspect initially avoids providing that information, shown in the pauses of lines 189, 191, 197 and 201; points at which he could have responded to or commented[33] on the content of witnesses statement (line

189), on his movements (line 191), or provided an account of the 'missing' time (lines 197 and 201). It is only when the officer explicitly enquires if the suspect has anything to say in response to his statements that the suspect then provides his response, in which he reveals the withheld information. The suspect's silence in response to the officer's turns is not a dispreferred action as he shows that he does not interpret the officer's turns as requests for a response. This is evidenced in the suspect's eventual response only being produced after the officer makes an explicit request for a response from the suspect. This highlights that there are mechanisms available to the suspect, similar to the findings of Johnson and Newbury (2006), through which he can avoid providing an account that contradicts his earlier statements without producing a dispreferred turn. It also reveals how the requirements of interaction compel the suspect to finally produce a response. Although the suspect used the potential ambiguity of the officer's implicit requests for a response or an explanation to avoid revealing the withheld information, it is clear that the officer's provision of witness statements and the juxtaposition of those statements to highlight incongruities with the suspect's version of events (for example 'having heard what you just said', line 193), was the catalyst for the suspect's production of an alternate account.

Both extracts 27 and 28 have shown the suspect altering their account while continuing to maintain their innocence, after a contradicting account is produced by the officer. In extract 27 the suspect provided an explanation as to why the witness would have mistakenly assumed that he had seen him strike the victim. In extract 28, however, the suspect altered his account under the premise that the witness statements were correct, and it was his own account that was deceptive, and the fear of his (withheld) information being mistakenly perceived as incriminating behaviour that prevented him from producing this account upon earlier questioning.[34]

The suspect in extract 29 had been arrested earlier that day on suspicion of possessing and then selling a stolen leather jacket. In a direct question on line 329, the officer asks whether the suspect had received any money for the sale of the jacket. After a pause the suspect denies receiving any money, to which, after a further pause, the officer partially repeats the question. In this partial repeat (line 333) the officer reformulates and frames his utterance as a statement in which he presents a contradictory scenario (that the suspect did receive money), and then asks the suspect to 'think carefully'.

Extract 29: I put it to you

```
325   P1   he didn't. <how much> did (.) <you offer> the jacket for [sale fo:r
326   S                                                            [one hundred
327   P1   one hundred po:unds
328        (0.8)
329   P1   did you receive any mone:y
330        (0.5)
331   S    °no°
332        (0.8)
333   P1→  I put it to you that you di:d receive some money think careful↓ully
334   S →  oh I did oka:y
335        (0.3)
336   P1   how much money did you re[ceive
337   S                            [eighty po:und
(T40-66-06)
```

The use of phrases such as 'think carefully' have been posited as tactics by Inbau *et al.* (1986). They present an impression that the officer already knows the truth, in order to elicit that truth from guilty suspects. The turn in the above extract implicitly suggests that the officer is party to some currently undisclosed knowledge about the sale of the jacket, of which the suspect is not aware. This, together with the officer's statement of an alternate, contradictory account ('I put it to you that you did receive some money', line 333) forms an implicit request for the suspect to reconsider his prior answer. The lowered intonation during the officer's production of 'think carefully' has a threatening undertone that also alludes to the potential consequences facing the suspect if he continues this denial.

This is supported by the suspect's complete reversal of his account in the following turn 'oh I did okay' (line 334), which suggests that the suspect has indeed interpreted the officer's turn as a claim to knowledge which contradicts his first answer ('no', line 331). The suspect's complete reversal of his answer suggests the officer's turn directly preceding that reversal (the officer's partially repeated request for an answer, line 333), performed an other-initiated self-repair on the suspect's response. The direct influence of the officer's statement on the suspect is also apparent in the suspect's use of 'oh' in his repaired answer of line 334. This use of 'oh', a 'change of state token' (Heritage 1984), highlights 'some kind of change in his or her locally current state of knowledge, information, orientation or awareness' (Heritage 1984: 299) has happened and that the suspect has undergone as a result of the officer's preceding utterance. The 'oh' prior to his production of his altered answer (line 334) therefore demonstrates the suspect's reinterpretation of the officer's original question (line 329) from an exploratory one, into one to which the officer already knows the answer. That the suspect produces this repaired turn (line 334) without the pauses that had characterized the interaction in this extract up until this point, demonstrates that the suspect is quick to remedy his earlier answer in response to the officer's implicit knowledge claim. This readiness is see alson in the suspect's next turn (line 337) where, in a complete contrast to his prior denial of receiving money, he is so quick to tell the officer the amount of money he received that he overlaps the officer's turn (lines 336–337).

The following extract (extract 30) is from the same interview that extracts 7 and 8 (Chapter 5) were taken. The suspect has been arrested following his departure from a petrol station without paying for the fuel. Up until this point in the interview, the suspect has made no comment to all of the officer's questions, including the officer's direct questions about whether the suspect[35] or another party[36] committed the offence. In common with extract 31, the confession is the suspect's departure from making no comment to producing a response to the officer's questions, rather than (as seen in the other extracts in this chapter) the suspect producing otherwise withheld information or confessing to the crime.

The officer, on line 118, responds to the solicitor's confirmation (line 117) of the suspect's intention to continue to answer 'no comment'. The officer responds to this prior turn by initiating the closing sequence of the interview by stating 'I've got no further questions I want to ask you at this stage'.[37] This indicates the interview is coming to a close as a result of the suspect's intention to not answer questions, and is followed by the officer stating it is the suspect's opportunity to put forward his side of the story, which is another statement typical of the closing sequence of the police interview. This statement gives the suspect a final opportunity to comment on the crime (lines 120–121 and 123–125) and any other aspect of what happened (line 127) prior to the interview being terminated.

Extract 30: Rat your mates out?

117 So   he will be exercising his right to silence officer ye̲:s
118 P1   okay thank yo̲u (0.9) in that case (0.8) ive got no further questions I want
119   to ask you at this stage y- (1.2) just to let you <u>know</u> (0.6) °>as if its not<°
120   obvious enough already that this is <your opportunity to: e:rr> (1.4) put
121   your side of the stor↑y
122   (1.5)

```
123  P1    give your version of eve:nts (0.4) on the record (0.3) °would you- would
124        you like to do that at a↑ll have you got anything to say at a:ll about what
125        happened that night?°
126  S     no=
127  P1    =the way you've been treated by police or anything ↓else
128  S     °no°
129  P1    no:
130        (0.4)
131  P2→   you sure you don't want to rat your brother and your mate out mate
132        (2.3)
133  S →   they're nothing to do with ↓it they weren't driving the °c↓ar° ..hh (1.3)
134        they were the ones saying stop
135        (0.3)
136  P2    were they aware that it was sto:len tho:ugh
137        (1.1)
138  S     ..hh yeah ...hh
```
(T10-77-06)

The officer emphasizes the interview as the suspect's 'opportunity to ... put your side of the story' (lines 120–121). The raised inflection at the conclusion of this turn reflects the intonation of a questioning turn, and suggests it was intended to indirectly request or elicit a response from the suspect. The silence on line 122 is indicative of the next turn not being taken by the suspect, and in the absence of a response from the suspect, the officer then, on line 123, restates his previous turn 'give your version of events', before then reframing that statement as direct questions (lines 123–125). The officer's production of these explicit questions on lines 123–125 shows that he has retroactively reformulated his prior turn as a result of that turn not being responded to by the suspect as intended. The officer's explicit questions do then accordingly both yield a response from the suspect. The responses, the suspect's 'no' on lines 126 and 128, would ordinarily signal the continuance of the closing sequence by the officer,[38] as the officer has stated he has no more questions to ask and the suspect has indicated he has nothing more to say. The second officer (P2), however, interrupts this process by asking a question (line 131).

Despite the suspect's prior, systematic refusal to provide details of the offence or of the suspected accomplices, and the solicitor's confirmation of the suspect's intention to continue doing so (line 117), the elicitation of information from the suspect is ultimately successful. The suspect begins to answer questions about the offence and his role in it after the second officer interjects with 'you sure you don't want to rat your brother and

your mate out' on line 131. This question implies the officer believes the
brother and the 'mate' of the suspect were responsible for the crime. That
this implication has been interpreted as such by the suspect is revealed in
his response, in which he defends the other possible suspects, and, in doing
so, implicates himself in the crime (lines 133–134). The pause prior to the
suspect's answer (line 132) appears indicative of the suspect's reticence to
produce that turn; however, its eventual production (on lines 133–134)
suggests the suspect's desire to protect himself is overridden by his desire
to protect those who were with him. The second officer's referral to the
possible culpability of the other two people involved (line 131) therefore
ultimately led to the suspect's confession of information both after his turn
and also continuing further through the interview. The suspect goes on
to provide further information about the crime, including admitting his
accomplices knew the car was stolen (line 138) and that he had been under
the influence of drugs during the episode (see extract 34).

The extracts so far have demonstrated how officers' references to third
or outside parties can elicit a confessionary response from a suspect.
However, extract 30 differs from the others in that the officer did not refer
to explicit or implicit knowledge sources such as witnesses, but instead
referred to the potential culpability of those who were in the car with him
at the time of the offence – accomplices which the suspect may 'give up'.
In this case the suspect provided information about his own involvement
in the crime in order to prevent this from happening, supported by the
suspect breaking his commitment to silence to defend the other parties,
on both lines 133–134 and later, on lines 224–225.[39]

Extract 31 is from the same interview from which extract 20 was taken,
where the suspect was arrested on suspicion of inflicting grievous bodily
harm on his neighbour. Similar to extract 30, the confessionary turn in
this final extract of this chapter is produced by the suspect breaking the
silence he had maintained throughout this part of the interview in order
to respond to the officer's question. The extract opens with the officer
stating he believes the suspect is withholding information about the crime
(lines 118–119). This statement does not generate a response from the
suspect; the silence on line 120 is indicative of the suspect not taking
his turn. That the officer's statement of line 117–119 was intended as an
implicit request for information is shown in the officer's next turn, which,
following the suspect's silence, then explicitly requests information about
'what happened' (line 121). The suspect, after a pause, responds to this
explicit request by stating 'no comment'. The officer then produces an else
statement,[40] which relies on the innocence of the suspect as a condition

upon which the suspect will be able to provide the officer with the requested information. In doing so the officer, although again issuing a less explicit request, implicitly insinuates that, conversely, if the suspect does *not* provide the officer with that information, then the suspect's innocence is called into question. The suspect's 'no comment' in the following turn (line 128) shows the officer's attempt has again failed to elicit a response other than 'no comment' from the suspect.

Extract 31: Innocent party

```
117  P1   L↑AST NIGHT, (0.5) h↑arry (.) peters was ass↓aulted (0.4) quite ba:dl↓y
118        (1.3) and I believe that you were the:re (.) and you (0.3) obviously (0.5) I
119        believe that you saw what went on
120        (1.5)
121  P1   >can you< tell us wha:t ha:ppened
122        (0.4)
123  S     no c↓omment
124        (1.0)
125  P1   this is obviously your opportunity, (0.5) because you were there, >if you<
126        were an innocent party, (0.5) now is your opportunity >to tell< us what
127        happe:ned
128  S     no c↓omment
129        (2.6)
130  P1   coz SPEAKING (0.3) to er (.) harry >I don't think you had much
131        involvement< in the actual assault.
132        (0.8)
133  S →   I didn't [have a:ny °involvement°
134  P1            [so
135        (0.6)
136  P1   well >that is< (.) that is why I'm ↑asking y↓ou (.) what ha:ppene:d (0.8)
137        now is YOUR opportunity, if you had no involvement in it, (.) to tell me
138        what ha:ppen↓ed
139        (1.4)
140  P1   it's not gonna help- (.) by: (0.5) you're (0.8) totally right by saying no
141        comment, you're quite entitled to say th↓at (1.0) but- (0.5) if you (.)
142        were there, and you had nothing to do with it, (0.8) t↑ell me
143        (0.9)
```

(T6-119-06)

Framing his next turn as a continuation of the previous one (signalled by the use of 'coz', a contracted form of 'because', line 130), the officer refers to the victim as a source of information ('speaking to Harry') – a source which has the potential to vindicate the suspect from being held solely responsible for the assault. The officer uses this knowledge to indirectly offer the suspect an opportunity to provide information and ascribe some of the blame to another person. The suspect responds to the officer's suggestion that he had little to do with the assault by applying an other-initiated other-repair (that is, a correction) of the officer's utterance. This serves to qualify the officer's statement by asserting he had *no*, rather than the *little* involvement posed by the officer (line 133). That the suspect produces a response to the officer's turn other than the 'no comment' he had currently produced throughout the interview suggests that the officer's knowledge claim based on the victim's statement had motivated the suspect to respond, if only to assert his innocence by repairing the officer's statement. If the suspect had not responded to this potentially vindicating utterance of the officer, it could implicitly suggest a lack of agreement with that utterance,[41] and therefore accordingly implicitly indicate that he *did* have an involvement in the assault. So the suspect uses his turn on line 133 to take the opportunity to respond to the claim of the victim, but also, in its repair, to show that his part in the assault was not only negligible, but in fact non-existent. However, although the officer's turn does generate a response other than 'no comment', the suspect does not provide details of the assault, or respond to the officer's subsequent requests to tell him what happened (lines 137–138 and line 142).

The officer continues, using the suspect's response in an attempt to elicit information about the assault ('well that is why I'm asking you', line 136); making the officer's attempt to get 'what happened' from the suspect explicit. His use of 'well' as a preface to this statement (line 136) also indicates that he has interpreted the suspect's immediately preceding answer as incomplete or insufficient (Lakoff 1973). The officer continues his turn by issuing partial repeats of his earlier else statement of 125–127; first on lines 137–138 and, after no response from the suspect is forth-coming on line 139, again on lines 141–142. The first of these further else statements incorporate the only response (other than 'no comment') the suspect has provided: 'I didn't have any involvement' (line 133), in the officer's response 'if you had no involvement' (line 137). This is an attempt to draw a response from the suspect by inviting him to 'prove' the truthfulness of his prior statement.[42] The silences on lines 139 and 143, however, show the suspect does not provide the information the officer has attempted to elicit through these turns.

Although the suspect's response is not a confession or the provision of previously withheld information, it does demonstrate the officer's use of outside knowledge educing a response from the suspect in an otherwise unfruitful interview. The elicitory nature of the knowledge claim is reinforced by the suspect's declination to respond, both prior to and following his provision of this response on line 133. The officer subsequently uses the suspect's response to attempt to draw out further responses, but the suspect does not provide the information the officer requests and returns to answering 'no comment' in response to the officer's questions. This illustrates the suspect's brief respite from not responding was used to address the knowledge claim by repairing it (line 133), and reasserting his innocence.

Discussion: Confessions – Knowledge Claims

This chapter has shown that knowledge claims are used successfully as an elicitory technique across differing types of confessionary turns. Similar to the findings of Komter (2003), knowledge claims are used by officers in the successful challenge of suspects' versions of events. The officers' references to outside sources of knowledge – for example, to witness or victim statements – is used to construct evidence. This, as claimed by Inbau *et al.* (1986) and shown in Watson's (1990) findings that the officer presents information from external sources as evidential fact, can draw previously withheld information from the suspect. The officers' claims to knowledge are particularly strong as they cite (with the exception of extracts 29 and 30) particular or named witnesses or victims, which is a technique suggested by Underwager and Wakefield (1990), Inbau *et al.* (1986) and FM (1987). In extracts 27 and 28, the elicited information comprises information withheld until the point at which the suspects were compelled to respond to the incongruities brought by the officers' presentation of contradicting accounts of witnesses. This identification of contradictions is posited by Kassin *et al.* (2007) as a favoured elicitory technique of officers.

This links to the techniques posited by Leo (1996) and Kassin *et al.* (2007), the officers' use of knowledge claims both identified and highlighted contradictions with the suspects' stories in order to attempt to elicit a response or the required information. The suspects in extracts 27, 28 and 29 altered their accounts to incorporate the claims of the witnesses, while maintaining their innocence. Extract 27 showed the suspect accounting for the witness' version by claiming he did swing for the victim, a previously undisclosed version of events, and the suspect in extract 28 acquiesced to the witness' accounts by admitting that he had in fact (innocently) left the location at the time the witness stated. Extract 29 demonstrated an implicit, rather than explicit knowledge claim by the officer. Nevertheless, the suspect responded to the implicit knowledge claim (which contradicted his own version of events) by similarly complying with the claimed knowledge and altering his answer in accordance with the contrary claim. Rather than (as in extracts 27 and 28), providing a scenario in which both his and the source's information could be mutually accurate without admitting the offence, the suspect in extract 29 abandoned his version of events for the version posited by the officer, and admitted the offence.

In extract 30 it was the suspect's vehement rejection of the officer's reference to the culpability of others that resulted in achieving a response (in an otherwise 'no comment' interview) from the suspect. Whereas in extract 31 the suspect, in a similar 'no comment' interview, finally responds to repair the officer's interpretation of the witness' account. In the case of extract 30, the officer's use of knowledge claims reflect the findings of Napier and Adams (2002), who posited apportioning blame to another party as a technique for eliciting information from a suspect. The officer's deference to the victim's statement in extract 31 is a similar attempt to obtain incriminating information about others present at the crime.

This chapter has shown how the officers' reference or deference to outside sources of knowledge is used to obtain responses from the suspect. It has provided an empirical insight into the elicitation of confessions and has presented evidence that knowledge claims are used, and can be used successfully, as elicitory techniques. The extracts have demonstrated their successful use in a variety of cases, from encouraging the suspect to talk to creating a position where the suspect retracts their previous statement and admits to having committed the crime.

Chapter 9

Confessions: Minimization

While the previous chapter has shown officers deferring to witness accounts or claims to knowledge as a way to challenge suspects' versions of events and draw confessionary turns from suspects, this chapter will illustrate how officers challenge suspects and elicit confessions through the use of minimization. This can take various forms, such as the officer providing justifications for the crime (extract 33) and softening references to the crime (extract 32) or its seriousness (extract 33). It is also evident in the officers' minimization of the consequences of confessing (extract 34) or the link between the suspect and the crime (extract 35).

The suspect in extract 32 has been arrested on suspicion of the theft of a leather jacket. In this extract the officer is attempting to draw from the suspect the name of the man to whom he had sold the stolen jacket. It opens on line 265 with the officer explicitly requesting the details of the man from the suspect. The pause on line 267 is indicative of the suspect's turn not being taken, suggesting the suspect's avoidance of answering the question, and indicating his unwillingness to provide the details requested by the officer (see endnote 41). This is supported by the suspect's subsequent turn on line 268, in which he, although fulfilling the interactional requirement to respond to the officer's question, avoids providing an 'exact' description of the 'gentleman' (as requested by the officer on line 265). Instead the suspect provides details of the man's occupation, an utterance qualified with an unsolicited assessment of the legitimacy of the man's business (line 268).

Although the suspect's turn fulfils the requirement for an answer as the second part of an adjacency pair, it does not attend to the implied semantic requirements of the officer's question. The suspect uses the potential ambiguity of the officer's 'who' (line 265) to mean 'who is the man as a person' rather than 'what is his name'. That the suspect does not provide the detail actually required by the officer is illustrated by the second of the officer's following two turns. While the first (on line 271) addresses the suspect's immediately prior answer by probing further into the topic of the man's employment, the second returns to his initial request for the suspect to provide an identification of the man (line 274). The explicitness of this request (of line 274) illustrates the officer's retroactive reformulation of his previous question (of line 265) into a direct, unambiguous and explicit request for the man's name, complete with the typical markers that identify this turn as a direct question, namely the wh- token 'what' at the beginning, and the politeness marker 'please' at the end. It is in this way that the officer avoids enabling, as his turn did on line 265, the suspect's production of another response that avoids directly addressing the request.

Extract 32: The gentleman

```
265   P1    =conce:rne[d who is this gentleman exactly
266   S              [that's it
267         (3.3)
268   S     he's a legi:t (.) pho:ne ma:n who does portable pho:nes=
269   P1    =°*mhm°
270         (1.1)
271   P1    and he works nearb↓y, y[es?
272   S                           [ye:ah
273         (0.9)
274   P1    what is his n↓ame pl↓ease
275         (2.8)
276   S     he wo:n't get into trouble will he was- *I: (0.2) >*it's got< I don't want
277         him [to °>get in trouble<°
278   P1        [he'll (.) he'll have to be spoken to about this ma:tter (0.3) we're talking
279         about a four hundred po:und leather ja[cke:t h↓ere
280   S                                           [°mhm°
281         (0.6)
282   P1→  alright, (0.2) >that< is: huhh (0.6) passed out of the possession (0.2) of
283         the true owne:r (0.5) into <someone's hands> who lets face it isn't the true
284         o:wner i:s i:t
285         (0.4)
286   S     mhm=
287   P1→  =so somehow we've gotto get this leather jacket ba:ck and I'd appreciate
288         the man's name so we can c[onduct the necessary enquirie:s
289   S                              [all I know him a:s
290         (0.2)
291   S →   his: (0.3) fi:rst name his nickname >and I< call him ra:b
292         (0.3)
293   P1    mhm
```

294   (0.3)
295   S   that's about it
(T40-66-06)

The pause on line 275 is indicative of the suspect's reluctance to provide an answer to the officer's now explicit request for the man's name. With the explicitness of the officer's request disabling the suspect's (previously enacted, on line 268) option to provide an alternate response, the suspect responds on lines 276–277 not with the corresponding answer, but by producing the first turn of an insertion sequence.[43] This takes the form of a question in which he voices his concerns about the consequences of meeting the officer's request and telling him the man's name. The suspect's initiation of an insertion sequence defers his production of his answer to the officer's question until the concerns that prevent him answering have been addressed. In other words, the officer has to answer the suspect's question before he can return to the topic of his question. This response also further supports the suggestion that the suspect's pause immediately prior to this turn (line 275) is an indication of his reluctance to answer the question. The officer's following two turns, in which he emphasizes his need for a dialogue with the man in order to facilitate the return of the jacket, are responded to by the suspect with minimal responses (lines 280 and 286). The officer's turn on lines 287–288 does, however, elicit the required, previously hidden (or not revealed)[44] answer, albeit in the form of the man's nickname (line 291).

The officer's turn (lines 287–288), linked to his prior turn by the use of 'so' (line 287), is the second part of the two stages of the elicitation. In the first part, on lines 282–284, in which the officer identifies the jacket possessed by the man as not his property, the officer uses the phrase 'passed out of the possession' rather than the more explicit term 'stolen', which is a minimization of the name of the criminal act. In the second (lines 287–288), the officer uses an emotional appeal (FM 1987; Shuy 1998) to the suspect; asking for his help to get the jacket back to the owner, and stating his appreciation for any help the suspect can provide. It is after this turn that the suspect produces the man's name, first as a failed overlap (line 289) and then as a full response on line 291. The officer's absence of further attempts to elicit the name indicates that the nickname provided by the suspect was satisfactory.

The series of turns leading to the suspect's production of the previously withheld information (the man's name) demonstrate the development of the elicitory tactics used by the officer. That prior to this extract the officer had failed to obtain the information from the suspect suggests it is this *particular* sequence of turns by the officer that resulted in the successful elicitation of the suspect's confession. The officer's implicit question, when avoided by the suspect, resulted in the officer's production of a more explicit question, to which the suspect's reticence to provide the required details was made explicit. In response to the suspect's initiation of an insertion sequence, the officer's elicitory tactics then changed from directly asking for the man's name, to emotionally appealing to the suspect by explaining how this information will be appreciated, and asking the suspect to be sensitive to his need for the information to return the jacket to the rightful owner. This frames the officer's request as one for the benefit of the wronged party (to return the jacket), but also to help the police ('I'd appreciate the man's name', lines 287–288), rather than to get the man 'into trouble' (line 277) as feared by the suspect. This demonstrates the officer reframing the emphasis of his request for the details, and using minimization and emotional appeal to draw the information from the suspect.

Extract 33 is later on in the interview shown in extract 10 (Chapter 5). It is of a suspect who has been arrested on suspicion of theft of a computer game and videos from a local video rental store. Prior to this extract the officer has asked the suspect both directly[45] and indirectly[46] if he has committed the crime, or has any knowledge of it, to which the suspect has consistently issued denials.[47] The extract shows the point at which, finally, after 17 minutes of the 20-minute interview, the suspect admits that he is indeed responsible for committing the crime. Similar to extract 32, the elicited utterance in extract 33 is negotiated over a series of turns. However, although the culmination of the elicitation in extract 32 was the suspect's provision of information that he had been previously unwilling to disclose, in the extract below, it is the suspect confessing to having committed the crime.

On lines 845–846 the officer first sums up the scope of the crime before going on, in his next turn, to provide a potential explanation for its committal. That the suspect must already possess awareness of the crime for which he is suspected[48] suggests the officer's turn (lines 845–846) is not designed to inform the suspect of the crime but to introduce his next turn (lines 849–852) in which he provides possible reasons for the crime being committed by the suspect. This is demonstrated in the officer's linking of those turns through the use of 'it' at the beginning of the second turn (line 849) in reference to the theft of videos discussed in his previous turn. The officer's use of 'yeah' on line 846 frames his turn as a question, to which the suspect minimally responds on line 847. This framework is similar to the interaction in extract 32, where the officer first provides the basics of the crime (lines 282–284) before producing the ultimately elicitory utterance (lines 287–288).

Extract 33: I will take them back

```
845   P1    >ri- wha:-< >e- at th↑is< sta:ge what I'll tell y↓er >I mean is< (.) basically
846         >what we're looking at< he:re is we've go:t (0.6) a theft of vide↓os yeah=
847   S     =°<m:hm:>°
848         (0.4)
849   P1→   I:t <c↑ould> >have been a< misunderstand↓ing (0.5) °right,° (0.3) so I'm
850         a:sking you n↓ow, (.) i:s it a misunderstand↓ing, (0.5) ha:ve you taken
851         those videos ↓out, (0.5) °>and<° not returned them for >what↑ever
852         re:ason< (.) be:st known °>to<° yours↓elf (0.7) and ↑if you ha:ve are you
853         prepared to take them b↓↓a (.) t- t- to give them b↓ack
854         (0.4)
855   S →   y↓es
856         (0.8)
857   P1    yes wh↓at
858         (0.4)
859   S     I will take them b↓ack
(T18-23-06)
```

The officer first minimizes the seriousness of the crime, shown in his use of 'basically' and the strong falling intonation during the word 'videos' (lines 845 and 846 respectively), both suggestive of the triviality of the items stolen. This is supported by the suspect's later admission that his earlier denials to the officer's elicitory attempts were lies[49] and his elaboration on why he confessed when he did: 'I've dropped myself in it now I've told you the truth *I could've carried on* [lying], *but it's getting a bit silly over a video*' (lines 1026–1027 of T18-23-06, see Appendix II, emphasis added). The officer, in addition to emphasizing the minor nature of the crime, also, by using 'at this stage' (line 845), then implies, although currently minor, the potential seriousness of the situation if it remains unresolved. Following a minimally positive response from the suspect on line 847, the officer (on lines 849–853) minimizes the suspect's committal of the crime by displaying the 'hypothetical situation' (Komter 2003) of the crime being the product of a misunderstanding. He offers the suspect an opportunity to confess either under that explanation or an alternate one he does not even need to disclose ('for whatever reason best known to yourself', lines

851–852) and return the stolen goods. After a pause, the suspect agrees with the officer, responding 'yes' (on line 855) to this turn. This response, however, is treated as ambiguous by the officer, as it is an unexpanded single affirmative utterance in response to the officer's multifaceted and presuppositional immediately prior turn. The suspect's response is also uttered despite the suspect's repeated denials that have typified his interview responses up until this point. This uncertainty is reflected in the officer's next turn (line 857), in which he indicates the inadequacy of the suspect's answer and directly requests a more explicit response 'yes what' (line 857).

The suspect responds on line 859 to the officer's request for a fuller answer by issuing a close repeat of the officer's earlier question 'I will take them back'. That this elicitation of the suspect's confessionary turn is linked to the officer's prior turns is made clear in this clarifying statement 'I will take them back' (line 859), which incorporates the previous utterance of the officer ('are you prepared to take them back', line 853). This response indicates the suspect has repaired the ambiguity of his first response by incorporating the part of the officer's prior question that his answer was addressing into the repaired response. This close repeat is also symptomatic of the effect of the officer's elicitory utterances on the suspect's utterance.

In the turn immediately prior to the confession, the officer frames the crime as a potential misunderstanding that can be resolved. Although this ultimately led to the suspect producing his confession, the fact that the suspect had not similarly responded with a confession to the officer's prior references to a possible reason for the crime[50] suggests that it was the combination of both this and the utterance prior to this confession-ultimate utterance (lines 845–846, in which he minimizes the seriousness of the crime), that contributed towards the suspect finally confessing. The suspect's reversal of his version of events at this point, rather than in the 17 minutes prior to this exchange, reflects the temporal immediacy implicit in this utterance. It also illustrates the effect of the officer's minimization of the scope of the theft, together with justifications of the crime's occurrence, where it is framed as a potential misunderstanding, rather than a deliberate criminal offence. These 'face-saving excuses' (Kassin and McNall 1991: 235) offered by the officer echo the minimization technique posited as an approach by which elicitations can be gleaned from non compliant suspects (Inbau *et al.* 1986, Napier and Adams 2002).

Extract 34 is from later on in the interview used in extract 30; occurring four turns after the suspect's initial confession of information (line 133, extract 30). On line 153 the suspect responds ambiguously but vaguely positively (as although 'yeah' is uttered, it is done so following the potentially negative component 'n') to the officer's question (line 152) of whether he had been taking anything. The interaction-to-come reveals the 'anything' the officer is referring to is implied by the officer, and interpreted by the suspect, to be a reference to drugs. The pause on line 154 is indicative of the officer's turn not taken, which, as explored throughout this book, indicates the suspect's turn being perceived by the officer as incomplete or unsatisfactory. This is supported, after no elaboration from the suspect is forthcoming, by the officer's explicit request for further details on line 155. The suspect's explicit refusal to elaborate exactly what drugs he had taken (line 157) is followed by a turn by the officer (line 159), which ultimately elicits this information from the suspect.

Extract 34: Not nicked for that as well

```
152   P2    have you been t↑aking anything earlier on
153   S     (1[.....hh].6) °ny↓eah°
154         (2.4)
155   P2    do̤: yo̤:u mi̤:nd te̤:ll ṳ:s wh↑at?
156         (0.6)
157   S     no not really
158         (0.8)
159   P2→   we̤:ll y̤:- you c↑an't get nicked for that as we̤:ll its gone inside ye̲:r
160         (1.0)
161   S →   °s:::::° smoke (0.2) el ess dee (0.6) >bit of< crack
162         (1.8)
163   P2    all on the one night
164         (0.5)
165   S     mm↑hm (0.2) since yesterday
(T10-77-06)
```

The officer's use of 'well' (line 159) links the officer's turn to the suspect's answer (line 157) as it is a marker that the statement-to-come does not align with the prior utterance (see endnote 52). The officer interprets the suspect's reticence to supply him with the information as a product of the suspect's desire to avoid implicating himself in a further crime. This interpretation of the officer is shown in his turn on line 159, in which he addresses this perceived concern of the suspect in minimizing, by eliminating, the negative consequences facing the suspect upon providing the details of the drugs. The suspect's willingness to then provide that information after the officer assures the suspect he 'can't get nicked for that as well' (line 159) reinforces the suspect's original reticence to answer was indeed a product of the fear of reprisal.

The officer therefore elicits a confession by devising a turn that minimizes the reasons preventing the suspect from confessing, which in this case involved removing the prospect of charges being brought in light of his admission of his drug use. This is similar to Irving (1980) and Irving and Hilgendorf (1980) who posited that reducing the factors preventing the suspect from confessing can then entice the suspect to confess. As a tactic, this is successful, for the suspect then does, in his next turn, tell the officer exactly what medley of drugs he had taken. Using this tactic as an elicitory tool does have its limits, however, as by virtue of the fact that the information the suspect is attempting to withhold is incriminating, there must be little or no advantage that can be gained in granting amnesty from arrest in order to secure the release of that information. In addition, it is doubtful that an officer actually has the authority to grant those kinds of assurances to a suspect. Indeed, the officer's claim that the suspect cannot be arrested for taking drugs at the time of contradicts the fact this is an offence under section 4 of the Road Traffic Act 1988. In addition to the confession evidence against the suspect, despite the officer claiming 'you can't get nicked for that as well its gone inside yer' (line 159), the interview takes place less than three hours after the offence was committed, and the law allows the officer to perform a saliva test for methamphetamine, cannabis or MDMA, all of which are subject to a legal limit of zero (Road Safety Act 1986: Sections 49, 55E and 55D).

The suspect in the following extract has been arrested on suspicion of breaking and entering LowPrice, a local budget convenience store that evening. The interaction in extract 35 opens after the suspect has repeatedly asserted that he was not near the parade of shops or the shop that was broken into,[51] but finishes with the suspect admitting that he was indeed outside the shop when the window was smashed.

On line 329 the officer asks the suspect if he had gone near LowPrice. Similar to extract 32, the suspect does not directly answer the officer's question, but asserts he was not *in* LowPrice rather than answering whether he was *near* the store as requested. The officer responds by partially repeating his question, and situating it more broadly (line 332), this time focusing not specifically on the suspect's proximity to LowPrice, but his proximity to the general vicinity. This broadening reflects the practice of obtaining 'mini confessions' as a starting point for the elicitation of further, more substantial information (Shuy 1998). In turn, the suspect's answers

to the officer's questions become successively less precise; from a straightforward denial on line 330, to an equivocal 'in a sense yeah but I didn't'
on line 334. The vagueness of the suspect's response, and that it does not
answer the officer's question is demonstrated in the officer's next turn in
which he issues a request for a further clarification from the suspect ('in
what sense', line 335).

Extract 35: In a sense yeah

```
329   P1    DID YOU GO NEAR LOWPRI[CE
330   S     °right° (0.3) no I h↑aven't been inside LowPrice and I haven't didn't (0.2)
331         dam[age LowPrice window or an[ything so
332   P1→      [did-                      [did you go near the parade of shops
333         (1.6)
334   S →   well ye:ah in a sense yeah but I didn't
335   P1    in what sense
336         (0.7)
337   S     °well in that I was° in the a:rea yeah (0.4) but it isn't (0. 4) is (0.2) it was
338         local
339         (3.0)
340   P1→ were you outside the shop when the window was smashed
341         (4.5)
342   P1→ [by Mark
343   S →   [yeah
344   S →   yeah
(T2-111-06)
```

The suspect's use of 'well' on line 334 and his long pause prior to that turn
are both markers of a forthcoming dispreferred turn shape. In this case the
dispreferred action about to be performed is the suspect's production of
an answer that contradicts his own prior turns; changing his response from
a categorical denial of being near the shops to then admitting he was. That
the suspect's answer (line 334) to the officer's request for clarification (line
332) is vaguer than his prior response (lines 330–331) could also be indicative of an attempt by the suspect to avoid conclusively aligning himself
with this contradictory and potentially incriminating answer. The suspect
uses 'well' in his utterances on lines 334 and 337–338, although these turns
do not disagree with the officer's turn. It is in this way that the suspect's use
of 'well' can be seen to mitigate the potential threat to his own 'face'[52] in
potentially implicating himself in positively responding to the (previously
denied) question of whether he had been near the parade of shops.

The officer's next turn (line 340), similar to line 274 of extract 32, removes any further opportunities for the suspect to provide a vague response, as he explicitly asks 'were you outside the shop when the window was smashed' (line 340). This is reminiscent of the elicitory technique posed by Napier and Adams (2002) which states the officer must first establish the suspect's close proximity to the scene of the crime or the victim, which, once established, can then (although not in this case) be used by 'practiced interviewers … as a wedge to open the door to additional incriminating statements' (Napier and Adams 2002: 4). In this turn the officer uses the past tense 'was' rather than an identifier such as 'you' in his question; stating 'were you outside the shop when the window was smashed' (line 340), rather than 'when *you* smashed the window'. The officer, by using the word 'was', focuses this question on the *locality* of the suspect in relation to the time the crime was being committed, and not the suspect's involvement in that crime. This minimization enabled the officer to avoid the accusatory stance he had employed earlier[53] that had failed to elicit a confession.

When the pause in the next turn (line 341) indicates a turn not taken by the suspect, the officer then reinforces this act of distancing by attributing the smashed window explicitly to another party ('by Mark' line 342). This retroactively emphasizes his earlier request (line 340) as an attempt to identify the suspect's location rather than his responsibility in the act of smashing the window. The suspect's turn on line 343 must have been produced in response to the officer's turn on line 340 rather than the turn on line 342, as it overlaps with the onset of the latter. The elicited confessionary turn was therefore produced by the suspect in response to the implicit minimization of the officer's first turn, and not the direct reference to the assumed window smasher of his second. The suspect then issues a repeat of his answer on line 344, which attends to the possibility that his overlapped speech was unheard, and possibly also in response to the officer's second turn.

The officer's attempt to elicit the disclosure of less incriminating information from the suspect, such as his presence near the parade of shops, is used (as discussed by Shuy 1998) as the starting point for a wider confession. The officer establishes the suspect's proximity to the crime as a starting point from which he can then attempt to elicit the suspect's admission to being one of the perpetrators (Napier and Adams 2002). This is made explicit (although ultimately unsuccessfully) in the questioning that follows this extract, in which the officer refers to the suspect's confessionary turn as the exposure of 'one lie' (line 366) and as the 'first lie out the way … so the rest isn't so hard now is it' (line 372).[54]

Discussion: Confessions – Minimization

The extracts in this chapter illustrate how minimization can be used in a range of ways to successfully obtain confessions from suspects. Corresponding with the literature, it is used in officers' avoidance of 'realistic' (Inbau *et al.* 1986) words to describe the crime (extract 32); in semantically distancing the suspect from their involvement in the crime (extract 35, Napier and Adams 2002; Inbau *et al.* 2004); providing rationalizations for the crime (extract 33, Komter 2003); and in removing the consequences of confessing (extract 34, Irving 1980; Irving and Hilgendorf 1980).

While extracts 27–31 and 32–35 demonstrate the use of varying degrees of, and concurrent types of, knowledge claims and minimization respectively, the data also reveals multiple uses of elicitory techniques. In extract 33 the officer uses two types of minimization by providing justifications for, and also downplaying the seriousness of the crime (as seen in Napier and Adams 2002), which suggests that these techniques can be used in various complementary combinations in order to achieve the desired effect. Extract 31 shows the officer issuing else statements in an attempt to draw information from the suspect, and in extract 32, although the officer minimizes the crime (Inbau *et al.* 2004), the officer also uses emotional appeal (FM 1987) as part of the elicitory turn. Multiple approaches are see alson in the officers' use of a two-part strategy in both extracts 32 and 33, where the officer first presents the details of the offence and then posits a reduced version of events. This version is used to either reduce the perceived consequences of the crime by directing the attention from the suspect's utterance potentially harming an associate, to instead helping the victim (extract 32), or to reduce the perceived criminality or immorality of theft by providing a potential justification for the offence (extract 33).

The use of 'well' featured heavily in the extracts, and as the analyses revealed, for a variety of uses similar to those posited in other interaction. 'Well' was shown to aid the ambiguity in the suspect's own reply and to save the suspect's own face (extract 35), as well as to mount challenges to the suspect's perception (discussed in Jucker 1993) through disagreement (extract 34) (as seen in Pomerantz 1984 and Holtgraves 1997, 2000). Echoing Lakoff (1973), it can also be used to mark the suspect's turn as insufficient in the contextual frame of their utterance (extract 34), rather than as a way to disambiguate the speaker's reply or save the face of the other by signalling a potential face-threatening utterance-to-come (Holtgraves 1992, 2000). In extract 35 the analysis shows the suspect uses 'well' to save his own face, which could be indicative of the constraints of this particular context, for example a suspect may potentially implicate himself by contradicting his earlier answers. The use of 'well' by the officers across these extracts reveals the shape of their role by showing how it is frequently used to contradict and challenge the suspects' prior assertion.

Conclusion to Part Three

The patterns of the officers' interactional behaviour prior to confessions illustrate the systematic and successful use of two specific techniques. It has revealed that the officers' use of knowledge claims and minimization can lead to the successful elicitation of confessions from the suspect in the police interview. The analyses indicate how these techniques facilitate the officers' challenges to, or contradictions of, a suspect's prior turn or version of events. These findings accord with the evidence posited by the range of research that suggests that a confession from a suspect is more likely when there is evidence presented against them or against their story (Moston *et al.* 1992; Sigurdsson and Gudjonsson 1996; Leo 1996; Gudjonsson and Sigurdsson 1999; Gudjonsson 2003; Kassin *et al.* 2007).

The extracts in Part Three have shown the suspect responding to the elicitory techniques of knowledge claims and minimization by producing otherwise withheld information, responses or admissions. This is despite the capability of these techniques having been called into question elsewhere (see Baldwin 1992b, 1993; Gudjonsson 1996). Many of the confessions were produced during interviews in which the suspect had denied or withheld that material for long periods of time, which illustrates that despite their rarity, the officer can indeed influence a suspect's decision to confess information in the police interview.

Successful elicitations do not necessarily comprise a single technique. The small proportion of successful elicitations present in the corpus, all of which are shown here, echo Baldwin's (1992b, 1993) statement that confessions are rare. It also suggests that the techniques found are unlikely to produce an artificially high rate of confessions. Additionally, although the purpose of the police interview is generally (mis)understood to be to extract confessions from suspects rather than to establish the facts and allow the suspect to put forward their version of events (see Chapter 2), the data shows that this does not necessarily translate to a high confession rate. As discussed in the opening section of Part Three, the definition of confessions in this work does differ from Baldwin's (1992b); however, the interaction in extract 33, in which a confession under Baldwin's (1992b) definition *is* produced, demonstrates that the general elicitory pattern posited in these chapters does apply across differently defined confessionary turns.

Failed uses of knowledge claims and minimization are also widespread in the wider corpus, that is, in interviews that do not lead to confessions. This illustrates that officers regularly employ these elicitory techniques both successfully and unsuccessfully. It highlights that knowledge claims and minimization are customary, as suggested through the wealth of literature on confession elicitation and officers' techniques. Unsuccessful examples followed a similar pattern of elicitory techniques to the successful ones. The absence of a confession after a particular technique, however, is not necessarily an indication of the failure of that elicitory attempt by the officer. Indeed, a successful elicitation must rely on the suspect being guilty of the crime or withholding information from the officer, something that this book cannot claim to discern.

Although the extracts in Chapters 8 and 9 demonstrate the presence of confession elicitation techniques outlined in the opening section of Part Three, certain techniques were notably absent, from both the immediate surroundings of the confessions and any other point in the extracts or in the unused data in the corpus. These techniques are prescribed and designed to produce confessions; many of which, such as intimidation or physical threat, are deemed inadmissible in a UK court of law. Their absence in the data reveals that such psychological or coercive techniques are not a condition on which the successful elicitation of confessions must rely, and therefore challenges the traditional perceptions, and favoured techniques, of confession elicitation described in Chapter 2 and in the introduction to Part Three. The data in which confessions were not produced also did not show evidence of these other tactics in the officers' (failed) attempts to draw out confessionary turns. A reason for this could be that many of the tactics would be prohibited under the PACE Act 1984. For those that may prove admissible, such as the implicit use of maximization of the offence, the maximization of the consequences of the crime, or the use of silence, it is problematic to identify or state with certainty whether an officer's turn is actually a failed elicitation attempt or simply another interactional turn in the interview (especially in non-verbal or more implicit cases). They may also be framed as the enactment of an administrative necessity as in extract 19 of Part Two, where the officer frames her otherwise adversarial elicitory technique as something she is required to do by a higher, legal authority. Alongside the more coercive tactics, the elicitory techniques that were found in the data have also come under criticism for leading to false confessions as well as producing their real counterparts (Kassin 1997, 2005; Gudjonsson 2002, 2003). These concerns of the validity of confessions as evidence cannot be assessed here as the scope of the data cannot determine whether the confessions obtained were falsely produced or not. It does, however, show an officer using the morally ambiguous practice of presenting a false representation (Kassin and McNall 1991) of the severity of the crime, opinion of the crime, and the severity of the consequences, in claiming that if the suspect admits his possession and use of drugs he 'can't get nicked' (line 159, extract 34).

These chapters have identified both similarities to and differences from the techniques suggested in training manuals and in research into this aspect of the police interview. Rather than stand-alone, abstractly employed devices for extracting confessions, the approach used in this work has allowed Part Three to explore officers' uses of these techniques, expose their inner workings and recognize them as part of a jointly constructed exchange with the suspect. It has found that the officers' references to sources of knowledge and use of minimization are ways in which officers can challenge suspects, their stories and denials, and has revealed the interactional work required in order to create an environment in which the suspect can confess.

Chapter 10

Conclusion

Police interview participants' interaction relies heavily, although in an extraordinary setting, on the fundamental rules of conversation. It also relies on the speaker's ability to use the interaction to ensure they are understood by the other participant. The findings draw out the modifications participants make to the interactional phenomena, and demonstrate how they are usefully employed in this context, rather than other institutional or ordinary conversation. In this final chapter recommendations and suggestions are made for police interview training and techniques while evidence is pulled together from across the three parts of this book to show how talk can be used to create a more relaxed and open environment, or be used in subtle manipulative ways that can manifest in unchallenged breaches of the codes of conduct.

There are myriad approaches to researching the police, policing and interaction, and these broad areas have been explored in a variety of contexts. Despite the wealth of analytic explorations of the operational, linguistic and structural properties of policing, from lab-based to empirical explorations, it is apparent that there remained scope and requirement for original research from a conversation analytic perspective. This work represents an undertaking of that opportunity; using conversation analytic tools, the previously under or unexplored details of the police interview are drawn into focus.

Part One highlighted the uses of laughter and revealed that officers and suspects use laughter in both similar and divergent ways as a tool to accomplish particular actions in accordance with their roles. The use of uninitiated third turns, and semantically and legally redundant utterances explored in Part Two then exposed the way in which officers negotiate their attendance to both the silent participant and to the immediate, local interaction of the interview with the suspect. The investigation of the lead-up to the suspects' production of confessionary turns in Part Three revealed the range of tools employed by the officer in their successful elicitation of a confession. Taken together, the findings illustrate how communicative phenomena such as third turns, laughter, minimization and knowledge claims are used as tools by both suspects and officers to accomplish a variety of actions in the police interview. For example, tools are relied on to ease neglect of the local interaction (seen in the officers' use of conversational utterances and accounts of their attendance to the silent participant), or a neglect of the legal requirements (such as the use of laughter to mitigate potential breaches of the PACE Act 1984). Distinctive insights have not only been provided into the construction and use of the chosen phenomena, but also into the construction and maintenance of police interview interaction, and into the participants' own navigation and understanding of talk in this particular context. The extracts reveal that the success of these tools relies, in part, on the recipients' interpretation of their use. This demonstrates how both the speaker and the listener are part of the interactional construction of these phenomena.

Part Three shows that the talk in the police interview is a joint accomplishment and is not, as typically understood, the product of the lone enterprise of a dominating officer, who draws information from an unwilling and non-compliant suspect. The difference between this conventional perception of police interviewing and its reality is made transparent, for example in the joint construction of the confession in extract 34, where the officer uses his interpretation of what is preventing the suspect from confessing, to elicit that confession. It is see alson in the suspect's interaction in extract 29, where he produces a confession in response to his interpretation of the officer's prior turn as a claim to knowledge. Throughout the analytic parts we can see the speaker often relying on the recipient interpreting their talk in a particular way, for example, encouraging the production of particular utterances such as a confession, laughter portraying a conversational state, or an utterance being directed to the silent participant and not to the suspect.

The three analytic parts reveal both consistencies with, and departures from the findings of methodologically and contextually comparable research. For example, in Chapter 7 the analyses demonstrated the correspondence between the use of uninitiated third turns to orient to the silent participant by officers in police interviews and attorneys in courtroom interaction. The uses of laughter explored in Part One revealed similarities to the uses of laughter found by Stokoe and Edwards (2008) such as in response to a 'silly' question, and similarities to managing complaints (Edwards 2005), albeit in the form of helping a suspect to correct an officer's version of events. Police interview laughter showed commonalities with laughter in other institutional contexts, for instance the asymmetry of laughter (West 1984; Haakana 2001), and its use to mitigate a dispreferred act (Jefferson 1984; Brown and Levinson 1987; Billig 2005). Part Three revealed that similarities are also apparent in the types of elicitory techniques that successfully led to confessions. Specifically, knowledge claims and minimization mirror techniques posited as techniques for that very purpose in training manuals (Inbau *et al.* 1986) and research (such as Watson 1990; Kassin and McNall 1991; Napier and Adams 2002).

Despite this, differences were also found across all the analytic parts; uninitiated third turns, discussed by Heydon (2005) as rare, were widely present in the data, and the mutual laughter explored by Stokoe and Edwards (2008) was only present in one instance (extract 17). Confession elicitation techniques such as the use of interruptions (FM 1897) and intimidating behaviour (Inbau *et al.* 1986) were absent from the data, and additionally the rarity of confessions also differed from general perceptions that they are obtainable and attained solely through the work of the officer. These differences between current understandings and the detail of the police interview revealed in this book highlight its contribution to sociological and criminological literature. It also reveals the reality of police interviewing in contrast to police and the public perceptions, and contributes to the general understanding of interaction in this setting.

Beyond exposing the similarities and differences between the detail of the interview found, and their academic, legislative or fictional counterparts, the analytic parts also revealed the officers' ability to circumvent the strictures of the PACE Act 1984 by using laughter to mitigate potentially breaching utterances (Chapter 5). The adherence to the Act (1984) was also found to be actually preventing the officer from adhering to the requirements of the suspect (Chapter 6). It is in examining the participants' communicative behaviours in their negotiation of and adherence to the requirements of their roles, that the internal and external constraints of this context and the participants' orientations to the conversational and institutional frameworks are revealed.

Conversational and Institutional Frames

The analytic chapters have shown the modifications that the uses of phenomena undergo when produced in police interviews, rather than as part of ordinary conversation or other institutional interaction. The manifestation of conversational and institutional orientations in the police interview reveals much about the differences between the interactional, social and legal requirements of the contexts. Analysing the interactional phenomena, the constraints (seen in the officers' adherence to the PACE Act 1984 overriding their need to orient to the suspect) and the interests (such as the suspects' use of laughter to project an image of innocence) of the individual participants make it possible not only to examine the utterances of the participants, but also the motivations and orientations that may lie behind them.

Although mostly adhering to the pre-allocated turn structure indicative of this institutional context, talk more typical of the structure of ordinary conversation does creep into the interaction in the police interview. The performance of interactional phenomenon may then simply be ordinary conversational phenomenon that happens to occur in an extraordinary setting, and has to adhere to the rules of the setting. However, the analytic parts have made clear that the use of conversation analytic talk in this context can be manipulated for real and specific ends. This conversational interaction can be employed by the officer as a tool to persuade, to mitigate breaches of the institutional interaction, and to perform subtle excursions from adhering to the suspects' rights (shown in Chapter 5). It can also orient utterances to the suspect or account for their lack of attendance to the local interaction (shown in Chapter 6), or to minimize the seriousness of the offence (shown in Chapter 9). The differences between the communicative requirements of the police interview and the communicative requirements of the institutional context are what underlie the extracts in Part Two. The differences between the requirements of the institutional context and those of the conversational contexts are shown in Part One, and both parts reveal the legislative and communicative boundaries of police interview interaction.

A considerable amount of research on laughter focuses on its use in ordinary interaction (Jefferson 1979, 1984; Jefferson *et al.* 1987; Sacks 1992; Glenn 1995), which possibly reflects its perceived status as a typically conversational phenomenon. The first analytic part showed how laughter is a prevalent and highly structured part of interaction in the police interview, which can be used in ways similar to laughter in ordinary conversation (such as to negotiate talk-in-trouble, Jefferson 1984).

Police interview interaction does not therefore exist on one end or at a certain point on the formal/informal continuum, where institutional interaction is at one end and ordinary conversation is at the other, as suggested by Sacks *et al.* (1974). Instead it consists of various shades of formality that change in accordance with the requirements of the exchange. These are dependent on many factors such as the role of the speaker and their intention for the utterance (including directing it towards a particular recipient), and can be employed regardless of the speaker's cognition. The use of typically conversational utterances, however, such as one participant overlapping another's talk, can be rebuked in the police interview. The following extract is an example of an officer explicitly sanctioning a suspect's overlapping response:

Extract 36: Let me finish

```
358   P1    coz th↑is w↓ire (0.3) looks like it's been attached (0.8) this is the red
359         wir[e
360   S        [yeah that's the live a[nd the plus innit
361   P1→                              [>°hang on hang on le:t me finish let me finish°<
(T3-112-06)
```

The use of laughter, interruptions and colloquialisms in the police interview generate responses that suggest they are both acceptable and unacceptable in this setting. Investigating these cases has exposed the unwritten interactional rules that combine to comprise the institutional structure of the police interview and what differentiates it from other contexts. That certain typically conversational utterances or orientations can remain unchallenged in this context suggests, contrary to traditional perceptions, there is a level of flexibility concerning acceptable communication in police interviews. This flexibility is made apparent in the ease with which recipients interpret and understand the constantly shifting frames (such as conversational, legal and institutional) that particular utterances are situated in at any particular moment. Difficulties in the construction of this delicate interactional work are nevertheless present, and show how the particularities of the phenomena must be navigated in order to successfully mitigate the production of utterances that breach the rules. This is how, despite its flexibility, the serious demands of the police interview codes of conduct are made visible in the officer's late use of laughter in extract 7 of Chapter 5. They are see alson in Chapter 6 where the officers' attendance to the institutional aspect is shown to take precedence over the conversational; even if this results in the officer neglecting the current, local interaction with the suspect. This unaccounted-for disregard of the content of suspects' utterances illustrates the need for the officer to seamlessly attend to both the legal institutional requirements of the context, and to the communicative requirements of the local interaction with the suspect.

The findings of Part One show how uses of laughter are tailored to the interactional requirements of the context and to the participants within it. Traditionally conversational uses of laughter in the police interview were shown to override the interactional rules of institutional talk and revert the talk to a more conversational framework. This use of laughter as a 'time out' from the ordinary rigours and rules of the interaction demonstrates how the conversational visage of laughter could be exploited to distance the talk from the institutional framework; in particular, in distancing from a breach of the PACE Act 1984. However, that officers' attendance to the silent participant overrides their attendance to the suspects' interaction also suggests that, although the conversational interaction circumvents some aspects of institutional interaction (in the adherence to the legal requirements), it is superseded by the officers' institutional interaction. These findings suggest that, paradoxically, police interview talk is at once interpreted as flexible and highly restricted. They demonstrate the tensions between the conversational and institutional aspects of the police interview, and make the conflict between the officers' adherence to the institutional aspect and their attendance to the conversational aspect transparent.

The findings reveal the detail of the interactional structure particular to the police interview, and contribute to the current understanding of the communication in this often closed and misrepresented setting, and to the existing understandings of institutional talk. Exploring the differences between the police interview and other contexts also exposes the need for further empirical research in this area. The ethnomethodological implications of this orientation to the institutional and conversational aspects by the officer and suspect are addressed in the following section.

Policing the Interaction, Participants' Perceptions and the Construction of Reality

Analysing and exploring these different aspects of talk in this restricted and heavily governed environment has exposed the practical accomplishment of police interviewing. The detailed line-by-line analyses of the structure of the interaction highlights the tools available to the officer and suspect in the production of that interaction, and explores the various uses of those tools. The use of empirical data will enable police interview training to be developed that is based on the results of this in-depth exploration and documentation of real-life communicative practices of the police officer and the suspect. Practitioners can use this to gain insights not only into how their interaction can affect the suspect, but also into the potential for suspects to use interactional phenomena for specific purposes, such as using laughter to present an alternative version of events.

Various communicative resources are available to the officer and suspect in the police interview. These phenomena can be employed systematically and for specific purposes, and are often differently tailored in their use from ordinary conversation and other institutional interaction, or in ways that depart from those traditionally expected. The participants' interaction creates, preserves and maintains their conception of both the boundaries and the shape of this specialist institutional context. Hester and Eglin (1992: 74) state, 'The law is made ... each time it is invoked or otherwise used.' This type of construction is enacted by the officer and the suspect in their interaction. The creation of the interactional boundaries provides an insight into and demonstration of the ethnomethodological performance of interaction, where the interaction creates and is created by the context in which it is uttered; it shapes and is shaped by its participants.

On a broad level, this self-policing of the talk by the participants and their shaping of the context is demonstrated through their own sanctioning of utterances that lie outside what they perceive to be the communicative requirements of the role or the context. Specific orientations to these interactionally, rather than legally, defined strictures of the context and the roles within it are a recurring theme across the analytic chapters. That the participants can be sanctioned by one another for their use of conversational (or non-institutional) talk in the police interview illustrates the participants' own perception of, and construction of, the interactional constraints of the context. The legal constraints, however, epitomized by the PACE Act 1984, are externally imposed codes that govern the officers' conduct in the police interview. It has been revealed here how these external protocols, or the officers' perception and projection of their reach, are internally managed by the officer in the interview in a similar way to the interaction protocols. This is illustrated in Chapter 6 where officers framed the constraints as wider-reaching or stricter than they actually were, by deferring to protocol where it was not legally required.

Both participants use laughter as a way to attend to, and account for deviations from the institutional constraints imposed upon their inter-action.[55] This is shown in both participants' uses of laughter in similar ways in order to avoid breaching their roles. Whereas in ordinary conversation, each participant is generally unrestrained by the context in their challenge of another (although such challenges can constitute a dispreferred action), indexically, in police interviews the talk is constrained or shaped both legally (by the Act 1984), and interactionally (by the self-policing of the participants). For example, while the Act (1984) restricts certain challenges the officer can make of the suspects' utterances (such as challenging a suspect in exercising their rights), the suspects' perception of their and the officers' roles may also restrict their ability to overtly challenge the officer. Indeed, the analytic parts suggest the suspect interprets their role as one where overt challenges to the officer are discouraged. This is supported by the fact that many such challenges are not directly produced but conveyed non-lexically, or mitigated through suspects' uses of laughter. However, it is only the officer that faces legal consequences for such breaches (for example, having the tape being ruled inadmissible as evidence or even facing possible criminal charges).

The importance of remaining within protocol is highlighted through the officers' over adherence to the codes of conduct, and also in their circumvention of certain institutional (legal) requisites by employing a conversational framework to their utterances. This shows that the officers' self-constructed restrictions on their interaction is based on their perception of these constraints, rather than the (in reality less restrictive) boundaries themselves. This illustrates that, while the suspect is restricted by their own understanding and by the officers' understanding of the perceived role of a suspect, it is the talk of the officer that is most heavily constrained as it is shaped by both the interactional *and* the legal strictures of the context.

The self-imposed, legally redundant boundaries are, nevertheless, a product of the overarching legal requirements of the PACE Act 1984, reinforced by the physical presence of the tape recorder in the interview. The suspects' interaction, as addressed earlier, is also a construction based upon their perceptions of their role but, unlike the officers' interaction, it is unlikely to be as a result of an attempt to maximize the admissibility of the interview, or be based on exposure to police interviews, the codes of conduct or police training. The suspects' perception of their and the officers' roles are in all probability forged from accessible representations of the police interview such as those in the media. This type of retro-spective interpretation (Sacks 1972), that is, acting in and interpreting a current situation on the basis of prior experiences, is evident in suspects' orientations to, and construction of their role based on representations of police interviewing on television. This is made explicit in the following extract, where a suspect explicitly defers to television portrayals of suspects under arrest. The suspect cites 'too much television' (line 34) as the reason for his earlier response 'best I make no reply' (quoted by the officer on lines 31–32) at the time of his caution and arrest. This illustrates how the suspect's media-informed perception of the police interview is drawn on and reproduced in the reality of his behaviour at his arrest. The extract also shows the officer's reaction to the suspect's reference to the media – it is perceived as unexceptional, indeed, 'fair enough' (line 35) by the officer.

Extract 37: Too much TV

```
30    P1    >I arrested you on that< on suspicion of
31          that assault, and when I cautioned yo:u (0.6) you replie:d (.) be:st I<make
32          no reply: I thi:nk> (.) >can you just< explain why you made that repl↓y
33    S →   I- I thought that >it< I should have °had- a° solicitor pres↓ent (.) °I don-°
34          re- >too much< televisio:n (.) khh. hh.
35    P1    right >oka:y< [that's >fair eno:ugh<
(T33-22-06)
```

This demonstrates the explicit role-taking that is central to the symbolic interactionist perspective (Hester and Eglin, 1992), the use of referring to roles as an interactional device (Halkowski 1990), and is an example of the suspects' construction and maintenance of their role in accordance with the media perception of that role. In effect, the suspects' performance is constructed by the representations of that role in the media.

Media representations and expectations of policing and police work also influence the way that officers view and carry out their duties (Perlmutter 2000). However, the majority of role-taking in the interviews used does not involve such explicit referral to, or interactional use of, the specific roles or expectations of those roles (with the exception of the opening sequences which are dictated by legislation and not the participants). The insights still provide 'greater understanding of how members of society organize their social worlds through the use of such notions [of roles]' (Hester and Eglin 1992: 222), as both participants demonstrate *implicit* self-labelling through the performance of their roles and the interpretation of those roles as 'typically officer' or 'typically suspect' behaviour. This is seen for instance in the suspects' use of laughter to support their position of innocence; this use of laughter suggests it is used as a non-verbal resource due to an expectation that particular utterances, as part of their role as a suspect, will not be believed. This repeated and systematic employment of laughter by suspects across the data illustrates the enactment of 'category predicates' (Sacks, 1974) in the participants' common understanding of, and orientation to, the accomplishment of what is 'properly and expectably done' (Hester and Eglin: 124) by a suspect in this setting.

The officers' shaping and perception of their role as an officer is demonstrated in Chapter 6 through their patterned adherence to the perception of the legal constraints imposed upon them, rather than the actual and often less restricting reality of the constraints of the codes of conduct. Officers' perceptions of their roles and that of the suspect are also made transparent in the officers' use of minimization in Chapter 9, which reflects their attempt to address the reasons they believe are preventing the suspect from confessing, such as potential condemnation by the officer. This minimization is achieved through officers lessening the moral or social culpability of the suspect, minimizing their own reaction to the alleged crime and its severity, or implicitly inferring leniency if the suspect confesses.

The three analytic parts therefore show how the suspect and the officer create their own communicative reality in the production and maintenance of their own and each other's roles. The uses of interactional tools illustrate the ethnomethodological premise that interaction is determined and reflected by the functions, requirements and strictures of the social context. It is also determined by the participants' interpretation of that context and their role within it. Hester and Eglin (1992: 96) state, 'The sociologist must "take the role of the other" in order to see how police perceive their circumstances and accordingly construct their actions'. The participants' own understandings of their roles, however, are revealed in the analyses through their interactional performance. The officers' and suspects' actions and interpretations are present in their own talk; requiring the sociologist not to take roles but instead make these orientations visible through the use of conversation analytic techniques.

Phenomena such as uninitiated third turns and the over adherence to protocols, laughter and minimization are used by the suspect and officer in accordance with their perception of their roles. Their jointly constructed talk-in-action has been revealed to be part of, and house, a series of tools through which the officer and suspect create and maintain the structure of the interaction. This suggests the officer and the suspect have a collaborative understanding of, and orientation to the interview; a construct at odds with the conflict with which it is traditionally associated. The objectives to which these phenomena are directed define and are defined by the prescribed roles and the context of the police interview.

Such objectives include attending to the silent participant, buttressing innocence, mitigating breaches of protocol or eliciting confessions. This supports the ethnomethodological premise discussed in Chapter 2 that members construct similar realities to each other through their adherence to and understanding of communicative processes through retrospective interpretation, and maintain those realities in accordance with the rule of economy (Sacks 1972). This fluid and interpretative understanding of the interactional roles by one another is reminiscent of the 'no apparent articulated shape...[but] a lore of understanding' (Goffman 1974: 21) of many interactional frameworks, unlike the more rigid framework of legal statutes which govern the officers' talk. However, as discussed by Hester and Eglin (1992), ethnomethodological investigations of policing typically involve analysing categories of criminals and criminal acts. Similarly, Atkinson and Drew (1979: 3–4) state, 'The main emphasis of courtroom studies has tended to be on what courts are claimed to do to defendants (e.g. intimidate, bewilder, oppress, alienate, label, stigmatise, etc.) *rather than on the details of how they work*' (emphasis added).

In revealing the interactional properties of the police interview on a participant level, the three analytic parts have identified the suspects' and the officers' talk-in-action as the primary focus, rather than the societal constructs of values, types of criminal actions, or the criminality of suspects, which are at the heart of symbolic interactionism. The detailed exploration of the interaction and the use of CA in the analytic parts of this work provide a different perspective from much research into this context and in the broader context of the criminal justice system (see Chapter 2). By applying and updating conversation analytic techniques (as discussed in Chapter 3), the detail of the interview could be examined through some of its under-explored and unexplored areas. In doing so this illustrates the continuing importance of CA to ethnomethodology, the study of criminology and to police interview practice and training. This contributes toward the general understanding of interaction in the police interview, the impact and understanding of the PACE Act 1984, and clarifies the reality of the police interview in light of media, police and general representations and perceptions of police interviewing. The following section explores the application and implications of these myths, theories and legal parameters of this interaction in the form of the Act (1984).

Myths, the PACE Act 1984 and Training: Putting the Results into Practice

Exploring the detail of police interview interaction has revealed similarities to and differences from the reality of police interviewing and perceptions of the police interview manifested in the media, wider academic literature and operational police interview training manuals. This has highlighted the differences between the legal premise of the police interview and the understanding of that premise by interviewing officers. This also reveals the concerns of the ability of the PACE Act 1984 to safeguard the suspects' rights.

The opening and closing sequences of the police interview are heavily regulated. However, there is a lack of guidance from the PACE Act 1984 regarding the content of the main body of the interview, for example, providing specific examples of inappropriate questioning techniques. The officers' use of minimization and knowledge claims, justifications and rationalizations prior to the successful elicitation of confessions correspond to the techniques suggested in police interview and interrogation manuals (such as Inbau *et al.* 1986; see Chapter 2). However, these techniques have been criticized by Kassin (1997), Kassin *et al.* (2003) and Gudjonsson (2002, 2003) as having the potential to elicit false confessions from suspects without explicit direction from the Act (1984) to highlight or minimize this possibility. The relative freedom of the officers' interactional capabilities during the main body of the interview could have implications in the ability of the Act (1984) to protect the premise of the police interview and the suspects' rights.

The unsuccessful enactment of the techniques present in the data corpus indicate a concord with criticisms of the success of specific elicitory techniques (Vrij *et al.* 2001) and officers' overconfidence in their ability to apply them (Powell 2002). Therefore, despite the third analytic part illustrating the officers' successful use of techniques advised in training manuals, such as downplaying the seriousness of the crime or the situation (Kassin and Wrightsman 1985, Kassin and McNall 1991, Pearce and Gudjonsson 1999) and providing justifications for the offence (Napier and Adams 2002; Inbau *et al.* 2004), the rarity of the confession still remains. It conflicts with traditional perceptions of the confession that it is easily obtainable and commonly occurring (see Chapter 2). This reinforces the need for police interview training to be an accurate reflection of the reality of the police interview in practice, and suggests there remains a requirement for current understandings of confessions and the police interview to be revisited with further empirically based, interactionally focused, value-free analyses.

The officers' use of laughter illustrates how non-verbal interaction could be used as a possible communicative device where other explicit and verbal ways may not be available or legally viable. The findings show the real possibility that some uses of these phenomena by interviewing officers, albeit framed as conversational asides or natural bursts of laughter, can mask or enable real breaches of the codes of conduct. This could be used to train officers to become aware of, and alerted to, the potential hazards in the use of such phenomena. Accordingly, they can be usefully employed by supervisory officers and other silent participants whose work it is to assess the legality of the interview. The presence of the silent participants can create its own difficulties, apparent in the officers' adherence to both the codes of conduct and the suspect, which is epitomized in their orientation to the silent participant overriding the requirements of the immediate interaction with the suspect. Such findings could likewise be used to inform practitioners and provide a catalyst for evidence-based changes in the administration of, and requirements of, the Act (1984). The results also revealed more positive applications of the phenomena; providing officers with insights into how using such tools can broaden their own communicative capabilities. These can be used, for example, to support communication with non-responsive or challenging suspects who may respond on this more conversational level. Indeed, Shuy (1998) describes a conversational approach to interviewing as more favourable than more interrogational styles when eliciting confessions. Such an approach is illustrated in extract 19 of Part Two, where the officer delicately and conversationally frames her adversarial attempt to stop the suspect from remaining silent as a 'daft' requirement placed upon her. In this way, officers' laughter could also be beneficial in reducing the difficulties associated with the (often perceived by the suspect as) adversarial and intimidating nature of the police interview setting.

Although in Part Two officers successfully account for legally or inter-actionally breaching behaviour by situating that behaviour as part of a conversational rather than institutional exchange, it still remains that both officers' and suspects' talk is produced in an institutional setting and bound by the legal and interactional rules of that context. The lack of reprimand in response to potential or actual breaches of protocol does not, however, rule out later sanctions that may occur after the interview or as a result of a later review of the tape. This may be regardless of the officer's skilful application of interactional tools to account for or mitigate that behaviour. While it is not known whether the officers' (mitigated) potential breaches of the PACE Act 1984 are rebuked at a later date, that they are not challenged by legal representatives in the immediate interaction at the time of the breach is important. These uncontested episodes coincide with the use of the communicative tools, which gives an indication of their power at that moment, in that interview, regardless of any later reprisal.

Officers' orientations to the silent participants are features that shape their interaction. This is evidence that tape recording creates an additional interactional dimension to the police interview. Even where this orientation is not responsible for an effect on the interaction, it can be used as if it has done so; the officer in extract 19 used deference to a non-existent requirement of the later listeners, and a potentially future courtroom audience, as an elicitory tool. The findings suggest that, whether produced as an actual effect of the silent participant, or as a tool to achieve particular ends (such as a confessionary turn), the officers' primary orientation has the appearance of being to the silent participant rather than to the interests of the suspect. This can be manifested in the often hurried administration of the suspect's rights, despite evidence (Bridges and Sanders 1990; Baldwin 1992a; 1993) that it is detrimental to a suspect's understanding of their rights. Indeed, rather than informing and providing the suspect with the knowledge to exercise their rights if they wish, it actually negatively impacts on their ability to accurately decide on a course of action. Delivering the suspects' rights to satisfy the legislative requirements of the interview rather than for the benefit and protection of the individual has important implications. It signals a move from the fundamental principle of the Act (1984), and shows officers rigidly adhering to the Act (1984) itself, rather than to the spirit of it. This is not to state that the officers themselves are responsible for this shift in perspective; it is only reporting the reality of the Act (1984) in practice. Obviously their concern must lie with adherence to the Act (1984), as non-compliance could result in disciplinary action against them and render the interview, or part of the interview, inadmissible as evidence. Officers are unable to tailor the delivery of the suspects' rights to the specific requirements of the individual. This suggests that it is possible that the needs of suspects can be disregarded during the process of officers completing the legal requirements. It is the rigidity of those codes of conduct that threaten to alter the reason for their production from the original principle of protecting the suspect, to that of protecting the officer and the evidential admissibility of the interview.

Despite demonstrating the officers' rigid and often over adherence to the PACE Act 1984 codes of conduct, flexibility is immediately apparent when we consider how interactional tools can be used by officers to circumvent its demands. This inconsistency in the levels of adherence to the Act (1984) must have a resulting effect on the consistency of legislative protection offered to the suspect in the police interview. Drawing on Moston *et al.* (1992), despite deemed compliance with the Act (1984), 80% of officers believe that the primary objective of the police interview is to elicit a confession. This opposes the concept of the interview as investigative, and an opportunity for the suspect to state their version of events. This gap between policy and the reality of practice is made clear by Craib (1992: 90), who explained: 'The rhetoric of the adversarial system may view the rights of suspects and their protection ... as desirable in securing reliable confession evidence, but the police do not.' This suggests that ensuring the suspect's rights is seen as separate and at odds with an officer's objective of securing a confession. Moreover, officers may sideline their duty to protect the suspect in favour of achieving that confession. As discussed in Chapter 2, the belief that the main objective of the interview is to secure a confession (Moston *et al.* 1992; Plimmer 1997) goes radically against the spirit of the Act (1984), and the presumption of innocence on which the criminal justice system is based.

Moving On: PACE (1984), CA and Beyond

Since the recording of the interviews in the corpus, the PEACE model of investigative interviewing has been created. Designed to complement, rather than supersede the legislative requirements, it provides a further framework to the police interview within which the investigative stages are made clear. The PEACE model separates the interview process into five stages: 'planning and preparation', 'engage and explain', 'account, clarification and challenge', 'closure' and 'evaluation'. The three middle stages are completed during the course of the interview. The PEACE model focuses the officer more on the motivations behind each stage of the interview, however many difficulties still remain. The inconsistency in the delivery of, and the lack of tailoring of, the interview to ensure the protection of suspects' rights across interviews still remains, as does the question concerning the ability of the PACE Act 1984 to deliver this protection. The PEACE model does attempt to address the 'poor techniques' (Baldwin 1992a; Powell 2002) of officers by encouraging them to address the needs of the suspect through self-reflective practices and explicitly orienting to the suspect. Indeed, any model designed as a supplementary interviewing tool may encourage officers to consider the suspects' needs in the police interview. For example, under PEACE, the officer is required to summarize in the closing section of the interview what had taken place and explain the possible next steps to the suspect; while officering some knowledge and reassurance to the suspect, this will, however, have limited utility if there has been no change in the officer's perception of the interview as a confession-elicitation exercise. This concern is raised by Plimmer (1997) and by Walsh (2006), who argue that officers and interviewers trained in the PEACE model still remain oriented to the guilt-presumptive objective of eliciting confessions.

If the inflexibility in the way the legislative requirements can be applied remains the same, the officer will ultimately remain compelled to adhere to those legal strictures over the needs of the suspect. It will still remain that the legislative framework itself, and the demands on the officer to adhere to that framework, to protect themselves and the admissibility of the interview, supersede this model. Therefore it can still render officers unable to (and facilitate those unwilling to) ensure the protection of suspects' rights. The concern, therefore, might be that additional interviewing procedures may simply add to the requirements of the officer rather than add to the protection of the suspect. Problems with the PEACE model are not restricted to the rigidity of the overarching legal statutes. It has itself been described by officers as inflexible (Clarke and Milne 2001), and, although interviewers endorse the PEACE model as an effective interviewing tool and claim improvements in their interviewing skills (Walsh 2006), they may not necessarily be relied on to judge their own interviewing ability or the effectiveness of their techniques (Fischer *et al.* 1987; Baldwin 1992b; Moston and Engelberg 1993).

The use of CA has provided this exploration of the police interview with an innovative view of the detail of the interaction that serves to complement and add to previous and current explorations. It has also presented an opportunity to expand its function beyond its more traditional uses seen in previous and recent work, through the focus on under and unexplored phenomena, and more practically, through the use of computer software. The use of Goldwave software has taken the application of CA beyond the audio interpretation of sounds traditionally associated with this methodology, to the use of digital formats that represent the audio as a visual waveform (spectrograph, see Chapter 3). This is an analytic technique intended to complement the purely audio-based methods of analysing sound that are currently used. This research used this augmented method to analyse the waveforms of speech in terms of timing pauses in the police interview interaction. As discussed in Chapter 3, this analytic development could strengthen this and other interactionally focused methodologies by adding another dimension to their analytic capacity, which is standardized, calculable, digitally accurate, comparable and replicable across contexts and research. It could be used to add another dimension to analysing pitch and volume by harnessing the digital representation of the sounds in terms of amplitude and frequency. Clearly this would be in addition to the original conversation analytic techniques and would not seek to replace them; indeed as explained in Chapter 3, the original techniques should take precedence over the mechanical, and the original premise of CA should be retained. But it does embark on a new way of thinking that would add to the analytical capabilities of this and other interactional methodologies. Having a calculable, measureable, replicable and more quantifiable aspect to the method would also be particularly useful if an analysis were required as expert evidence. While this type of work is not traditionally associated with the conversation analytic technique, and it may appear to be moving away from its original premise, I see this as part of its natural progression. This view may be met with some resistance; however, similar resistance has also been encountered with many developments within academic disciplines, one of the most striking examples being the move from white collar crime being initially seen as outside the criminological sphere to now being part of the mainstream.

This work has demonstrated the deep understandings that can be gleaned from using conversation analytic techniques on police interview data; nuances and the transfer of meaning and understandings that would be lost from the data if it had been transcribed without using conversation analytic techniques. Each of the analytic parts have demonstrated officers and suspects communicating on a level deeper than words; the way these words were spoken, and, where there were no words at all, phenomena such as the hesitations, laughs and turntaking. It is well established that these all contribute toward the overall meaning of 'what was said'. Therefore it is clear to see the difficulty associated with the current mechanisms of presenting police interviews as evidence in court; it is usually the transcript of the interaction rather than the tape that is presented in court as evidence, and the extra-interactional detail discussed above is typically absent from this version. These difficulties are illustrated in extracts 9 and 18 of the analytic parts; extract 9 shows the officer using laughter as a non-lexical tool to challenge the suspect exercising their rights; however, if this were presented as a transcript in court, the laughter particles would most likely not be represented on the transcript. Indeed, the officer even says 'ok ok', which, without the bubbling-through laughter that accompanies it, would appear to show the officer agreeing with the suspect's use of 'no comment.' This is not the case upon listening to the audio record: it is clear the officer is actually challenging it, something that is brought out in the CA transcription. Juxtaposed with extracts 7 and 8 for example, the officers' challenge to the suspects' rights is similar, but in these cases it is verbalized; the meaning would remain whether transcribed conversation analytically or otherwise. Extract 18 illustrated an officer's rapid production of the suspect's rights, and, upon analysis, showed how the speed at which a police caution is produced can be against the spirit of PACE (1984). Again, as evidence in court, the extra-interactional markers such as speed at which talk is delivered would be stripped from the transcript. These examples highlight that, if the police interview is used as evidence in court without the possibility of the tape itself being played, it is essential that conversation analytic transcriptions, or those with some indication of how the words were spoken, are used. They more accurately represent not just what was said, but the way it was said, and capture those extra-interactional parts of speech that this book has demonstrated are essential in understanding the construction and maintenance of interaction, and have so much to do with conveying meaning far beyond the words that accompany them.

This investigation into the detail of the interview has produced findings that are useful to broadening the understanding of the police interview, applications of CA, and offers a contribution to the fields of sociology, criminology and forensic linguistics. It is also relevant to the practice of interviewing; offering potential application in training for police officers as well as other officers who are authorized under the PACE Act 1984, such as local government Trading Standards Officers. This research is going to be further developed with the use of audio-visual police interview DVDs of current cases; these can be aligned to the current legislative mechanisms, and alongside the use of the PEACE model. This can also start to incorporate the visual cues that are present alongside the extra-lexical cues analysed in the current work. By broadening the scope of CA, future applications could include analysing phenomena used by officers and suspects in relation to the type of crime (for example acquisitive or violent) or on a scale of the seriousness of the offence. Research could also compare the differences in the participants' use of interactional tools in accordance with the presence of a legal representative, translator or responsible adult in the interview. Other avenues include exploring what links exist between the type and frequency of confessions, and analysing elicitation techniques by the type of offence. The power dynamics in the police interview could be exposed in this setting by using police interviews with witnesses as a comparator; as the participants in witness interviews are not subject to the Act (1984)[56] and the interaction is seen as a collaborative process.

This could provide insights that enable officers to further tailor their use of phenomena to enhance and maximize the usefulness of the interview, protect the suspects' rights and maintain an interactional bond. It would also provide rich sociological insights into the participants' perceptions of different crimes and those who commit them, by analysing the interaction and by analysing the officers' and suspects' performance of their roles. In addition, this would offer rich understandings into the way their talk changes when faced with differing levels of formality and seriousness, and the potential consequences associated with the most serious crimes. It could also be used to compare similar types of crimes from a sociological perspective, for example in examining and comparing the participants' construction and maintenance of their roles in cases of benefit fraud and tax evasion.

This book has taken an investigative journey through the police interview, from the stereotypically expected phenomena of confessions, and the multilateral effect of the silent participant, to the traditionally unexpected presence of laughter in this setting. It has identified the presence and structure of these phenomena as interactional tools that can be used to achieve various objectives, and it has shown how the talk is deeply ordered on a level that supersedes contextual differences. The constant fluctuation between the institutional and conversational aspects of the interaction reflects the differing orientations of the suspect as a non-institutional outsider and the officer as a representative of the institution. The conflicting obligations of the officer require their often skilful use of interactional tools; that it is possible for this vacillating orientation to occur seamlessly illustrates the joint and implicit communicative understanding between the suspect and the officer.

On a practical level, the insights into the deeper intricacies of police-suspect interaction, and the performance of the unwritten interactional rules and roles to achieve certain objectives, can also be used to supplement interviewing techniques and provide a resource to enhance communicative understandings. There are benefits to be gleaned from evidence that shows the real potential for officers to use laughter in their circumvention of the PACE Act 1984, and that such phenomena can be used as tools rather than being understood as simply naturally occurring events or conversational additions that are beyond legal scrutiny. It could increase officers' awareness of the dangers of cursorily reciting the police caution and the potential for neglecting the suspects' rights through adherence to the Act (1984), and for the potential for officers to breach without rebuke or challenge. Fundamentally, this work has begun to address the officers' ability to circumvent the constraints while also being restricted in their ability to adapt them, and has identified the misalignment that can exist when attempting to balance the institutional concerns with the interactional needs of the suspect.

Appendix I

Transcription Conventions (adapted from Hutchby and Wooffitt 1998)

P1	Interviewing police officer.
P2	Second interviewing police officer.
S	Suspect.
So	Solicitor.
(TNN-NN-NN)	Transcript identifier number.
(0.5)	The number in brackets indicates a time gap in tenths of seconds.
(.)	A dot enclosed in brackets indicates a pause in the talk of less than two-tenths of a second.
=	The equals sign indicates latching between utterances. For a definition of latching, see Appendix III.
[	An open square bracket between adjacent lines of concurrent speech indicate the onset of a spate of overlapping talk.
..hh	Two dots before an 'h' indicates speaker in-breath. The more 'h's the longer the breath.
hh..	Two dots following an 'h' indicates an out-breath. The more 'h's the longer the breath.
y(hh)es	An 'h' or collection of 'h's in brackets indicates 'bubbling through laughter'. The more 'h's the longer the laugh. This laughter occurs mid-word; its placement denotes the placement and length of laughter.

hh haha heh	The variety of sounds occurring as a result of types of full laughter are onomatopoeically denoted by a variety of letters in order to render as literal a transcription as possible. This result in a collection of 'h's, 'hah's, 'heh's, 'hih's and variants thereof.
((coughs))	A description enclosed in a double bracket indicates a non-verbal activity.
–	A dash indicates a sharp cut-off of the prior word or sound.
:	Colons indicate that the speaker has stretched the preceding sound or letter. The more colons, the greater the extent of the stretching.
!	Exclamation marks are used to indicate an animated or emphatic tone.
( )	Empty parenthesis with a large gap indicate the presence of an unclear fragment on the tape.
(guess)	The words within a single bracket indicate the transcriber's best guess at an unclear utterance.
.	A full stop indicates a stopping fall in tone. It does not necessarily indicate the end of a sentence.
,	A comma indicates a 'continuing' intonation.
?	A question mark indicates a rising inflection. It does not necessarily indicate a question.
*	An asterisk indicates a 'croaky' pronunciation of the utterance that immediately follows.
↑↓	Pointed arrows indicate a marked rising or falling intonational shift. They are placed immediately before the onset of the shift.
a:	Less marked falls in pitch can be indicated by using underlining immediately preceding a colon.
a:	Less marked rises in pitch can be indicated by using a colon which itself is underlined.
under	Underlined fragments indicate speaker emphasis.

CAPITALS	Words in capitals mark a section of speech as noticeably louder than that surrounding it.
° °	Degree signs are used to indicate the talk they encompass is spoken noticeably quieter than the surrounding talk,
°° °°	while double degree signs indicate the talk they encompass is even quieter.
Thaght	A 'gh' indicates that the word in which it is placed had a guttural pronunciation.
> <	'More than' and 'less than' signs indicate that the talk they encompass is produced noticeably quicker than the surrounding talk.
< >	'Less than' and 'more than' signs indicate that the talk they encompass is produced noticeably slower than the surrounding talk.
→	Arrows in the left margin point to specific parts of an extract discussed in the text.
...	Three dots to the left of the first word in an extract indicate that the speech is a continuation of a turn that is not included in the example. Three dots to the right of the last word in an extract indicate there is further speech in that turn that is not detailed in the extract.
16 . . . 22	Three dots in the margin in the place of line numbers indicate that turns have occurred but are not shown in that particular extract. The line numbers give an indication of the number of lines that have been omitted.

Appendix II

Additional Transcript Extracts

Extracts Referred to in Chapters 4 and 5

Line from T22-20-06

166 S   I (.) >I didn't even know it was< the:re

Lines from T11-80-06

252 S   ...statement that ni:ght (0.4) but everyone here was saying I was too
253   drunk to make a sta:tement >and as there was already too many
254 →   pe:ople making a sta:tement I weren't even drunk<

Lines from T11-80-06

309 P1   ...>we kno:w< you were >feeling the effects of
311   alcohol because a< doctor said (.) that you were (.) too drunk to be
312   intervie:wed
313 → S   >yeah but I< we:ren't tho:ugh
314   (0.5)
315 → S   well its up to him I suppo:se but I we:ren't (.) I know when I'm drunk

Lines from T18-23-06

603 P1   >a:ll it is is< (.) >I mean< (0.6) >for the sake of< two: video games and a
604   compu:ter g↓ame, >I mean< I dunno if you forgot to return them, ↓or
605   (1.3) you've passed them o:n to somebody else, (0.6) or you've >just
606   thought< w↓ell >you know< I'll keep the:se I'm going on holiday fairly
607   soon,

Lines from T18-23-06

612 → P1   >le:ts just< get this a:ll cleared ↓u[p

613   S   [ye[ah yeah I've you kno:w ↓I've

614   P1   [>I thi:nk (.) I thi:nk< you know

615   wha:t

616 → P1   I th↑ink you know what it's ab↓out

Lines from T18-23-06

849   P1   i:t <c↑ould> >have been a< misunderstand↓ing (0.5) °right,° (0.3) so I'm

850   a:sking you n↓ow, (.) i:s it a misunderstand↓ing, (0.5) ha:ve you taken

851   those videos ↓out, (0.5) °>and<° not returned them for >what↑ever

852   re:ason< (.) be:st known °>to<° yours↓elf (0.7) and ↑if you ha:ve are you

853   prepared to take them b↓↓a (.) t- t- to give them b↓ack

Extracts Referred to in Chapters 6 and 7

Line from T22-20-06

1   P1   >thi:s interview< is being tape recorde̲:d (.) I:'m (.) <wpc> frances green...

Lines from T11-80-06

387   P1   but er (0.2) >wh↑o was< the (.) <the e:rr> (0.4) the black guy >who...

.

.

.

393   P1   never se:en him before

.

.

.

402   P1   you didn't see one

Line from T29-31-06

355   P1   f↑irst of all she says that you've been living at a separate addre:ss

Lines from T1-67-06

239   P1   >°an y-°< you've got no s- you've got no signs outside saying garage or

240   anything like tha:t

241		(0.6)
242	S	no there's loads down there though >you know warri mean<
243	P1	and (0.7) you're quite far down green la:ne
244		(0.3)
245	S	yeah
246 →	P1	and you've only been there a couple of weeks
247		(1.1)
248 →	P1	..hhh so you're saying that a (0.6) a bloke hh.. (0.6) out the blu:e (0.3)
249		turns up in a fifteen grand car (1.2) comes down green lane (0.7) stops by
250		some (0.2) tatty old worksho:ps (0.4) with no signs saying garage (0.5)
251		comes up to you (0.8) to a garage where there's no (0.7) machi:nes inside
252		and says can you do some work on a ca:r

Lines from T1-67-06

160	P1	it's a few bob though that its still for you though (.) about twelve fifteen
161		grand

Lines from T1-67-06

203	P1	what have you got there
204 →		(0.9)
205	S	erm: (0.6) >wo↑rkshops old workshops< beaten up ones an that

Lines from T1-67-06

207	P1	what (0.3) equipment have you got in there yourse:lf
208	S	nothing at the moment
209		(0.2)
210	P1	nothing
211		(1.0)
212 →	P1	°ri:ght°
213 →		(1.1)

Lines from T1-67-06

261	P1	so a bloke with a fifteen grand car comes to a place where there's (0.4)
262		>there's l< (0.7) ..hh there's (.) a lot of (0.4) car- (0.5) repair places down
263		there and then he comes to a bloke who hasn't got any

Lines from T1-67-06

579 P1   dave (1.2) never met before (1.3) turned up at your derelict (0.8)
580   workshop (0.9) with no (.) car equipment in it at all (1.5) with fifteen
581   grand car (0.8) and says to you (0.5) >°i want the plate< I want the car
582   sprayed° (1.7) he then leaves a fifteen grand car with a total stranger (.)
583   with the keys (0.6) not at a proper garage (0.5) yeah=

Line from T1-67-06

601 P1   ..hhh SOUNDS A BIT FU[NNY: TO ME DUNNIT

Extracts Referred to in Chapters 8 and 9

Lines from T18-23-06

1026 S   I've dropped myse:lf in it no:w I've told you the tr↓uth (0.5) d- I
1027   could've carried on, °b↓ut° (0.2) it's getting a bit silly: (0.2) over a video:°

Lines from T33-22-06

107 S   =(0.3) coz when I'm upset I am loud, (0.5) but <as for an assau:lt> no
108   assault °ever took pl↓ace°

Lines from T33-22-06

211 S   the >alleged assault< is a l↓ie (.) because I never (.) I never (.) <come into
212   contact with him> *er- (.) other than pushing hi:m

Lines from T33-22-06

237 S   [>I didn't hi:t-hi:m< (0.3) never °h-° never
238   t↓ouched him

Lines from T33-22-06

221 → P1   >right thi:s is< a statement from a witness, (0.5) °called° fre:derick stuart,
222 S   y:ep
223   (2.0)
224 P1   quoting a bit fro:m his stateme:nt (6.3) tk- >its got< here the ski:p driver
225   got <into his> ca:b by the drivers si:de which was nearest m↓e (0.3) the

226   ro:ver driver was standing by the damage on his ca:r and appeared to be
227   writing something do:wn (0.4) the:n the skip driver ju:mped out of his cab
228   (0.3) appro:ached the other driver and pu:shed the rover driver in the
229   che:st (0.3) back against his ca:r (0.2) and with a <ri:ght hand> hi:t the
230 →   rover dri:ve:r (0.3) t[o the left side of his face [or ne:ck (0.5[) <I [saw=
231   S   [°n↓o°   [°*n:↓ah°   [°no°
232 → P1   =him hi:t him o:nce> (0.5) I'm no:t sure definitely if it was with a
233 →   cle:nched fi:st <but it was> (0.4) in my thought a deliberate p↓unch

Lines from T7-120-06

49   P1   ri:ght (0.2) >can you tell me where< you've been tonight,
.
.
.

58   P1   and what happened then
.
.
.

70   P1   tell me the route you took home

Lines from T7-120-08

206   P1   I'd asked you before
207 → S   yeah but it wasn't sort of (0.3) the only reason I didn't sort of say it
208 →   because if I's said it it would've looked sort of more suspicious

Lines from T7-120-08

231   S   [the only reason I said that because if I said that I'd sort of
232   like gone to monolo and then gone back that way again it sort of looks
233   more suspicious [than what im being accused for

Line from T10-77-06

54   P1   yeah (1.6) you were driving that car were you

Lines from T10-77-06

87   o'clock in the morn↓ing (.) are you responsible for the theft of that
88   vehicle?

Lines from T10-77-06

96   P1   also last night (1.4) som:e (.) little while before (.) the vehicle was chased
97   by police (0.[..h]6) ..hh and stopped (0.3) on the bee twelve (1.3) the car
98   was involved in (0.8) what we call a drive out >a theft of petrol< (1.3) that
99   was on the petrol station (.) at (4.0) cresswells heath (.) or cresswell heath
100   (1.2) by the southbank carriage of the bee tw↓elve

Line from T10-77-06

102 P1   yeah? were you the driver of the vehi:cle at that time

Lines from T10-77-06

90   P1   do you know who was responsible for the theft of that vehicle:

.

.

.

110   >did anybody else< drive that car at all.

Lines from T10-77-06

238 P1   okay mate >is there anything else you want to sa:y at all<
239   (0.3)
240 S   n↓o
241   (5.2)
242 P1   any observations you got to make ma'a:[m
243 So   [°°n↓o thanks°°
244 P1   okay (0.3) in that case (1.7) I'll terminate the interview now the time (0.3)
245   >by the clock on the wall< is: (0.4) two fifty three (0.9) p↓m

Lines from T10-77-06

220 P1   have you got anything else you wanna sa:y
221   (0.7)
222 P1   percy
223   (1.1)
224 S → °no° (0.3) apart from peter and michael (0.9) they weren't (0.5) >nothing
225   to do with it<

Lines from T40-66-06

218   P1   about what time (0.6) did you make arrangeme:nts to sell this j↓acket

219   (2.4)

220   S   soon as I had it in my posse:ssi:on

221   (0.9)

222   P1   ri:ght so as so:on as you saw the jacket you made that instantaneous

223   decisi:on (0.2) that you were gonna sell it

224   (0.4)

225   P1   [so presu:mably you had someone in m↓ind who wanted to bu:y this=

226   S   [yeah

227   P1   =j↓acket

228 → S   no:t in mind, I thought I'd try him and he was (0.5) interested at the time

229   so I'd so:ld it

Lines from T40-66-06

237   P1   so <is this> gentlema:n wasn't interested in purch- >presumably it's a<

238   gentleman we're talking ab↓[out

239 → S   [mhm

Lines from T40-66-06

265   P1   =conce:rne[d who is this gentleman exactly

266   S   [that's it

267   (3.3)

268 → S   he's a legi:t (.) pho:ne ma:n who does portable pho:nes=

Lines from T40-66-06

274   P1   what is his n↓ame pl↓ease

275   (2.8)

276 → S   he wo:n't get into trouble will he was- *I: (0.2) >*it's got< I don't want

277   him [to °>get in trouble<°

Lines from T18-23-06

257 → P1   °↓erm° (0.2) and <someone> produced ide:ntificati:on (0.9) for <three

258   e:lm ro↓ad>

259   (1.7)

260 → P1   wa:s that yours↓elf

261 → S   no

Lines from T18-23-06

312   P1   °a-° and >you are< (.) denyi:ng that its yourse:lf
313   (1.0)
314 → S   ye:s >I am< °deny:ing ↓it°

Lines from T18-23-06

593 → P1 °you've hired the comp↑uter ga:me°, (0.4) and for some reason I don't
594   know why, (0.4) you just haven't bothered retu:rning the:m
595   (0.2)
596   S   mhm:
597   P1 °I mean°
598   (3.2)
599   S   ((clears throat))
600   (1.0)
601 → P1 >wha:t have you to< say about th↓at

Line from T18-23-06

637   P1 >you're sa:ying that you< don't know a:nything about it at ↓all

Lines from T18-23-06

139   P1 >wh↑at it i:s< (0.4) >↑I've had a< repo:rt from monolo vid↓eo, (2.9) that
140   two: videos, namely <sa:dfilm and funnyfilm,> (0.6) >↓and a< computer g
141   console ga:me (.) fungame two? (0.6) were hired (1.3) on the twe:nty
142   si:xth of ma:rch nineteen ninety four. (0.4) do you know anything about
143   thi:s at ↓a[ll
144 → S   [no I d↓on't

Lines from T18-23-06

263 → P1 who: would it be: (0.2) who: would have identification for three elm roa:d
264 →   if it wasn't (.) yo:u
265   (0.5)
266 → S   no ide:a

Lines from T18-23-06

582   P1 >I'll t↑ell you< what I thi:nk, (0.2) I thi:nk you've hi:red these vide:os
583   (0.5) yourse:lf

Lines from T18-23-06

593 P1 °you've hired the comp↑uter ga:me°, (0.4) and for some reason I don't
594   know why, (0.4) you just haven't bothered retu:rning the:m

Lines from T18-23-06

603 P1 >a:ll it is is< (.) >I mean< (0.6) >for the sake of< two: video games and a
604   compu:ter g↓ame, >I mean< I dunno if you forgot to return them, ↓or
605   (1.3) you've passed them o:n to somebody else, (0.6) or you've >just
606   thought< w↓ell >you know< I'll keep the:se I'm going on holiday fairly
607   soon,

Lines from T18-23-06

612 → P1 >le:ts just< get this a:ll cleared ↓u[p
613 S   [ye[ah yeah I've you kno:w ↓I've
614 P1   [>I thi:nk (.) I thi:nk< you know
615   wha:t
616 → P1 I th↑ink you know what it's ab↓out

Lines from T18-23-06

630 → P1 °I° just wa:nna get this matter cleared u:p and I th↑ink you know a bit
631 →   more abo:ut i:t tha:n what you're >letting o:n<
632   (4.0)
633 → P1 don't ya:
634   (0.3)
635 → S   n(h)o:

Lines from T18-23-06

616 P1 I th↑ink you know what it's ab↓out
617   (1.5)
618 → S   no:, [I (.) <I find it> very ann↓oying that I've been dragged out of b↓ed

Lines from T18-23-06

875 P1 [so: (.) you to↑ok the games (.) [you to:ok the games o:ut >yo:u've been<=
876 → S [ye:s I've been l↓ying   [yes

Lines from T2-111-06

147 → S   no (0.4) not anyw(h)here at all near there
148   (0.2)
149   P1   not anywhere at all
150 → S   no (0.5) jus (0.8) out of the subway and round the co:rner

Lines from T2-111-06

262 → S   very familiar but someone si:milar looking to me< like but it wasn't m(h)e
263   that he sa(h)w come out (0.[3) in or near any shops
264   P1   [did you g↑o near lowprice
265 → S   no I d↑idn't I came down (1.[4) all I did was come (0.2) up from the=
266   P1   [((COUGH cough))
267 → S   =subwa:y (.) across the parade but and along turner roa:d (.) I didn't go
268   anywhere near the (0.7) d- I know the (.) the shops the dry cleaners and
269   (0.4) there's a carpet shop I think[( )
270   P1   [(((COUGH cough [cough))
271 → S   [and a newsagents as
272   we[ll and lowprice up there (.) >no: and I< (0.5) d(h)idn't go=
273   P1   [yeah
274 → S   =a:nywhere near them or kirkdon gr↑een (2.1) its not- (.) >if you-<

Lines from T2-111-06

247 → P1   tk- (0.3) an he saw (0.2) you (0.5) and mark being stopped by police
248   (2.1)
249   S   °yeah°
250   (0.6)
251 → P1   so he's not only seen you walking out the shop or coming out the shop (.)
252   they've both seen you coming out the shop (1.2) they've also both seen
253   (0.3) the same person i.e. you being stopped by police

Lines from T2-111-06

366 → P1   so we've established one l↓ie (.) that you did go over to the shop and you
367   were stood outside when the window was sma:shed (3.2) y↑eah
368   S   yeah
369   (0.5)
370   P1   °right°
371   (1.3)
372 → P1   that's the first lie out the way with so the rest isn't so hard now is it

Lines from T2-111-06

498 P1 °m↑m: you should've told the truth in the first place shouldn't you° (2.6)
499   because I think you're still lying I think you did go into that shop

Glossary of Technical Terms

Approximants

Speech sounds that involve the narrowing of the vocal tract, often described as inbetween vowels and consonants, and form sounds such as 'l' and 'w'.

Bubbling-through laughter

Plosive aspiration within a word – that is, laughter that occurs during the production of a word. See the transcription convention glossary in Appendix I for its corresponding symbol.

Content level

Pertaining to an analytical level on which the content of the interview is the significant factor and point of interest.

Dispreferred action/turn

These are 'unexpected' or non-standard responses to the first of an adjacency pair. Some examples of adjacency pairs are greeting-greeting, request-compliance, or summons-answer (see Schegloff 1988, Hutchby and Wooffitt 1998). In the case of request-compliance, the request of one participant is 'expected' to be met with a certain response – namely compliance from the other participant, as shown in the following:

A: How about you pop over for coffee later?
B: Sure.

A dispreferred action can be identified by the behaviour that accompanies the action (for example, the use of 'well', hesitancy, hedging and pre-rejection accounts):

A: How about you pop over for coffee later?

B: Well (pause) tha- that's awfully kind of you but I won't be able to today. In the context of the police interview, a suspect's rejection or challenge of an officer's turn is a dispreferred action, as in ordinary conversation. However, the suspect is additionally constrained by the sequential organization and turn allocation of the police interview (Drew and Heritage 1992, Heydon 2005).

Full laughter

Laughter that is not attached to any lexical item or produced during lexical construction. See the transcription convention glossary in Appendix I for its corresponding symbol.

Institutional interaction

Pertaining to the interaction in institutional settings such as medical consultations, courtrooms, the media and psychiatric interviews.

Latching

An utterance is 'latched' onto another's utterance if its onset coincides with the other's conclusion without overlapping. See the transcription convention glossary in Appendix I for its corresponding symbol.

Lexical level

Pertaining to an analytical level on which the words used are the significant factor and point of interest.

Nasal consonant

A term that relates to the physical production of sounds by the body. A nasal sound is produced by directing the flow of air through the nasal passages, forming sounds such as 'm' and 'n'.

Non-lexical item/tool

Refers to a part of speech that is not expressed in words – for example a sigh, laugh or a 'tut'.

Participant

A person taking part in the interaction or an overhearer of that interaction.

Plosive

A term that relates to the physical production of sounds by the body. A plosive sound is produced primarily through the rapid release of a build up of air in the mouth, forming sounds such as 'p' and 't'.

Redundancy (semantic and legal)

Semantically redundant utterances are utterances rendered superfluous due to the physical surroundings of the talk. Legally redundant utterances are those that are not required by law; legally redundant utterances of interest are those framed as legally required.

Repair

A generic term in CA that covers a range of correction activities within talk. Repair can be carried out on a speaker's interaction by the speaker themselves (self-initiated repair) or by another participant (other-initiated repair). Accordingly, there are various permutations of this phenomenon, for instance other-initiated self-repair is where the speaker repairs their utterance at the suggestion of another, and other-initiated other-repair is where another participant repairs the speaker's utterance themselves. (See Hutchby and Wooffitt 1998: 61).

Talk-in-trouble

A generic term in CA that refers to a range of difficulties arising during the production of an utterance.

Token/Phenomenon

The part of interaction of interest – for example, laughter.

Turn

An utterance of any length attributed to the current speaker. The next turn will be the utterance by the next speaker. CA transcripts are not organized or numbered by turn but by line, and the current speaker is identified by their code (such as P1 and S for officer and suspect respectively; see the transcription convention glossary in Appendix I).

Appendix IV

Extract from *The Bill* Script

Episode 513: 'A Perfect Murder', Part Two[57]

13.02.07 – Shooting – Episode 513 – Scene 35, page 92

JO   Larry ... we also have a witness who claims that you assaulted him near City's house at around 11.30 on Wednesday night.

LARRY (nervous laugh) You're winding me up now.

JO   Our witness says you were 'hysterical'.

LARRY Do I look the hysterical type?

JO   Would you like to explain what you were doing there?

LARRY (shaky) Your witness must be confusing me with somebody else. That wasn't me, I'm sorry.

JO CAN SEE SHE'S TOUCHED A NERVE. SHE MOVES ON.

STUART Let's move on to the phone conversation you had with your sister late on Wednesday night ...

LARRY I already told you. I thanked her for the meal. And that was that.

STUART Alison's got a very different recollection now. She told us that you called in an awful state ...

13.02.07 – Shooting – Episode 513 – Scene 38B, page 101

LARRY SUDDENLY REALISES HE'S SAID TOO MUCH

JO   (softly) Go on.

LARRY SHAKES HIS HEAD, LIKE A CHILD. HE STARTS TO CRY.

LARRY I've said too much. Cindy will never forgive me! I've let her down again ...

JO	She needs to know the truth, Larry. We need to know the truth.
LARRY	It's my fault. It's my fault Cindy's dead.
JO	Are you telling me you killed Cindy?
LARRY	I will never forget that. Being there with her. Sharing those final…beautiful moments.
STUART	How did you do it Larry?
LARRY	I hit her over the head.
STUART	Why did you do that?
LARRY	Cindy was too good for this world. Whenever I saw her, she looked like a trapped animal. I could see it in her eyes, you know? The longing to escape … I was the only person who understood …

References

Agnew, S., Powell, M. and Snow, P. (2006) 'An examination of the questioning styles of police officers and caregivers when interviewing children with intellectual disabilities'. *Legal and Criminal Psychology*. Vol. 11(1): 35–53.

Alexander, D. and W. Wells (1991) 'Reactions of police officers to body-handling after a major disaster: A before and after comparison'. *British Journal of Psychiatry*. Vol. 159: 547–555.

Ashes to Ashes. Police procedural drama television series. First broadcast 2008. British Broadcasting Corporation (BBC1). London: Kudos Film & Television.

A Touch of Frost. Police procedural drama television series. First broadcast 1992.

Atkinson, J. M. (1992) 'Displaying neutrality: formal aspects of informal court proceedings'. In: Drew, P. and Heritage, J. (eds) *Talk at work: Interaction in institutional settings*. Cambridge: Cambridge University Press: 199–211.

Atkinson, J. M. and Drew, P. (1979) *Order in court: The organization of verbal interaction in judicial settings* (Oxford sociolegal studies series). London: Macmillan.

Atkinson, M. A., Cuff, E. C. and Lee, J. R. E. (1978) 'The Recommencement of a Meeting as a Member's Accomplishment'. In: J. Schenkein (ed.) *Studies in the Organization of Conversational Interaction*. London: Academic Press: 113–153.

Bain, S. A. and Baxter, J. S. (2000) 'Interrogative suggestibility: The role of interviewer behaviour'. *Legal and Criminal Psychology*. Vol. 5: 123–133.

Baldwin, J. (1992a) *The conduct of police investigations: records of interview, the defence lawyer's role and standards of supervision*. London: Her Majesty's Stationery Office.

Baldwin, J. (1992b) 'Video taping police interviews with suspects: A national evaluation'. *Police Research Series*. Paper No. 1. London: Home Office Police Department.

Baldwin, J. (1993) 'Police interview techniques: Establishing truth or proof?' *British Journal of Criminology*. Vol. 33(3), 325–352.

Billig, M. (2005) *Laughter and ridicule: Towards a social critique of humour*. London: Sage.

Black, D. J. (1970) 'The production of crime rates'. *American Sociological Review*. Vol. 35(4): 733–48.

Black, D. J. (1971) 'The social organisation of arrest'. *Stanford Law Review*. Vol. 23 (June): 1087–1111.

Boden, D. (1994) *The Business of Talk: Organizations in Action*. London: Polity Press.

Brandon, R. and Davies, C. (1973) *Wrongful imprisonment: Mistaken convictions and their consequences*. Hamden, CT: Archon Books.

Bridges, L. and Sanders, A. (1990) 'Access to legal advice and police malpractice'. *Criminal Law Review*. July: 494–509.

Brown, P. and Levinson, S. C. (1987) *Politeness: Some universals in language use.* Cambridge: Cambridge University Press.

Bucke, T. (1994) 'Equal opportunities and the fire service'. *Home Office Research and Statistics Department, Research findings.* No. 13 (September).

Buckley (2003) Cited in: Tyler, T. (2003) 'Why they lie and confess: false confessions studied' Sunday Star Sunday Special, 10 August 2003. *http://www.williams.edu/Psychology/Faculty/Kassin/files/Toronto_Star_8_03.pdf* (last accessed 30/03/11).

Butters R. R. (1993) 'Forensic linguistics comes of age: Review of language and the judicial process' edited by J. N. Levi and A. G. W. (New York, NY: Plenum, 1990) *American Speech.* Vol. 68(1): 109–112.

Buttny, R. (2001) 'Therapeutic humor in retelling the client's tellings'. *Text.* Vol. 21(3): 303–326.

Carrabine, E. (2008) *Crime, Culture and the Media.* Cambridge: Polity Press.

Carter, E. K. (2003) *Policing Interviews: The analysis of turntaking in the police interview on a conversation analytic level.* University of Essex unpublished master's dissertation.

Carter, E. K. (2005) *The laughing policeman: An analysis into the production and management of laughter in the police interview on a conversation analytic level.* University of Essex unpublished master's dissertation.

Caso, L., Gnisci, A., Vrij, A. and Mann, S. (2005) Processes underlying deception: An empirical analysis of truths and lies when manipulating the stakes. *Journal of Interviewing and Offender Profiling.* Vol. 2(3): 195–202.

Chomsky, N. (1965) *Aspects of the theory of syntax.* Massachusetts, MA: Massachusetts Institute of Technology.

Cicourel, A. (1968) *The social organisation of juvenile justice.* New York, NY: Wiley.

Clark and Sykes (1974) 'Some determinants of police organization and practice'. In: D. Glaser (ed.) *Handbook of criminology.* Chicago, IL: Rand McNally College Publishing Company: 455–494.

Clarke, C. and Milne, R. (2001) National evaluation of the PEACE investigative interviewing course *Police Research Award Scheme.* London: Home Office.

Craib, I. (1992) *Modern Social Theory: From Parsons to Habermas.* Harvester Wheatsheaf: Hemel Hempstead.

Criminal Justice Act (1967) c.80. London: Her Majesty's Stationery Office.

Criminal Justice and Public Order Act (1994) c.33. *http://www.uk-legislation.hmso.gov.uk/acts/acts1994/ukpga_19940033_en_1* (last accessed 30/03/11).

Critchley, S. (2002) *On humour.* London: Sage.

Data Protection Act (1998) (c. 29). London: Her Majesty's Stationery Office. *http://www.opsi.gov.uk/acts/acts1998/ukpga_19980029_en_1* (last accessed 30/03/11).

Davies, C. (1982) 'Ethnic jokes, moral values and social boundaries'. *British Journal of Sociology.* Vol. 33(3): 383–403.

Davies, C. (1988) 'Irish Joke as a Social Phenomenon'. In: J. Durant and J. Miller: *Laughing matters: A serious look at humour.* Harlow: Longman Scientific and Technical: 44–65.

Davies, C. (1991) 'Fooltowns: Traditional and modern local, regional, and ethnic jokes about stupidity'. In: G. Bennett (ed.) *Spoken in jest.* Sheffield: Academic Press: 215–236.

Davis, M., Markus, K. A., Walters, S. B., Vorus, N. and Connors, B. (2005) 'Behavioral cues to deception vs. topic incriminating potential in criminal confessions'. *Law and Human Behavior.* Vol. 26(6): 683–704.

Dent, H. R. and Stevenson, G. M. (1979) 'An experimental study of the effectiveness of different techniques of interviewing child witnesses'. *British Journal of Social and Clinical Psychology.* Vol. 18: 41–51.

Drew, P. (1987) 'Po-faced receipts of teases'. *Linguistics.* Vol. 25(1): 219–253.

Drew, P. (1992) 'Contested evidence in courtroom cross-examination: the case of a trial for rape'. In: P. Drew and J. Heritage (eds) *Talk at work: Interaction in institutional settings.* Cambridge: Cambridge University Press: 470–520.

Drew, P. and Heritage, J. (eds) (1992) *Talk at work: Interaction in institutional settings.* Cambridge: Cambridge University Press.

Edwards, D. (2005) 'Moaning, whinging and laughing: the subjective side of complaints'. *Discourse Studies.* Vol. 7(1): 5–29.

Ekman, P. (1985) *Telling lies: clues to deceit in the marketplace, politics, and marriage.* New York, NY: Norton.

Ekman, P. and Friesen, W. V. (1971) 'Constants across culture in the face and emotion'. *Journal of Personality and Social Psychology.* Vol. 17(2): 124–129.

Ekman, P. and O'Sullivan, M. (1991) 'Who can catch a liar?' *American Psychologist* 46(9): 913–920.

Field Manual (1987) *FM 34–52 Intelligence Interrogation.* Washington, DC: US Government Printing Office.

Fischer, R. P. and Geiselman, R. E. (1992) *Memory-enhancing techniques for investigative interviewing: The cognitive interview.* Springfield, IL: Thomas.

Fischer, R. P. Geiselman, R. E. and Raymond, D. S. (1987) 'Critical analysis of police interview techniques'. *Journal of Police Science and Administration.* Vol. 15(3): 177–185.

Foster, H. H. (1969) 'Confessions and the station house syndrome'. *DePaul Law Review* 18: 683–701.

Freedom of Information Act (2000) (c. 36) London: Her Majesty's Stationery Office. *http://www.opsi.gov.uk/acts/acts2000/ukpga_20000036_en_1* (last accessed 30/03/11).

Garfinkel, H. (1967) *Studies in Ethnomethodology.* Englewood Cliffs, NJ: Prentice Hall.

Garret, N. (2006) 'The cost of telling the truth'. *The Guardian* (15/05/06). Guardian News and Media Limited 2007. *http://www.guardian.co.uk/menezes/story/0,,1774680,00.html* (last accessed 30/03/11).

Giles, H. and Oxford, G. S. (1970) 'Towards a multidimensional theory of laughter causation and its social implications'. *Bulletin of the British Psychological Society.* Vol. 23: 97–105.

Glenn, Ph. J. (1989) 'Initiating shared laughter in multi-party conversations'. *Western Journal of Speech Communications.* Vol. 53: 126–149.

Glenn, Ph. J. (1991) 'Current speaker initiation of two-party shared laughter'. *Research on Language and Social Interaction.* Vol. 25: 139–162.

Glenn, Ph. J. (1995) 'Laughing at and laughing with: Negotiations of participant ailments through conversational laughter'. In: P. Ten Have, G. Psathas (eds) *Situated order: Studies in the social organization of talk and embodied activities.* Washington DC: University Press of America: 43–56.

Goffman, E. (1959) *The Presentation of self in everyday life.* New York, NY: Doubleday.

Goffman, E. (1974) *Frame analysis: An essay on the organization of experience.* New York, NY: Harper and Row.

Goffman, E. (1981) *Forms of talk.* Oxford: Blackwell.

GoldWave Inc. Available from *http://www.goldwave.com/* (last accessed 30/03/11).

Goodwin, C. (1981) *Conversational organization: Interaction between speakers and hearers.* London: Academic Press.

Graham, E., Papa, M. and Brooks G. (1992) 'Functions of humor in conversation: conceptualization and measurement'. *Western Journal of Communication.* Vol. 56(2): 161–183.

Greatbatch, D. (1988) 'A turn-taking system for British news interviews'. *Language in Society.* Vol. 17(3): 401–430.

Greatbatch, D. (1992) 'On the management of disagreement between news interviewees'. In: P. Drew and J. Heritage (eds) *Talk at work: Interaction in institutional settings.* Cambridge: Cambridge University Press: 268–301.

Greer, S. (1994) 'The right to silence, defence disclosure, and confession evidence' *Journal of Law and Society.* Vol. 21(1), The Royal Commission on Criminal Justice (March 1994): 102–118.

Grenhag, P. A. and Stromwall, L. A. (2004) *The detection of deception in forensic contexts.* Cambridge: Cambridge University Press.

Gronnerod, J. S. (2004) 'On the meanings and uses of laughter in research interviews: Relationships between interviewed men and a woman interviewer'. *Young.* Vol. 12(1) 31–49.

Gudjonsson, G. H. (1996) *Gudjonsson suggestibility scales.* Solihull: Helion and Company Ltd.

Gudjonsson, G. H. (2002) 'Unreliable confessions and miscarriages of justice in Britain'. *International Journal of Police Science and Management.* Vol. 4(4): 332–343.

Gudjonsson, G. H. (2003) *The psychology of interrogations and confessions: a handbook.* Chichester: John Wiley and Sons.

Gudjonsson, G. and MacKeith, J. A. C. (1982) 'False confessions. Psychological effects of interrogation. A discussion paper'. In: A. Trankell (ed.) *Reconstructing the past.* Deventer: Kluwer: 253–269.

Gudjonsson, G. H. and Sigurdsson, J. F. (1999) 'The Gudjonsson confession questionnaire revised (GCQ-R): Factor structure and its relationship with personality'. *Personality and Individual Differences.* Vol. 27(5): 953–968.

Haakana, M. (2001) 'Laughter as a patient's resource: Dealing with delicate aspects of medical interaction'. *Text.* Vol. 21(1–2): 187–219.

Halford, A. (1993) *No way up the greasy pole.* London: Constable.

Halkowski, T. (1990) '"Role" as an interactional device'. *Social Problems* 37(4): 564–577.

Have, P. Ten, (1989) 'The consultation as a genre'. In: B. Torode (ed.) *Text and talk as social practice.* Dordrecht/Providence: Foris Publications: 115–35.

Have, P. Ten (2007) (2nd edn) *Doing conversation analysis: A practical guide.* Thousand Oaks, CA: Sage.

Haworth, K (2006) 'The dynamics of power and resistance in police interview discourse'. *Discourse and Society* November 2006. Vol. 17(6): 739–759.

Hayward, K. (2004) *City limits: crime, consumer culture and the urban experience.* London: Glasshouse.

Heartbeat. Police procedural drama television series. Independent Television Plc (ITV1). Yorkshire Television.

Heath, C. (1981) 'The opening sequence in doctor-patient interaction'. In: P. Atkinson and C. Heath (eds) *Medical work: Realities and routines.* Gower: Farnborough: 71–90.

Heidensohn, F. (2002) 'Gender and crime'. In: M. Maguire, R. Morgan and R. Reiner (eds) *The Oxford Handbook of Criminology.* Oxford: Oxford University Press: 491–530.

Heidensohn, F. (2003) 'Gender and policing'. In: T. Newburn (ed.) *Handbook of Policing.* Devon: Willan Publishing: 556–577.

Heritage, J. (1984) 'A change-of-state token and aspects of its sequential placement. In J. M. Atkinson and J. Heritage (1984) *Our masters' voices: The language and body language of politics.* London: Methuen: 299–345.

Heritage, J. (1985) 'Analyzing news interviews: aspects of the production of talk for an "overhearing" audience'. In: T. A. Van Dijk (ed.) *Handbook of Discourse Analysis.* Vol. 3. London: Academic Press: 95–119.

Heritage, J. and Greatbatch, D. (1991) 'On the institutional character of institutional talk: The case of news interviews'. In: D. Boden and D. Zimmerman (eds) *Talk and social structure: Studies in ethnomethodology and conversation analysis.* Cambridge: Polity Press: 93–137.

Hester, S. and Eglin, P. (1992) *A sociology of crime.* London: Routledge.

Heydon, G, (2005) *The language of police interviewing.* Hampshire: Palgrave Macmillan.

Hochschild, A. R. (1979) 'Emotion work, feeling rules and social structure'. *American Journal of Sociology.* Vol. 85(3): 551–575.

Hodgson, J. (1994) 'Adding injury to injustice: The suspect at the police station' *Journal of Law and Society.* Vol. 21(1). The Royal Commission on Criminal Justice: 85–101.

Holby Blue. BBC police drama, 2007–present. *http://www.bbc.co.uk/drama/holbyblue.*

Holdaway, S. (1983) *Inside the British police.* Oxford: Blackwell.

Holdaway, S. (1996) *The radicalisation of British policing.* Basingstoke: Macmillan.

Holdaway, S. (1997) 'Constructing and sustaining "race" within the police workforce'. *British Journal of Sociology.* Vol. 48(1): 18–34.

Holdaway, S. and Rock, P. (1998) *Thinking about criminology.* London: University College London.

Holt, E. and Johnson, A. (2006) 'Formulating the facts: Responses to storytelling in police/suspect interviews' Paper presented at the *International Conference on Conversation Analysis,* Helsinki.

Holtgraves, T. M. (1992) 'The linguistic realization of face management: Implications for language production and comprehension, person perception, and cross-cultural communication'. *Social Psychology Quarterly.* Vol. 55: 141–159.

Holtgraves, T. M. (1997) 'Yes, but ...Positive politeness in conversation arguments' *Journal of Language and Social Psychology.* Vol. 16: 222–239.

Holtgraves, T. M. (2000) 'Preference organisation and reply comprehension' *Discourse Processes.* Vol. 30(2): 87–106.

Horselenberg, R., Merckelbach, H., Smeets, T., Franssens, D. Peters, G. J. and Zeles, G. (2006) 'False confessions in the lab – do plausibility and consequences matter?' *Psychology, Crime and Law*. Vol. 12(1): 61–75.

Hutchby, I. and Wooffitt, R. (1998) *Conversation analysis: principles, practices and applications*. Cambridge: Polity Press.

Inbau, F. E., Reid, J. E. and Buckley, P. (1986) *Criminal interrogation and confessions*. Baltimore, MD: Williams and Wilkins.

Inbau F. E., Reid, J. E., Buckley, J. P. and Jayne, B. C. (2001) (3rd edn) *Criminal interrogation and confessions*. Gaithersburg, MD: Aspen.

Inbau, F. E., Reid, J. E., Buckley, J. P. and Jayne, B. C. (2004) (4th edn) *Criminal interrogation and confessions*. Massachusetts, MA: Jones and Bartlett.

Independent Police Complaints Commission. *http://www.ipcc.gov.uk* (last accessed 30/03/11).

Irving, B. (1980) 'Police interrogation'. *Royal Commission on Criminal Procedure Research Study* no. 1. London: H.M. Stationery Office.

Irving, B. and Hilgendorf, L. (1980) *Police interrogation: The psychological approach*. *Research Studies No. 1*. London: Her Majesty's Stationery Office.

Jaishankar, K. (2007) 'Cyber Criminology: Evolving a novel discipline with a new journal'. *International Journal of Cyber Criminology*. Vol. 1(1): 1–6.

Jefferson, G. (1979) 'A technique for inviting laughter and its subsequent acceptance declination' In: G. Psathas (ed.) *Everyday language: Studies in ethnomethodology*. Hillsdale, N.J.: Erlbaum: 79–96.

Jefferson, G. (1984) 'On the organization of laughter in talk about troubles'. In: J. M. Atkinson and J. Heritage (eds) *Structures of social action: Studies in conversation analysis*. Cambridge: Cambridge University Press: 346–369.

Jefferson, G. (1985) 'An exercise in the transcription and analysis of laughter'. In: T. A. Van Dijk (ed.) *Handbook of discourse analysis*, Vol. 3. London: Academic Press.

Jefferson, G. (1989) 'Notes on a possible metric which provides for a 'standard maximum silence' of one second in conversation'. In: Roger, D. and Bull, P. (eds) *Conversation: an interdisciplinary perspective*. Clevedon: Multilingual Matters: 166–196.

Jefferson, G., Sacks, H. and Schegloff, E. A. (1987) 'Notes on Laughter in the Pursuit of Intimacy', in G. Button and J. R. E. Lee (eds) *Talk and Social Organization*: 187–188. Clevedon: Multilingual Matters: 152–205.

Jewkes, Y. (2003) 'Policing cybercrime'. In: T. Newburn (ed.) *Handbook of Policing*. Devon: Willan Publishing: 501–524.

Johnson, A. and Newbury, P. (2006) 'Suspects' resistance to constraining and coercive questioning strategies in the police interview. *International Journal of Speech, Language and the Law*. Vol. 13(2): 213–240.

Jones, C. (2008) 'UK police interviews: A linguistic analysis of Afro-Caribbean and white British suspect interviews'. PhD: University of Essex.

Jucker, A. H. (1993) 'The discourse marker "well": A relevance theoretical account' *Journal of Pragmatics*. Vol. 19(5): 435–452.

Kassin, S. M. (1997) 'The psychology of confession evidence' *American Psychologist*. Vol. 52: 221–223.

Kassin, S. M. (2005) 'On the psychology of confessions: Does innocence put innocents at risk?' *American Psychologist*. Vol. 60(3): 215–228.

Kassin, S. M. (2006) 'A critical appraisal of modern police interrogations'. In: T. Williamson (ed.) *Investigative interviewing: Rights, research, regulation.* Devon: Willan Publishing: 207–228.

Kassin, S. M. and Fong, C. T. (1999) '"I'm Innocent!": Effects of training on judgments of truth and deception in the interrogation Room'. *Law and Human Behavior.* Vol. 23(5): 499–516.

Kassin, S. M., Goldstein, C. C. and Savitsky, K. (2003) 'Behavioral confirmation in the interrogation room: On the dangers of presuming guilt'. *Law and Human Behavior.* Vol. 27(2): 187–203.

Kassin, S. M. and Gudjonsson, G. H. (2004) 'The psychology of confessions: a review of the literature and issues'. *Psychological Science in the Public Interest.* Vol. 5(2): 35–59.

Kassin, S. M. and Kiechel, K. L. (1996) 'The social psychology of false confessions: Compliance, internalization, and confabulation'. *Psychological Science.* Vol. 7(3): 125–128.

Kassin, S. M. and McNall, K. (1991) 'Police interrogations and confessions: Communicating promises and threats by pragmatic implication'. *Law and Human Behavior.* Vol. 15(3): 233–251.

Kassin, S. M. and Neumann, K. (1997) 'On the power of confession evidence: An experimental test on the fundamental difference hypobook'. *Law and Human Behavior.* Vol. 21(5): 469–484.

Kassin, S. M. and Wrightsman, L. S. (1985) 'Confession evidence'. In S. M. Kassin and L. S. Wrightsman (eds) *The psychology of evidence and trial procedure.* Thousand Oaks, CA: Sage Publications: 67–94.

Kassin, S. M., Leo, R. A., Meissner, C. A., Richman, K. D., Colwell, L. H., Leach, A., La Fon, D. (2007) 'Police interviewing and interrogation: A self-report survey of police practices and beliefs'. *Law and Human Behavior.* Vol. 31(4): 381–400.

Katz, J. (1988) *Seductions of crime: moral and sensual attractions in doing evil.* New York, NY: Basic Books.

Kebbell, M. R. and Wagstaff, G. F. (1996) 'Enhancing the practicality of the cognitive interview in forensic situations'. *Psycholoquy* 7. Vol. (16): 155–170.

Kidwell, M. and González Martínez, E. (2010) 'Let me tell you about myself ': A method for suppressing subject talk in a 'soft accusation' interrogation. *Discourse Studies.* February 2010: Vol. 12: 65–89.

Komter, M. (2003) 'The interactional dynamics of eliciting a confession in a Dutch police interrogation'. *Research on Language and Social Interaction.* Vol. 36(4): 433–470.

Krippendorff, K. (2004) (2nd edn) *Content analysis: An introduction to its methodology.* Thousand Oaks, CA: Sage.

Lakoff, R. (1973) 'The logic of politeness; or, minding your P's and Q's'. *Chicago Linguistic Society.* Vol. 9: 292–305.

Lavin, D. and Maynard, D. W. (2001) 'Standardization vs. rapport: Respondent laughter and interviewer reaction during telephone surveys' *American Sociological Review.* Vol. 66(3): 453–479.

Law Reform Commission of Canada (1988). In: J. Baldwin (1992a) *The conduct of police investigations: records of interview, the defence lawyer's role and standards of supervision.* London: Her Majesty's Stationery Office: 1–31.

Lee, D. (1997) 'Interviewing men: Vulnerabilities and dilemmas' *Women's Studies International Forum.* Vol. 20(4): 553–564.

Leo, R. A. (1996) 'Inside the interrogation room'. *Journal of Criminal Law and Criminology.* Vol. 86(2): 266–297.

Leo, R. A. (2008) "Police Interrogation and American Justice". Harvard, MA: Harvard University Press.

Leo, R. and Ofshe, R. J. (1998) 'The consequences of false confessions: Deprivations of liberty and miscarriages of justice in the age of psychological interrogation'. *The Journal of Criminal Law and Criminology.* Vol. 88(2): 429–496.

Life on Mars. Police procedural drama television series. British Broadcasting Corporation (BBC1). London: Kudos Film & Television.

Liddicoat, A. (2007) *An introduction to conversation analysis.* London: Continuum.

Lord Denning (1980) *McIlkenny v Chief Constable of the West Midlands* QB 283, at 323D.

Macpherson, W. (1999) *The Stephen Lawrence Inquiry: Report of an inquiry* (CM4262). London: Her Majesty's Stationery Office. *http://www.archive.official-documents. co.uk/document/cm42/4262/sli-00.htm* (last accessed 30/03/11).

Maguire, M. (2003) 'Criminal investigation and crime control'. T. Newburn (ed.) *Handbook of Policing.* Devon: Willan Publishing: 363–393.

Maguire, M. and Norris, C. (1994) 'Police investigations: Practice and malpractice'. *Journal of Law and Society.* Vol. 21(1): 72–84.

Malone, Paul B. III (1980) 'Humor: A double-edged tool for today's managers?' *The Academy of Management Review.* Vol. 5(3): 357–360.

Manning, P. K. (1980) 'Violence and the police role'. *Annals of the American Academy of Political and Social Science.* Vol. 452(1): 135–144.

Manning, P. K. (1997) (2nd edn) *Police work: The social organization of policing.* Illinois, IL: Waveland Press, Inc.

Mansfield, M. (1993) 'The presumption of innocence: Silence is golden' *Violations of rights in Britain (12).* London: Charter 88 Enterprises Ltd.

Marshall, G. (1998) (ed.) *A dictionary of sociology.* Oxford: Oxford University Press.

Martin, S. E. (1980) *Breaking and entering: policewomen on patrol.* Berkley, CA: University of California Press.

Matassa, M. and Newburn, T. (2003) In: T. Newburn (ed.) *Handbook of Policing.* Devon: Willan Publishing: 467–500.

Matza, D. (1964) *Delinquency and drift.* New York, NY: John Wiley and Sons, Inc.

Maynard, D. (1989) 'On the ethnography and analysis of discourse in institutional settings'. *Perspectives on Social Problems.* Vol. 1: 127–146.

McAlhone, C. and Stockdale, M. (1999) (2nd edn) *Evidence in a nutshell.* London: Sweet and Maxwell.

McCormick, C. T. (1972) (2nd edn) *Handbook of the law of evidence.* St. Paul, MN: West.

Meissner, C. A. and Kassin, S. M. (2002) '"He's guilty!": Investigator bias in judgments of truth and deception'. *Law and Human Behavior.* Vol. 26(5): 469–480.

Memon, A. Bull, R. and Smith, M. (1995) 'Improving the quality of the police interview: can training in the use of cognitive techniques help?'. *Policing and Society.* Vol. 5: 53–68.

Memon, A., Vrij, A. and Bull, R. (2003) (2nd edn) *Psychology and law: Truthfulness, accuracy and credibility of victims, witnesses and suspects.* Chichester: Wiley.

Merton, R. and Barber, E. (2004) *The travels and adventures of serendipity: A study in sociological semantics and the sociology of science.* Princeton, NJ: Princeton University Press.

Miller, G. R. and Stiff, J. B. (1993) *Deceptive communication.* Thousand Oaks, CA: Sage Publications.

Mills, C. W. (1940) 'Situated actions and vocabularies of motive'. *American Sociological Review.* Vol. 5 (December): 904–913.

Mirfield, P. (1985) *Confessions.* London: Sweet and Maxwell Ltd.

Morreal, J. (1983) *Taking laughter seriously.* New York, NY: State University of New York Press.

Mortimer, A. and Shepherd, E. (1999) 'Frames of mind: Schemata guiding cognition and conduct in the interviewing of suspected offenders'. In Memon, A. and R. Bell (eds) *Handbook of the psychology of interviewing.* Chichester: Wiley: 293–315.

Moston, S. and Engelberg, T. (1993) 'Police questioning techniques in tape recorded interviews with criminal suspects'. *Policing and Society.* Vol. 3: 223–237.

Moston, S., Stephenson, G. and Williamson, T. M. (1992) 'The effects of case characteristics on suspect behavior during questioning'. *British Journal of Criminology* 32(1): 23–40.

Moston, S. Stephenson, S. M. and Williamson, T. M. (1993) 'The incidence, antecedents and consequences of the use of right to silence during police questioning'. *British Journal of Criminology.* Vol. 32: 23–40.

Mulkay, M. (1988) *On humor.* New York, NY: Blackwell.

Napier, M. R. and Adams, S. H. (2002) 'Criminal confessions: overcoming the challenges – interview and interrogation techniques' *The FBI law enforcement bulletin* November 2002. Washington, DC: Federal Bureau of Investigation.

Newburn, T. (ed.) (2003a) *Handbook of policing.* Devon: Willan Publishing.

Newburn, T. (2003b) 'Introduction: understanding policing'. In: T. Newburn (ed.) *Handbook of Policing.* Devon: Willan Publishing: 1–10.

Norrick, N. (1993) *Conversational joking: Humor in everyday talk.* Bloomington, IN: Indiana University Press.

O'Quin, K. and Aronoff, J. (1981) 'Humor as a tool of social influence' *Social Psychology Quarterly.* Vol. 44(4): 349–357.

Osvaldsson, K. (2004) 'On laughter and disagreement in multiparty assessment talk' *Text.* Vol. 24(4): 517–545.

Oxburgh, G. E., Myklebust, T. and Grant, T. (2010) 'The question of question types in police interviews: A review of the literature from a psychological and linguistic perspective', *International Journal of Speech Language and the Law.* Vol. 17(1): 46–66. *http://www.equinoxjournals.com/IJSLL/article/view/6721 (last accessed 24/10/10).*

Pearce J. and Gudjonsson, G. H. (1999) 'Measuring influential police interviewing tactics: A factor analytic approach'. *Legal and Criminal Psychology.* Vol. 4: 221–238.

Perlmutter, D. (2000) *Policing the Media: Street Cops and Public Perceptions of Law Enforcement.* London: Sage.

Plimmer, J. (1997) 'Confession Rate'. *Police Review* (February): 16–18.

Police and Criminal Evidence Act (PACE) (1984) Codes of Practice. Order 1988. London: Her Majesty's Stationery Office.

Pomerantz, A. (1984) 'agreeing and disagreeing with assessments: some features of preferred/dispreferred turn-shapes'. In: J. M. Atkinson and J. Heritage (eds) (1984). *Structures of social action: Studies in conversation analysis*. Cambridge: Cambridge University Press: 79–112.

Powell, M. B. (2002) 'Specialist training in investigative and evidential interviewing: Is it having any effect on the behaviour of professionals in the field?'. *Psychiatry, Psychology and Law*. Vol. 9(1): 44–55.

Powell, M. B. and Roberts, K. P. (2002) 'The effect of repeated experience on children's suggestibility across two question types'. *Applied Cognitive Psychology*. Vol. 16: 367–386.

Presdee, M. (2000) *Cultural criminology and the carnival of crime*. London: Routledge.

Price, C. and Caplan, J. (1977) *The Confait confessions*. London: Marion Boyars Ltd.

Provine, R. R. (1997) 'Yawns, laughs, smiles, tickles and talking'. In: J. A. Russell and J. M. Fernandez-Dols (eds) *The psychology of facial expression*. Cambridge: Cambridge University Press and Paris: Editions de la Maison des Sciences de l'Homme: 158–175.

Psathas, G. and Anderson, T. (1990) 'The 'practices' of transcription in conversation analysis'. *Semiotica*. Vol. 78(1/2): 75–99.

Rafky, D. M. (1973) 'Police race attitudes and labelling'. *Journal of Police Science and Administration* 1(1): 65–86.

Redlich, A. D., Ghetti, S., Quas, J. A. (2008) 'Perceptions of Children During a Police Interview: A Comparison of Alleged Victims and Suspects' *Journal of Applied Social Psychology*. Vol. 38(3): 705–735.

Reiner, R. (1992) (2nd edn) *The politics of the police*. Hemel Hempstead: Harvester Wheatsheaf.

Reiner, R. (1993) 'Police accountability: Principles, patterns and practices'. In: R. Reiner and S. Spencer (eds) *Accountable policing: Effectiveness, empowerment and equity*. London: Institute for public policy research: 1–23.

Reiner, R. (2000) (3rd edn) *The politics of the police*. Oxford: Oxford University Press.

Reiner, R. (2003) 'Policing and the media'. In: T. Newburn (ed.) *Handbook of Policing*. Devon: Willan Publishing: 259–282.

Reiner, Robert (2010) (4th edn) *The politics of the police*. Oxford: Oxford University Press.

Road Safety Act (1986) (revised 2006) London: Her Majesty's Stationery Office.

Road Traffic Act (1988). *http://www.legislation.gov.uk/ukpga/1988/52/contents* (last accessed 30/03/11).

Robinson, W. P. (1996) *Deceit, delusion, and detection*. Thousand Oaks, CA: Sage Publications.

Report of the Royal Commission on Criminal Justice (1993, CM2263; Chair, Lord Runciman), Terms of reference i.

Roberts, B. (2006) *Micro social theory*. Basingstoke: Palgrave Macmillan.

Rutter, J. (1997) *Stand up as interaction: Performance and audience in comedy venues*. PhD: University of Salford.

Sacks, H. (1972) 'An initial investigation of the usability of conversational data for doing sociology'. In: D. Sudnow (ed.) *Studies in social interaction.* New York, NY: Free Press: 31–74.

Sacks, H. (1974) 'On the analyzability of stories by children'. In: R. Turner (ed.) *Ethnomethodology: selected readings.* Harmondsworth: Penguin: 216–232.

Sacks, H. (1984) 'Notes on methodology'. In: Atkinson and Heritage (eds) *Structures of social action: Studies in conversation analysis.* Cambridge: Cambridge University Press: 413–429.

Sacks, H. (1992) *Lectures on conversation.* Volume I and II. Oxford: Blackwell.

Sacks, H. and Garfinkel, H. (1970) 'On formal structures of practical action'. In: J. C. McKinney and E. A. Tiryakian (eds) *Theoretical sociology.* New York, NY: Appleton-Century-Crofts: 337–66.

Sacks, H., Schegloff, E. A. and Jefferson, G. (1974) 'A simplest systematics for the organization of turn-taking for conversation'. *Language.* Vol. 50: 696–735.

Sanders, T. (2004) 'Controllable laughter: Managing sex work through humour'. *Sociology.* Vol. 38(2): 273–291.

Sarangi, S. and Roberts, C. (1999) (eds) *Talk, work and institutional order.* Mouton: Berlin.

Scheck, B., Neufeld, P. Dwyer, J. (2000) *Actual innocence.* New York, NY: Doubleday.

Schegloff, E. A. (1992) 'Repair after next turn: The last structurally provided defense of intersubjectivity in conversation' American Journal of Sociology. Vol. 98: 1295–1345.

Schegloff, E. A. (1998) 'On an actual virtual servo-mechanism for guessing bad news: A single case conjecture' *Social Problems.* Vol. 35(4): 442–457.

Schegloff, E. A. and Sacks, H. (1973) 'Opening up closings'. *Semiotica.* Vol. 7: 289–327.

Schenkein, J. N. (1972) 'Towards an analysis of conversation and the sense of heheh'. *Semiotica* 6: 344–377.

Schenkein, J. N. (ed.) (1978) *Studies in the organization of conversational interaction.* London: Academic Press.

Serious Organised Crime and Police Act (2005) *http://www.england-legislation.hmso. gov.uk/legislation/scotland/ssi2007/ssi_20070241_en_1* (last accessed 30/03/11).

Shakespeare, W. (2000) *As you like it.* Act II, Scene vii. Cambridge: Cambridge University Press.

Sharrock, W. W. and Turner, R. (1978) 'On a conversational environment for equivocality'. In: Schenkein, J. (ed.) *Studies in the organization of conversational interaction.* London: Academic Press: 173–197.

Shearing, C. (1998) 'Theorizing–sotto voce'. In: S. Holdaway and P. Rock (1998) *Thinking about criminology.* London: University College London: 15–33.

Shuy, R. W. (1993) *Language crimes: The use and abuse of language evidence in the courtroom.* Oxford: Blackwell.

Shuy, R. W. (1998) *The language of confession, interrogation, and deception.* Thousand Oaks, CA: Sage.

Sigurdsson, J. F. and Gudjonsson G. H. (1996) 'The psychological characteristics of 'false confessors'. A study among Icelandic prison inmates and juvenile offenders'. *Personality and Individual Differences.* Vol. 20(3): 321–329.

Smith, J. A. and Osborn, M. (2003) 'Interpretative phenomenological analysis'. In: J. A. Smith (ed.) *Qualitative psychology: A practical guide to methods.* London: Sage: 51–80.

Speier, H. (1998) 'Wit and politics: An essay on laughter and power'. *The American Journal of Sociology.* Vol. 103(5): 1352–1401.

Stokoe, E. (2009a) '"For the benefit of the tape": Formulating embodied conduct in designedly uni-modal recorded police–suspect interrogations'. *Journal of Pragmatics.* Vol. 41(2009): 1887–1904.

Stokoe, E. (2009b) '"I've got a girlfriend" Police officers doing 'self disclosure' in interviews with suspects. *Narrative Enquiry.* Vol. 19: 1.

Stokoe, E. (2010) '"I'm not gonna hit a lady': Conversation analysis, membership categorization and men's denial of violence against women". *Discourse and Society.* January 2010: Vol. 21(1): 59–82.

Stokoe, E. and Edwards, D. (2007) '`Black this, black that': racial insults and reported speech in neighbour complaints and police interrogations' *Discourse & Society* 2007 (18): 337.

Stokoe, E. and Edwards, D. (2008) "Did you have permission to smash your neighbour's door?' Silly questions and their answers in police–suspect interrogations'. *Discourse Studies.* Vol. 10(1): 89–111.

Sutherland, E. (1949) *White collar crime.* New York, NY: Dryden Press.

Sykes, G. and Matza, D. (1957) 'Techniques of neutralization' *American Sociological Review.* Vol. 22(6): 664–670.

The Crown Prosecution Service *http://www.cps.gov.uk/legal/l_to_o/offences_against_ the_person/index.html#P92_3540* (last accessed 30/03/11).

The Police Reform Act (2002) (c. 30) *http://www.opsi.gov.uk/Acts/acts2002/ ukpga_20020030_en_6* (last accessed 30/03/11).

The Terrorism Act (2000) *http://www.opsi.gov.uk/acts/acts2000/ukpga_20000011_ en_1* (last accessed 30/03/11).

The Bill. Police procedural drama television series. First broadcast 1984. Independent Television Plc (ITV1), London: talkbackTHAMES.

Trowbridge, B. (2003) 'Suggestibility and confessions'. *American Journal of Forensic Psychology.* Vol. 21(1): 5–23.

Uildriks, N. and Mastrigt, Van H. (1991) *Policing police violence.* Aberdeen: Aberdeen University Press.

Underwager, R. and Wakefield, H. (1990) *The real world of child interrogations.* Illinois, IL: C. C. Thomas Ltd.

United States Supreme Court (1967) (Mr. Justice Goldberg) ESCOBEDO v STATE OF ILLINOIS (1964). In: C. Price and J. Caplan (1977) *The Confait confessions.* London: Marion Boyars Ltd.

Vrij, A. (2000) *Detecting lies and deceit: The psychology of lying and the implications for professional practice.* London: Wiley.

Vrij, A., Edward, K. and Bull, R. (2001) 'Police officers' ability to detect deceit: The benefit of indirect deception detection measures'. *Legal and Criminal Psychology* 6: 185–196.

Waddington, P. J. (1999) 'Police (canteen) subculture: an appreciation'. *British Journal of Criminology* Vol. 39(2): 286–309.

Walsh, D. (2006) 'Giving P.E.A.C.E. a chance?' Paper presented at the *Second*

International Conference on Investigative Interviewing (iii2). Portsmouth: University of Portsmouth.

Walklate, S. (1995) 'Equal opportunities and the future of policing'. In: F. Leishman, B. Loveday and S. P. Savage (eds) *Core issues in policing*. London: Longman.

Walters, S. B. (2005a) *The Interview Room*. Vol. 4(7). Versailles, KY: The Third Degree Publishing.

Walters, S. B. (2005b) *The Interview Room*. Vol. 4(8). Versailles, KY: The Third Degree Publishing.

Walters, S. B. (2005c) *The Interview Room*. Vol. 4(8). Versailles, KY: The Third Degree Publishing.

Watson, D. R. (1990) 'Some features of the elicitation of confessions in murder interrogations'. In: G. Psathas (ed.) *Interaction competence*. International Institute for Ethnomethodology and Conversation Analysis, Washington, DC: University Press of America: 263–295.

West, C. (1984) Medical misfires: Mishearings, misgivings and misunderstandings in physician patient dialogues. *Discourse Processes*. Vol. 7(2): 107–134.

Westmarland, L. (2001) *Gender and policing*. Devon: Willan Publishing.

Zimbardo. P. G. (1967a) 'The psychology of police confessions'. *Psychology Today*. Vol. 1(2): 17–27.

Zimbardo, P. G. (1967b) 'Toward a more perfect justice'. *Psychology Today*. Vol. 1(3): 44–4. *http://news.bbc.co.uk/onthisday/hi/dates/stories/march/14/newsid_2543000/2543613.stm* (last accessed 30/03/11).

Notes

1. Turntaking is discussed in more detail in the later section 'CA in Practice: Turntaking'.
2. See Appendix IV for an example of a fictional confession in an extract from a script from British television programme *The Bill*. The script shows the suspect ultimately confessing to a crime following several denials.
3. Sacks' first lectures on CA in the 1960s and 1970s were published posthumously.
4. For a definition of repair types, see Appendix III.
5. GoldWave screenshots courtesy of GoldWave Inc.
6. A dispreferred action is an action that is a rejection of, or 'unexpected' response to, the prior turn. For example, a denial in response to a request is the dispreferred turn shape, whereas an acceptance is the preferred turn shape. In the context of the police interview, the suspect's rejection of, or challenge of, the officer's turn constitutes a dispreferred action, as in ordinary conversation. However, the suspect is additionally constrained by the sequential organization and turn allocation (Drew and Heritage 1992; Heydon 2005) of the police interview and their perception of the power distribution between the officer and the suspect. See Appendix III for further detail.
7. Line 166 of T22-20-06, see Appendix II.
8. Contradicting a police officer is a dispreferred action – that is, one that does not affiliate with the social action being accomplished in this context. Laughter as a method of displaying disaffiliation is also addressed in Carter (2005). Although contradiction and the provision of contrasting accounts by the suspect and the officer may appear indicative of police interview interaction, they remain dispreferred turn shapes, particularly (in accordance with the power relations indicative of this context) concerning the suspects' interaction.
9. Lines 254, 313 and 315, T11-80-06; see Appendix II.
10. Line 612 of T18-23-06; see Appendix II.
11. Other examples of this are seen on lines 603–607, lines 612/616 and lines 849–853; see Appendix II.
12. For a definition of semantic and legal redundancy, see Appendix III.
13. The suspect is informed of their rights prior to the interview both verbally and in writing (the PACE Act 1984 Code C, section 3(a), paragraphs 1.1 and 3.2). The suspect is also cautioned, prior to its administration in the police interview, upon arrest (The PACE Act 1984 Code C, section 10(b), paragraph 10.5(a) and Code G, section 2, paragraph 2.2).
14. The PACE Act 1984 Code E, section 11.2.
15. The PACE Act 1984 Code E, section 10C.
16. The PACE Act 1984 Code E, section 16.3.

[17] On line 1 of the interview, T22-20-06; see Appendix II.

[18] The constraints of the opening and closing sequences in the police interview, such as the requirement of the officer to administer the suspect's rights, are addressed by Carter (2003) and Heydon (2005), and discussed in Chapter 3.

[19] Lines 387, 393 and 402 of T11-80-06; see Appendix II.

[20] Line 355 of T29-31-06; see Appendix II.

[21] Lines 239/252 of T1-67-06; see Appendix II.

[22] Lines 160, 239, 242 and 245 of T1-67-06; see Appendix II.

[23] Lines 204 and 212–213 respectively of T1-67-06; see Appendix II.

[24] Lines 248/252, 261/263, 579/583 and 601 of T1-67-06; see Appendix II.

[25] Before a suspect can be questioned about a particular offence, s/he must first be cautioned (the PACE Act 1984 Code C, section 10(a), paragraph 10.1), and informed about the nature of the offence(s) for which they are suspected (the PACE Act 1984 Code C, section 11(a), paragraph 11.1A).

[26] For example, this motivation is made explicit by the suspects in extracts 28 (lines 207–208) and 32 (lines 276–277).

[27] Maximization refers to the officers' use of tactics such as maximizing the consequences of the crime, references to the crime and the seriousness of the offence to elicit information from a suspect.

[28] As outlined in Chapter 3, extra-interactional information such as that which identifies suspects with learning or language difficulties were not provided with the data. Although certain conclusions may be drawn from the presence of a health worker or translator in the interview (no data in this book involved the presence of either), the reason for their presence would remain purely a deduction, and therefore the role or influence of language or other difficulties in the elicitation of confessions lie outside of the scope of this research.

[29] Lines 107–108, 211–212 and 237–238 of T33-22-06, see Appendix II.

[30] Lines 221, 230 and 232/233 of T33-22-06, see Appendix II.

[31] The 'swinging a punch and missing' the suspect claims to have done, which is an attempted assault, does not carry a prison sentence, while common assault, which is what this offence would be classed as if the suspect had admitted striking the victim, carries a maximum penalty of six months' imprisonment (The Crown Prosecution Service 2007).

[32] The suspect had withheld this information on prior occasions throughout the interview; see lines 49, 58 and 70 of T7-120-06, in Appendix II.

[33] A break in interaction is a type of transition relevance place (TRP), which is a moment in talk where the speaker can nominate the next speaker or a participant can self-select themselves as the next speaker and take the floor (TRPs are discussed in Liddicoat 2007).

[34] Lines 207–208 and lines 231–233 of T7-120-06; see Appendix II.

[35] Lines 54, 87–88, 96–100 and 102 of T10-77-06; see Appendix II.

[36] Lines 90 and 110 of T10-77-06; see Appendix II.

[37] The officer's statement that they have no further questions is recognized as the first stage of the closing of the police interview (Carter 2003: 40).

[38] The next, and final, stages in the closing sequence of the police interview would typically be: confirm the end of the interview (for example: 'Are you happy to end the interview at this time?') and note the time of its termination (for

example 'the time is now two thirty and the interview is terminated') (Carter 2003). This is shown later in the interview, on lines 238/245 of T10-77-06 (see Appendix II), when the sequence is re-initiated and completed.

39 See T10-77-06, Appendix II.

40 Else statements take the form 'if [condition] then [statement]'. The officer's statement on lines 125–126 translates to 'if [you are innocent] then [you must tell us what happened]'. Further else statements are also uttered on lines 137–138 and 141–142.

41 According to Hutchby and Wooffitt (1998), a delay after one part of the adjacency pair is produced (e.g. the officer's request for information) suggests that a dispreferred turn shape will be produced by the recipient, instead of the preferred, corresponding turn shape (e.g. the suspect's provision of information). Pomerantz (1984) and Holtgraves (1997, 2000) also discuss silence prior to a turn as a signal of disagreement.

42 Using the else statement principle, the officer's turn translates to 'if [what you said in the last turn was true] then [you can tell me what happened/who was responsible]'.

43 For a comprehensive account of insertion sequences see Hutchby and Wooffitt (1998).

44 Lines 228–229, 239, 268 and 276–277, T40-66-06; see Appendix II.

45 Lines 257–258 and 260, 312, 601 and 637 of T18-23-06; see Appendix II.

46 Lines 139–143, 263–264, 582–583, 593–594, 603–607, 612/616, 630–631 and 633 of T18-23-06; see Appendix II.

47 Lines 144, 261, 266, 314, 618 and 635 of T18-23-06; see Appendix II.

48 Before a suspect can be questioned about a particular offence, they must first be informed about the nature of the offence(s) of which they are suspected (the PACE Act 1984 Code C, section 11(a), paragraph 11.1A).

49 Line 876 of T18-23-06; see Appendix II.

50 Lines 593–594, and 603–607 of T18-23-06; see Appendix II.

51 Lines 147, 150, 262–263, 265, 267/269, 271–272 and 274 of T2-111-06; see Appendix II.

52 The use of dispreferred turn shape markers such as 'well' as a face-saving tool is posited by Holtgraves (1992).

53 Lines 247 and 251/253 of T2-111-06; see Appendix II.

54 Lines 366 and 372, from T2-111-06; see Appendix II. See also lines 498–499 of T2-111-06; see Appendix II.

55 For example, producing utterances that potentially breach the role of the officer, such as violating the requirements of the PACE Act 1984, or the suspect, such as challenging the officer's utterance.

56 Interviews with witnesses are conducted under section 9 of the Criminal Justice Act (1967).

57 Reproduced with permission from A. P. Watt Ltd on behalf of P. G. Morgan.

Index

ambiguity/ies 41, 50, 79, 94–6, 101,
    120, 129, 134, 139
ambiguous 93, 130, 134–5, 143
analysis
    content analysis 15, 19
    conversation analysis/analytic 1–2,
        5, 15, 16–17, 19, 21–3, 25, 27,
        29–31, 33–4, 36, 39, 72, 87–8,
        107, 144, 147, 153–4, 160–1 *see
        also* Conversation Analysis
    deductive 15, 21
    discourse analysis/analytic 19, 34
    inductive 15, 21, 29
    spectrograph 23, 28, 159
    waveform 23–4, 26–8, 159–60
approximants 24, 27, 37, 87, 147, 150,
    178

boundaries 6, 24–5, 151

change of state token 121
class *see* social class
coercion/coercive 108, 113–14, 142
communicative strategies 29
confession 1–4, 7, 10, 11 *see also*
        confessionary turn
    behavioural cues 111
    'The confession issue' 107
    elicitation 2–3, 14, 111, 142, 146, 159
        admissible/admissibility 1, 72–4,
            79–80, 83, 88–9, 104, 108, 142,
            151, 157, 159
        inadmissible 11, 54, 72, 74, 86, 88,
            142, 151, 157
        interrupt/interruption/
            interrupted 11, 36, 55–6, 75, 79,
            109, 123, 146, 148
        justify/justification 18, 75, 109–11,
            129, 134, 139, 155
        knowledge claim 109–11, 116–17,

119, 121–3, 125–8, 139, 141–2,
    145–6, 155
maximize/maximization/
    maximizing 21, 28, 73, 108, 110,
    142, 151, 162, 198
minimize/minimization/
    minimizing 30, 86, 88, 101, 105,
    108–11, 115, 118, 129, 131–9,
    141–3, 145–7, 153, 155
successful 56, 101, 104, 106, 109,
    123, 127–8, 132, 136, 139, 141–2,
    145–6, 148, 155–6
techniques 14, 110, 142, 146, 161
unsuccessful 91–3, 104, 138, 142,
    155
evidence 107, 113, 136, 158
    unreliable as 113
'The exclusion issue' 107
confessionary turn 21–2, 101, 116, 124,
    127, 129, 134, 138, 142, 145, 157
    see also confession
continuers 108
Conversation Analysis (CA)
    accountability 18
    dispreferred action 34, 37–8, 40,
        44, 47–8, 51–2, 60, 87, 108, 112,
        120, 137, 151, 178, 179, 197
    dispreferred turn 46, 66, 120, 137,
        197, 199
    next-turn proof procedure 34, 50
    overlap/overlapped 24, 32, 63, 76,
        122, 131, 138, 148, 164, 179
    pause 22, 24, 27–8, 36, 42–3, 45–50,
        57, 65, 78, 80, 82, 91, 94–5,
        98–9, 112, 118–20, 122, 124,
        129, 131, 134–5, 137–8, 160, 164
        see also silence
    timing 22, 24, 27–8, 160
    repair 18, 33–4, 42, 44, 48, 76, 80,
        90, 92–5, 97–101, 116, 119,

121–2, 124, 126–8, 134, 180, 197

other-initiated other repair 94, 180

other-initiated self repair 92, 94, 121, 180

self-initiated repair 180

self-initiated self repair 42

silence 7, 18, 24–8, 41, 43–4, 46, 48, 50, 55–6, 85, 93, 96, 100–1, 106, 108–9, 112, 120, 122–4, 126, 142, 199 *see also* pause

transcription 2, 15–16, 19–23, 36, 68, 161, 165, 178, 197, 181

cyclic process of 21

turntaking 11, 31–4, 36–7, 65, 70, 112, 160, 197

culpability 41–2, 51, 110, 124, 128, 153

moral or social 153

culture 1, 9, 12, 110 *see also* police culture

false 5, 13, 29, 107, 111, 113–14, 143, 155

involuntary 108

joint construction of 145

likelihood of 12, 109, 111, 114

part-confessions 13, 107

rationalisations 108, 110, 139, 155

reprisal 110, 136, 157

resistance/resisting 34, 106, 160,

sequence 108

withheld information 106, 115, 117–20, 122, 126–7, 131, 141

context

conversational 147

institutional 3, 32, 37–9, 67, 70, 72, 95, 146, 147, 150

local 15, 86

context-specific 110

contextual differences 162

deception 4, 29, 57, 106, 111–14

cues 111–12

detection 112

demographic details 29

denial 19, 35, 45–6, 49, 51, 59, 63, 109–10, 117, 121–2, 132–4, 137, 143, 197

sub-types of 110

disagreement 24, 37, 39, 45, 52, 61, 101, 112, 139, 199

disambiguate 94, 139

dispreferred 34, 37–8, 40–1, 44, 46–8, 51–2, 60, 66, 87, 108, 112, 120, 137, 146, 151, 178–9, 197, 199

dissafiliative 43, 51, 52

dominant 38–9

else statement 124, 126, 139, 199

emotional appeal 108, 131–2, 139

emotions 112

emotion work 38

ethnic origin 29

ethnomethodology/ ethnomethodological 16–17, 149–50, 153–4

evidence 1, 6, 10, 12–13, 20, 41, 54, 57, 68, 72, 74, 79–80, 82, 85–6, 88, 93, 98, 104, 107–10, 113–18, 120, 127–8, 136, 141–4, 151, 156–8, 160–2

construct/constructing 110, 127

empirical 1, 104

evidence-based 12, 67, 156

false 114

extra-interactional 29, 82, 160–1, 198 *see also* interactional

face 18, 38, 134, 137, 139–40

floor 36, 113, 198

gender 8, 29

guilt/guilty 10, 13–14, 29, 44, 48, 72, 107, 112–14, 121, 142, 159

humour 27, 36–9, 48–50, 52, 58, 66–7

identity/identities 1, 30, 32–3, 57, 93

incriminating 41, 47, 50–1, 93, 100, 109, 112, 118, 120, 128, 136–8

incrimination *see* self-incrimination

incriminatory 66

innocent/innocence 13, 113

innocently 127

intellectual 11

intelligence 11

interact
interaction
  client-therapist 38
  comedy club 37–8
  counsellor-client 69
  courtroom 33, 70–3, 93, 97, 99,
    100–2, 145
  doctor-patient 19, 33, 66, 69
  institutional 32, 35, 38–9, 52, 70, 75,
    102, 147, 149–50, 179
  newsroom 90
  ordinary conversation 3, 17–18,
    31–2, 35–6, 38–9, 45, 51–2, 55,
    65–6, 70–1, 87, 90, 95, 100–1,
    144, 147, 150, 179, 197
  police emergency calls 4
  police interview *see* police interview
  sex workers 38
  telephone 16–17, 20, 38
interactive 17
interview/interviewing *see also* police
    interview
  technique/s 5, 11–13, 35, 107, 111,
    114, 162
  training 5, 11, 12, 14, 67, 144, 149, 155
intimidate/intimidating 109–10, 146,
    154
intimidation 109, 142

joke/joking 37, 48, 51, 80 *see also*
    non-serious
joke-telling 37
jury/juries 69–70, 72, 88, 90, 96, 108,
    110, 113

labelling/self-labelling 34, 152
language difficulties 114
latching 164, 179
laughter
  asymmetry 39, 67, 146
  bubbling-through 36, 47, 61, 161, 178
  full 36, 165, 179
  invitation 39, 45, 65
  reciprocal 36, 44, 51, 63–5, 80
learning difficulties 29
linguistic turn 17

media 1–3, 8–10, 14, 21, 33, 151–2,
    154–5, 179

mental health 29, 114
minimal responses 11, 108, 131
miscarriages of justice 6, 10

negotiation 1, 3, 15, 37, 87, 95, 115,
    146
no comment 54–8, 64, 71, 85, 91, 122,
    124–8, 161
non-lexical 42, 52, 68, 72, 151, 160, 179
non-serious 48, 50, 58, 64
non-verbal communication 31
  body language 31, 112
  eye gaze 31, 37
  microexpressions 112
  verbal leakage 113

overhearing audience 69, 73, 90, 105
    see also silent participant

pattern/s 2, 18, 24, 26, 30, 39, 70, 77,
    141–2, 153
plosive 24, 178, 180
police culture 9 *see also* culture
police interview *see also* interview
  adversarial 85, 88, 103, 142, 156, 158
  American 13, 107
  British 13, 107
  caution 28, 33, 81–2, 85, 161, 163,
    197–8
  children 11
  closing 33, 54, 122–3, 155, 159, 198
  constraints 4, 38–9, 54, 60, 68, 71,
    73–5, 77, 79–81, 83, 85–90, 95,
    102, 140, 146–7, 150–1, 153, 163,
    198
  design 69–71, 73, 90–1, 96–7,
    99–101, 104, 110, 112, 119, 132,
    142, 159
  evidence-based 12, 156
  flexibility/flexible 11, 148, 149, 158,
    159
  guilt-presumptive 159 *see also*
    presumption of innocence
  interrogation/s 1, 11, 13, 108–12,
    114, 155–6
  investigative interviewing 158
  myths 1–4, 11–14, 111, 154
  opening 33, 57, 69, 76–7, 80–1, 83,
    88, 104, 141–2, 152, 155

protocol 6–7, 54, 64, 73–8, 80–3,
    85–7, 103, 150–1, 153–4, 156
restrictions 5, 107, 151
role/s 1–2, 4, 7–9, 13, 30, 38–41,
    52, 54, 59–60, 66–8, 71, 87, 106,
    111, 123, 140, 144, 146, 148,
    150–4, 162, 198–9
rules 1, 17, 30, 34, 37–9, 52, 54,
    56, 64, 66–7, 69, 82, 86–8, 144,
    147–9, 156, 162
self-policing 150–1
status 36, 52, 66–7, 85, 110, 147
tape recording 3, 5–6, 8, 104, 157
training 2, 5, 11–12, 14, 16, 40, 52,
    67, 89, 105, 107, 111, 143–4,
    146, 149, 151, 154–5, 161
'truth-finding activities' 108
police subculture 9 *see also* subculture
power/powerful 33–4, 39, 41, 51, 57,
    110, 157, 162, 187, 197
powerlessness 87
preference organization 108
presumption of innocence 13–14,
    158 *see also* guilt presumptive
    process
prosody

question-answer 33, 71, 93, 94, 101
question types 5
    closed 11–12
    direct 48, 120, 122–3, 130
    leading 47–8
    open-ended 11, 114
    specific 12, 15

redundant/redundancy
    legal/legally 73, 78, 80, 83–6, 89–90,
        144, 151, 180, 197
    semantic/semantically 72, 74–5,
        77–8, 83–4, 86–7, 103, 180
rights 6–7, 9, 13–14, 30, 33, 35, 54, 57,

66–8, 71–2, 74, 76–7, 81–2, 88,
    103–4, 107–9, 113–14, 147, 151,
    155, 157–63, 197–8
ritual 4, 18
rushed speech 112–13

self-implication/self-implicatory 49, 99
self-incrimination 48, 66
silent participant 3, 6–7, 21, 32, 34,
    36, 52, 69–80, 82–90, 93, 95–6,
    98–105, 144–5, 149, 154, 156–7,
    162
social class 29–30
social etiquette 37, 52
solicitor 55–6, 74–8, 83, 85, 122–3, 164
spectrograph 23, 28, 159
storytelling 19, 108
subculture 9, 110 *see also* police
    subculture
subordinate/subordinating/
    subordination 39, 67
suggestible/suggestibility 5, 111,
    113–15
syntax 19

talk about troubles 36, 112
talk-in-trouble 147, 180
third turn 47, 70, 90–100, 103 *see also*
    uninitiated third turn
time out 56, 64, 66, 149
topic 3, 33, 43, 56, 107, 130–1,
truth 4, 13, 29, 108, 111–12, 114, 121,
    133, 177, 183,
turn shape 46, 66, 108, 117, 137, 197,
    199
turn-type pre-allocation 32–3

unambiguous 130
uninitiated third turn 70–2, 91, 93–4,
    99 *see also* third turn